Phillip Bonosky

Afghanistan — Washington's *Secret* War

International Publishers, New York

Also by Phillip Bonosky
Burning Valley (1952)
Brother Bill McKie (1952)
The Magic Fern (1960)
Dragon Pink on Old White (1962)
Beyond the Borders of Myth: from Vilnius to Hanoi (1967)
Two Cultures (1978)
Are Our Moscow Reporters Giving Us the Facts About the USSR (1981)
A Bird in Her Hair (short stories) (1987)
Devils in Amber—The Baltics (1992)
Brother Bill McKie - 2nd Ed. (2000)

© International Publishers, New York, 1985
All rights reserved.
Text printed in the USSR
Covers printed and bound in the USA

© 2nd edition, 2001
Text and cover printed in USA
All rights reserved

For the 1st edition:
Library of Congress Cataloging in Publication Data
Bonosky, Phillip.
Afghanistan, Washington's Secret War Against

1. Afghanistan—History—Current status,—1979
I. Title. II. Title.
DS371.2.B66 1984   958'.1044 84-19139
ISBN 0 — 7178 — 0618 — 9
ISBN 0 — 7178 — 0617 — 9 (pbk.)

For the 2nd edition:
Bonosky, Phillip.
Afghanistan—Washington's *Secret* War

Includes bibliographical references and index

Contents

Preface

Since the horrific events of Sept. 11, 2001, much has been said about the desperate situation of the Afghani people now crushed under the heel of the theocratic, dictatorial Taliban, and about the role of the Northern Alliance and other Taliban opponents who now figure in Washington's plans for the region.

There has been talk, most of it distorted, about the role of the Soviet Union in the years from 1978 to 1989. There has been talk, most of it understated, about the role of the U.S. in building up the Mujahadeen forces, including the Taliban. But almost no one talks about the effort the Afghan people made in the late 1970s and '80s to pull free of the legacy of incessantly warring tribes and feudal fiefdoms and start to build a modern democratic state. Or about the Soviet Union's role long before 1978.

Some background helps shed light on the current crisis. Afghanistan was a geopolitical prize for 19th century empire builders, contested by both czarist Russia and the British Empire. It was finally forced by the British into semi-dependency.

When he came to power in 1921, Amanullah Khan—sometimes referred to as "Afghanistan's Kemal Ataturk"—sought to reassert his country's sovereignty and move it toward the modern world. As part of this effort, he approached the new revolutionary government in Moscow, which responded by recognizing Afghanistan's independence, and concluding the first Afghan-Soviet friendship treaty.

From 1921 until 1929—when reactionary elements, aided by the British, forced Amanullah to abdicate—the Soviet union helped launch the beginnings of economic infrastructure projects such as power plants, water resources, transport and communications. Thousands of Afghani students attended Soviet technical schools and universities. After Amanullah's forced departure, the projects languished, but the relationship between the Soviet and Afghan people would later re-emerge.

In the 1960s, a resurgence of joint Afghan-Soviet projects included the Kabul Polytechnic Institute—the country's prime educational resource for engineers, geologists and other specialists.

Nor was Afghanistan immune from the political and social ferment that characterized the developing world in the last century. From the 1920s on, many progressive currents of struggle took note of the experiences of the USSR, where a new, more equitable society was emerging on the lands of the former Russian empire. Afghanistan was no exception. By the mid '60s, national democratic revolutionary currents had coalesced to form the People's Democratic Party (PDP).

In 1973, local bourgeois forces, aided by some PDP elements, overthrew the 40-year reign of Mohammad Zahir Shah—the man who now, at age 86, is being promoted by U.S. right-wing Republicans as the personage around which Afghanis can unite.

When the PDP assumed power in 1978, they started to work for a more equitable distribution of economic and social resources. Among their goals were the continuing emancipation of women and girls from the age-old tribal bondage (a process begun under Zahir Shah), equal rights for minority nationalities, including the country's most oppressed group, the Hazara, and increasing access for ordinary people to education, medical care, decent housing and sanitation. During two visits in 1980-81, 1 saw the beginnings of progress: women working together in handicraft co-ops, where for the first time they could be paid decently for their work and control the money they earned. Adults, both women and men, learning to read. Women working as professionals and holding leading government positions, including Minister of Education. Poor working families able to afford a doctor, and to send their children—girls and boys—to school. The cancellation of peasant debt and the start of land reform. Fledgling peasant cooperatives. Price controls and price reductions on some key foods. Aid to nomads interested in a settled life. I also saw the bitter results of Mujahadeen attacks by the same groups that now make up the "Northern Alliance"—in those years aimed especially at schools and teachers in rural areas.

The post-1978 developments also included Soviet aid to economic and social projects on a much larger scale, with a new Afghan-Soviet Friendship Treaty and a variety of new projects, including infrastructure, resource prospecting and mining, health services, education and agricultural demonstration projects. After December 1978 that role also came to include the limited presence of Soviet troops, at the request of a PDP government increasingly beset by the displaced feudal and tribal warlords who were aided and organized by the U.S. and Pakistan.

The rest, as they say, is history. But it is significant that after Soviet troops were withdrawn in 1989, the PDP government continued to function, though increasingly beleaguered, for nearly three more years.

Somewhere, beneath the ruins of today's torn and bloodied Afghanistan, are the seeds that remain even in the direst times within the hearts of people who know there is a better future for humanity. In a world struggling for economic and social justice—not revenge—those seeds will sprout again.

The publication of this updated edition of Phillip Bonosky s book is much needed now. It is a serious, valuable study of Afghanistan's history as well as a well-documented, persuasive exposure of the role of the CIA and the Pentagon serving the aims of U.S. imperialism.

Marilyn Bechtel*

---

* Marilyn Bechtel is a writer on international issues for the *People's Weekly World* and former editor of *New World Review*

Afghanistan — Washington's *Secret* War

NOTE:

    The dates cited for news stories are taken, up to mid-1981, from the *International Herald-Tribune*, which is jointly owned by the *New York Times* and the *Washington Post*, but is published in Paris. It is the only daily newspaper available to English-speaking Europeans and to Americans living abroad, including those correspondents stationed in Moscow.

    Because of time differences and editorial reasons, the datelines in some news stories in the IHT differ by a day or two from the date of publication in the NYT or the WP. There is a wider gap in dates for feature stories and editorial comment. Thus the dates cited, unless otherwise noted, are the IHT dates.

A Word to the Reader

1985

Although this is a book about Afghanistan, it is inevitably as much a book about Soviet-American relations. There is no question for our times that looms larger than that and all other questions ultimately defer to it.

In taking up the question of Afghanistan, I have chosen to deal with a problem that, from the official American point of view, seems to be an open-and-shut case. Whatever other issues divide Americans, most seem agreed—or at least the media seems to agree for them—that there is no difference of opinion there. And yet, as an eyewitness to those events, a close observer of what took place in Afghanistan before and after December, 1979, I saw an entirely different Afghanistan than the one most Americans believe they saw.

And there is the crux of the matter.

What precisely is involved here? How can perceptions of the same phenomena vary so widely? As William Blake had noted in his day:

> *Both read the Bible day and night,*
> *But thou read'st black where I read white.*

Does an objective reality reign over conflicting forces *anyhow*? And is it possible to find what it is, even in the middle of the storm as the winds howl and the heavens rage? On what rock can you stand that does not itself shake?

In this book I have attempted to seek that reality that survives the storm, to find that rock on which to stand, not away from the storm, but *inside* the storm itself: there only to rest on judgment.

ANTIQUE LAND

They are the nameless poor who have been marching
Out of the dark, to that exact moment when history
Crosses the tracks of our time.
Thomas McGrath, *Nocturne Militaire*

There are several hundred secret passageways (one account puts it) through the mountain range dividing (with the help of the Durand Line) but not separating Afghanistan from Pakistan. Every Fall, through these ancient passageways, which curl upon each other like veins in an old cheese, tens of thousands of nomads, mainly Pushtun, but including Baluchi, follow the ghosts of their ancestors to the grazing grounds of what is known to us as Pakistan, and the following Spring, back to what is known to us as Afghanistan.

But if you were to ask them who they are—Afghans or Pakistanis—they would look blankly at you, shaking their heads, for to them, whose allegiance today, as it had been for centuries, is to a tribal leader, neither Afghanistan nor Pakistan is a clear reality. They have no state. They recognize no Durand Line. Their "state" is where the grass grows green.

So it was when Marco Polo found them over 700 years ago: "The mountains afford pasture for an innumerable quantity of sheep, which ramble about in flocks..." So it still was to Karl Marx in 1857 who said that Afghanistan was a mere poetical term for various tribes and states...

Pushing their herds before them—sheep, horses, camels, cattle—they go from pasture to pasture, and on their way they are waylaid by history, which comes to them as a violent and alien intrusion. Out of those mysterious spaces beyond the mountains, strange monsters periodically leap at them: an Alexander of Greece, who admired their horses; a Tamerlane, a Genghis Khan from far-off Mongolia—tormented them for a time and then were gone. They resumed, then, their timeless caravanserai during which infants of every variety were dropped from humans, sheep and camels without stopping the motion of their lives. All they knew of history was that it came to them as an interruption in this back-and-forth shuttling between green and green.

In the 19th century other historic monsters from British India leaped out on them—this time their names were Lord Palmerston, Disraeli, Winston Churchill, Lord Curzon, Sir Mortimer Durand; and after these had been shaken off again they went their way, anxious to get out of the mountains and to pasture before the first snows fell.

6

But these Pushtun shepherds were equal to all of history's surprises, cruelties and treacheries. They were to know kings and emperors. Traders from far Cathay and the near Indies had passed through their valleys along the "silk route." Hellenic culture had touched them. Buddhism arrived from India but had fallen to Islam by the 7th century. But good or bad, whatever befell them, these nomadic, pastoral peoples understood how to deal with it, and in the end they absorbed their tormentors as the immemorial movement of time absorbed their own history. Their country was a vast, natural fortress with "many narrow defiles" which, as Marco Polo had noted, protected them against "any foreign power entering with hostile intentions." They shook all of the past centuries away like water. . .

Except this one, the 20th.

This most formidable of all centuries broke open the cocoon of time in which they had been wrapped by silence and spilled the contents of their lives—only half-real, still merged with myth—into the pitiless glare of klieg lights and TV cameras and confronted them with their own history as an accusation. They had slumbered too long. They had come into the modern world too late. They would now be fearfully punished for it.

These new, 20th-century marauders demanded their souls as down payment for allowing them entry into what had become the private century of America—trade-marked "The American Century." The ritual of passage into this American-owned century proved to be a harrowing gauntlet to be run on the red-hot coals of social torment toward a destination signaled by the two morbid towers of smoke over Hiroshima and Nagasaki!

In the race of the various "revolutions" set loose on the world in our times, the scientific-technological revolution descended on Afghanistan before its social revolution arrived, and in the tension set up between them Afghanistan itself was pulled into a shape it no longer recognized. Hardly had those shepherds reached the 20th century, within touch of indoor plumbing and telestar, when they were told that they most likely would not reach the 21st. The herdsmen who push their sheep and cattle and camels through valleys that sometimes narrow to where animals are threaded through one by one, work by a time that has not changed in ages: by sunlight and dark, dawn and dusk, snow and ice, grass beginning to grow and grass beginning to die.

At night, wrapped in blankets which they drape over their shoulders during the day, they sit, descendants of Sufi poets, beside campfires and tell tales to each other of times gone by. These images of the past have grown old in their heads as they traveled from father to son, each century interweaving its own hopes and fears with the hopes and fears of the previous century, until what has now been produced, like one of their rugs, is an image of their own souls, with the thousand strands of their life woven to-

7

gether into a single pattern. But this "weaving" has abruptly ended with our times. Fable has given way to hard fact—which has become a strange new fable. Technology replaces those tales at the campfire. For they lie down at night now not to listen again to the old tales of their fathers but to press their ears against the modern radios they had brought with them all the way from Kabul or Herat or Kandahar. In those mountains "it seems time has stopped still over our campfires," a herdsman has noted, on his way some 1,200 kilometers and 60 days from rest, "but we hear sounds of our century over our transistor radios."

It is these "sounds" which have interrupted their eternal tales so abruptly and put an end to the even flow of the past. The present is noisy and drowns out the whispers of their ancestors. They eavesdrop on their own century, as though they were intruders themselves. They tune in on the world in those mountains where they are resting, and it is through this chromium box that they discovered one day that there was no way back to the pastures of Afghanistan again: they are exiled from Spring, perhaps forever.

Let them unroll their prayer mats, facing East to Allah and to Mecca in Saudi Arabia where they planned to make a *Hajj*, but meanwhile there is no going back to Spring for them this year. They are no longer Afghans, nor Pakistanis, nor Pushtuns, nor Baluchi, nor anything they recognize. That little metal box informs them that they are now "refugees," and new threats spring out at them from it: Carter, Brzezinski, Reagan, Mohammad Zia ul-Haq, strange generals who have enlisted them in that mysterious war of the Past against the Future without having asked them which they prefer. Unfree, they are dubbed "freedom fighters."

Alexander of Greece, at 25, had wept to his presumably Afghan mistress Roxanne that there were no more worlds to conquer, unaware that in the conquest of geography he had merely carried the war to History itself. The freeing or unfreeing of space had become a pretext. It was the motion of History that his after-warriors wanted to conquer—to freeze into immobility at the point of their conquest of space, stiffening social relationships like the carved figures in a stone frieze just as they formed them: now the master as eternal ideal standing over the slave who, on bended knee, in the quiet stone offers him his ravaged heart forever.

As the herdsmen sleep by campfires at night, beyond them speed Peugeots and Cadillacs to the Khyber Pass and on to Peshawar to deposit their passengers in a warm bath already drawn and waiting for them at the deluxe Khyber Hotel. This night those men who intermingle sheep and shepherds in their calculating machines will sleep in beds of Hashish comfort with American dollars and American bombs cascading through their opium dreams. In the prints of the world they will be hailed as *Mujahiddin,* those fierce "holy warriors" who, from their havens in Pakistan, will direct the war against the infidel, interrupting their labors only for quick *Hajj* to London and Washington, which has effectually replaced Mecca for them.

Those foreigners who tried to breach Afghanistan's historic loneliness, which they cultivated behind the Durand Line, had come as marauders. They came for booty, and getting it, left. It was the British alone who stayed. The British were not content, as were Genghis Khan's warriors, to speed their horses through camp, sweep up what riches they could as they went by, and then speed out into oblivion again. The British wanted not only the booty of the present but of the future. They wanted to *grow* their slaves. And it was they whom the Afghans could not forget nor forgive.

To the British the Afghans were "savages," "barbarous." A hundred years later the American writer Paul Theroux, setting out to go around the world by train, was astounded to discover, in 1975, that there were no trains in Afghanistan because there were no railroads in Afghanistan.*

For him "Afghanistan is a nuisance. Formerly it was cheap and barbarous, and people went there to buy lumps of hashish—they would spend weeks in the filthy hotels of Herat and Kabul, staying high. . . Now Afghanistan is expensive but just as barbarous as before. Even the hippies have begun to find it intolerable. The food smells of cholera, travel there is always uncomfortable and sometimes dangerous, and the Afghans are lazy, idle and violent." (*The Great Railway Bazaar*, by Paul Theroux.)

Amazing as that is, still more amazing than what was known about Afghanistan before December 1979—when Americans at least still had no awareness of the country at all—is what became "known" subsequently. "The trouble with people," Josh Billings had remarked in his day, "is not that they don't know but that they know so much that ain't so."

In April 1979, when Zbigniew Brzezinski, then President Carter's National Security Adviser, though not exactly Adviser to Cyrus Vance, was asked by an interviewer from the *U.S. News & World Report* why "the Carter administration has been afraid to use American military power in crisis areas," the National Security Adviser very reasonably, not yet having seen arcs that were unstable in that area of the world, replied: "I feel it [the criticism of cowardice] was not well founded. The fact of the matter is that in the crises of the last two years, circumstances clearly mitigated against a direct display of presence of American power ... as in the case of Afghanistan, the area was remote from the reach of U.S. power."

But that same year the Afghanistan that had been "remote" in April had miraculously—mainly through the "miracle" of television—become near and menacing, "the greatest threat to peace since World War II" (Carter),

---

* Except one small narrow-gauge railroad constructed by the Germans but soon discontinued. Later the Soviets began to build one across Amu Darya.

by December. The question arises therefore: what had happened to chase the hippies out of Afghanistan one year and bring Carter in soon after?

Why did Afghanistan become such a swelling wound allegedly poisoning the conscience of the world precisely on the night of December 27th, 1979? On that night a certain Hafizullah Amin, known in the prints of the Western world as a "hard-core Communist," who had come to power over the body of Noor Mohammad Taraki, also a "hard-core Communist," a scant four months before, had himself "gone to his God," as Kipling would put it at an earlier time, before a firing squad. Oddly enough, there were very few in Afghanistan itself to mourn his going. In fact, there had been dancing in the streets of Kabul when his death became known. But, surprisingly, there was one man in far-off America who had never been to Afghanistan, who hated all Communists but now shed a public tear for one, and a "hard-core" Communist at that! He was an unlikely mourner at that bier, but his grief was genuine. His name was Jimmy Carter.

"Why," as Artemus Ward asked at an earlier occasion, "these weeps?" Why should the capitalist-minded Carter weep for the Communist-minded Amin?

This was surprising—indeed as surprising as to be told that a "defender of Islam" had been born in that born-again Baptist, and surprising too to hear him declare that Amin was the "legitimate" president of Afghanistan, at whose demise the free world should stand at respectful attention, though it was Amin who had obviously murdered his "friend and teacher," Noor Mohammad Taraki, only months before, the man who had had a hand in the assassination of Adolph Dubs, the American ambassador to Afghanistan.

Taraki's widow, released from prison, had cried bitterly in a letter to President Carter: "I am angered and shocked ... by the fact that you are trying to protect this criminal and murderer, Amin ... this plotter, this apostate, who was not averse to using most insidious methods... *He killed my husband!"*

That same evening of the day when Babrak Karmal gave his first interview to the Western press in Chelsutoon Palace, in January 1980 I watched a replay of that interview (in which I had asked a strange question) on television at the Kabul Hotel.

When Babrak Karmal cried to the men from BBC: "You are the face of British imperialism! Three times you got a bloody nose from the Afghans" —a cheer broke out from the small group of hotel workers who had left their tables uncleared and floors unwashed to come and listen. The fears of real people explain ghosts. The ghost of British imperialism had been conjured up by Karmal not because he feared the British. The British no longer had their old power. A new power had come to haunt them.

LOOKING FOR A WAR

> Take up the White Man's burden—
>   Send forth the best ye breed—
> Go bind your sons to exile
>   To serve your captives' neea;
> To wait in heavy harness,
>   On fluttered and wild—
> Your new-caught, sullen people,
>   Half-devil, half-child...
> Take up the White Man's burden
>   And reap his old reward :
> The blame of those ye better,
>   The hate of those ye guard—
> The cry of hosts ye humor
>   (Ah, slowly!) toward the light—
> "Why brought ye us from bondage,
>   Our loved Egyptian night?"

Rudyard Kipling,
The White Man's Burden

Why did Great Britain try, not once but three times, to bring "the light" to the Afghans, to take on the "hate" of these ungrateful people, half-devil, half-child, who for over 100 years resisted with all their being those glowing gifts of British imperialism that a noble people, headed by a "gracious Queen," in all their generosity yearned to bestow on them?

True, perfidious Albion in the end gave up trying—but only after shifting the burden of empire onto the shoulders of Americans who carry it so much more eagerly today. But why did the British come at all, so far from home, and why did they keep on coming, taking one "bloody nose" after the other —and does this past of theirs have anything to teach us about our present?

Most Americans, it's true, know very little of what took place in their own past, let alone the British. They tend to agree with Henry Ford that "history is bunk." So perhaps they take on trust Kipling's rhymed version of historical event, content to check his view against Hollywood's at the local cinema, where sooner or later (or on TV's Late Show) Gary Cooper, or Errol Flynn, or Clark Gable (still working though long dead) will show up at the Khyber Pass and explain it all to us again as the "Great Game that never ceases day or night."

So, for most of the "world" (in mid-19th century), Afghanistan had no real existence of its own. There was no reason to watch it. Britain's excessive interest in it seemed, from afar, hardly more than the assumed "burden" it had chosen to carry in its zeal to "serve" the ends of civilization, and however untidy the process, nobody could question the nobility of the aim.

It would have taken a hardy soul indeed to have stated, in the mid-19th century, that unknown Afghanistan would one day move extraordinarily close to America and become known to it in a most unforeseen way.

And yet there was such a hardy soul. From London he was writing for the *New York Daily Tribune,* and among the many mysteries and secrets of current and past events that he was unraveling for his inattentive American readers (including why at the height of the Confederate victories, the Southern oligarchy of slaveowners—already historically out of date—would inevitably lose the war) the mystery of why the British had gone into Afghanistan in the 19th century and why, if we had read him closely then, we would understand that we should *not* in the 20th.

He, of course, was Karl Marx who, with his closest collaborator and friend Frederick Engels, kept a sharp watch on events everywhere. Uncannily prophetic, Marx found the future not in studying the entrails of chickens or in the stars but in concrete reality as it unfolded itself before his eyes. In explaining to the world what Britain's Lord Palmerston was made up of he would be explaining to us *(mutatis mutandis)* what made up a Carter, a Brzezinski, a Zia ul-Haq, even a Mao Tse-tung.

Then (in the mid-1800s) as now, candor about the real motives of politicians was hard to come by. Swathed in the robes of the most altruistic and high-minded rhetoric, the reality of imperialist necessity was almost impossible for contemporaries to discern. But so overwhelming was this *need* —this drive for empire—quite independent of individual motives, morality and home-town behavior, and even in defiance of them, this need demanded its way. The rapist's overwhelming need pays no attention to custom or law: it makes its own law. Imperialism is also rape.

Thus it was that when it was deemed necessary to go into Afghanistan— an unoffending nation tucked behind and among the grimmest of mountains —Lord Palmerston could not afford to let his countrymen know the real reason why he sent British soldiers so far from home to die (as many of them did!). In fact, he never told the British people at all what had happened nor why. Marx, however, was not bound by British imperial needs, and he told his American readers of the *Tribune* precisely what, in fact, had happened—Palmerston justified the invasion of Afghanistan by saying Sir Alexander Burnes had advised this to be done as a means of countering Russian intrigue in Central Asia...

Amazingly enough, even then this charge, made over 150 years ago and though made against Czarist Russia for which Marx had no love, was nevertheless a lie. Sir Alexander Burnes, sent as a special envoy on an imperial mission to the warring Afghan chiefs, had said no such thing. This charge had been invented by Palmerston, who needed a pretext. Thus, Palmerston's first war (1838-42), undertaken without the knowledge of Parliament, was the Afghan war, mitigated and justified by forged documents. (See the article, "The London 'Times' and Lord Palmerston" by Karl Marx, published in the *New-York Daily Tribune*, Oct. 21, 1861.)

So the British learned that gentlemen can—and do—lie: history is replete with instances of the most squalid lying perpetrated by men in high places for ends that were low. This particular instance, when it finally broke upon the British people, shocked them, much as the American people would be shocked a century later by similar instances of malfeasance in high office.

A special commission, investigating the "hidden" war that was waged while England slept (and whose conscience was awakened no doubt because the war had ended in disaster, much as was the Americans' by a war in Vietnam which also ended in disaster), came up with this unprecedentedly scathing report: "This war of robbery is waged by the English Government through the intervention of the Government of India (without the knowledge of England, or of Parliament and the Court of Directors); thereby evading the check placed by the Constitution on the exercise of the prerogative of the Crown in declaring war. It presents, therefore, a new crime in the annals of nations—*a secret war*! It has been made by a people without their knowledge, against another people who had committed no offense."* (From "Report of the East India Committee on Causes and Consequences of the First Afghan War"—1838-1842. Italics in the original.)

So, trying to fix what Afghanistan was, and how one should see its people, and one's own relationship to them, had been part of a fierce ideological struggle in which *forgery* and slanted *interpretation* based on forgery, and newspaper reports that did not report the facts, played important roles in Great Britain a hundred years ago.

As to reports from later journalists on the later scene (there would be other clashes), they would arrive at the British breakfast table under the by-line of the young journalist Winston Churchill (1897), who summed Afghans all up as "...dangerous and as sensible as mad dogs, fit to be treated as such." (*The Story of the Malaband Field Force* by Winston Churchill.)

Countered Frederick Engels, the other pair of eyes watching the British in Afghanistan: "...Afghans are a courageous, vigorous and freedom-loving people..." (*New American Cyclopedia*, 1958.)

Explaining: "The supreme necessity of never-ceasing expansion of trade —this *fatum* which spectre-like haunts England..."

---

* Like the secret war conducted by the U.S.A. in Laos for a decade.

Said Theroux, the latest of the modern "travelers" whom we have met again more than once since Marco Polo and listened to their marvelous tales: ". . . Afghans are lazy, idle and violent."

But Karl Marx wrote that on the walls of Jalalabad . . . the sentries espied a man in tattered English uniform, on a miserable pony, horse and man desperately wounded. . . And another commentator would note that the British colonel waiting eagerly for news of the 15,000-man expedition that had left Kabul believed this man in a tattered uniform was bringing him good news: "Here comes the messenger!" he cried.

But this "messenger" was all that was left of the 15,000 British soldiers who had set out from Kabul weeks before. "It was Dr. Brydon, the sole survivor. . ." Marx noted, and he was dying of starvation.*

Wrote Kipling bitterly:

> *When you're wounded and left on the plains*
> *An' the women come out to cut up what remains*
> *Just roll to your rifle and blow out your brains*
> *An' go to your God like a soldier.*

That is the message for imperialism which the Doctor brought.

---

* *Notes on Indian History* by Karl Marx. Actually there were other survivors, prisoners, 35 officers and 51 soldiers, as well as some European civilians. There were also survivors among the Sepoy infantry which accompanied the British. As for Dr. Brydon, he went on to become Surgeon William Brydon, Commander of the Bath.

FURNISHING A WAR

> Everything is quiet. There is no trouble here.
> There will be no war. I wish to return.
>
> Remington (from Havana, 1897)

> Please remain. You furnish the pictures and I'll
> furnish the war.
>
> W. R. Hearst
(Editor & owner of New York Journal,
in an exchange of cablegrams)

In 1897 Frederick Remington, a newspaper cartoonist who had been sent to Cuba by William Randolph Hearst, Sr. to find a war, had cabled back to his boss in New York that he could find no war.

Unperturbed, Hearst nevertheless ordered him to stay in Cuba and assured him that he would be duly furnished with a war. The U.S. battleship *Maine* was forthwith blown up (Feb. 18, 1898) and, "By Jingo!" Remington had his war. Dewey took Manila and Theodore Roosevelt took Cuba. And meanwhile the pictures kept on coming.

"Where the hell is the war?" Jim Gallagher of the *New York Daily News* cried in January 1980 with mixed anger and frustration once he had landed in Kabul and had found the city alive with cars, buses and trollies, and people hustling back and forth, but no soldiers, no "red animal war." The 200 or so other foreign correspondents stationed in Kabul's best hotel, the Intercontinental, were also just as confused, and couldn't tell him either.

Meanwhile Carter in Washington was clamoring for the press to "build a chorus" of condemnation of the Soviets for "invading" Afghanistan, and the presumption was that Kabul, the capital, was now under armed occupation and the war was raging everywhere. Surely nobody can hide a whole war in our day: total electronic surveillance–the way Palmerston could in his? The army of foreign correspondents had come expecting to see it right there in front of them: how could you miss seeing tanks rushing against a terrified but heroically resisting populace? They had been told to expect to see Soviet soldiers, bullies in uniform, armed to the teeth, crowding the sidewalks, butting the sullen people out of the way, shooting down children— tyrants from the land of the working class!

And yet, "Where the hell is the war?"

Meanwhile the *New York Daily News* was champing at the bit: it wanted "pictures," and quickly. But where could you get them? Where was the war hiding? Kabul was as quiet as Sunday at home. How could you build a chorus when there were no notes to build it with?

I, too, came looking for a war. On my way to Kabul I read in my copy of the *International Herald Tribune* (owned jointly by *The Washington Post* and *The New York Times,* published in Paris or, when Paris is on strike, in London—simulcasting itself in five other printing plants, as far off as Hong Kong) that since I landed in Kabul I would find no Afghan soldier with his own gun.

This is what I read on my plane: "Two travelers, arriving in New Delhi reported ... that the few Afghan soldiers that they had seen guarding the airport and public buildings in Kabul in the last two days..."—This was dated Jan. 9 and I arrived next morning—"were conspicuously unarmed. The travelers, both businessmen, said that this seemed to support reports that Afghan units had been disarmed." And this dispatch was datelined New Delhi.

The first thing I saw—almost falling into his arms—as I came down the steps of the plane that had just landed at Kabul airport (I checked to see that it *was* Kabul airport), drowsy-footed and grainy-eyed from a sleepless night's ride, was an Afghan soldier standing on the tarmac, his bayonet-gleaming rifle at ready. This bared bayonet made him seem conspicuously armed, I thought.

The second thing I saw when I entered the airport waiting room was another Afghan, but this one in civilian clothes though he was obviously no mere civilian. Whoever he was he carried a submachine gun slung over his shoulder as carelessly as a schoolboy slings his satchel of books. Nevertheless he looked conspicuously armed, and unmistakably Afghan.

The third thing I saw when I entered the air terminal, but which I was not supposed to see at all, here or anywhere, was an old peasant unroll his prayer mat and, spreading it on the stone floor facing Mecca (which is how I deduced where Saudi Arabia was), fell on his knees, bending low until his forehead touched the mat. And so he prayed. You could hear the faint calls of the mullahs from the mosques somewhere not too far away. We would learn later that we were hearing *azan*—the call to prayer which would be made every morning, and four more times during the day until night fell. "Allah-o-Akhbar—God is great. There is no God but Allah. Mohammed is the Messenger of God. Come to pray, come to prosper!"

So, with one foot hardly firmly planted on Kabul soil, I had experienced three surprises.

But the fourth thing, which I was supposed to see *first,* I did not see at all. *I saw no Soviet soldier* (that is, "the war"). Those watching Kabul from New York and Washington saw Soviet soldiers jamming the city streets. In Kabul itself I saw none. To reassure the reader that my eyesight is normal enough (and even to reassure myself) I cite this story from the same *Herald Tribune:*

> Journalists entering the country found few signs of the large Soviet military presence, however. Afghan troops patrolled the streets in sub-zero weather with the Soviet troops and tanks presence at a minimum. (IHT, Jan. 7, 1980, from Kabul.)

So it was the very first day. So it would be for the eight days I spent in Kabul in January, and for the almost two weeks I would spend there again in July: searching for a war, searching for the Russians, searching for an oppressed and tyrannized populace.

It was then that I made my first acquaintance with those extraordinary sources of information about Afghanistan whose reliability was to be as unquestioned as their anonymity was absolute: "travelers," "diplomats," "area specialists," "businessmen," "experts," all of whom managed to pass back and forth between Peshawar in Pakistan and Kabul in Afghanistan through the fiercest of battles, tank encirclements and an entire Soviet army encamped in Kabul itself, with greater ease than one can get past the guard at the New York Fifth Avenue library!

Later we will learn more precisely why newsmen were so coy about revealing the identity of their sources—why the "diplomat" they cited remained so tactfully unnamed and why, in fact, "Western diplomats" remained in Kabul at all, especially the Americans after the assassination of Ambassador Adolph Dubs in 1979.

Meanwhile we were in Kabul, and what is Kabul? It is a city of indeterminate population—estimated at 800,000 to a million—and is tucked inside a valley of the Hindu Kush mountain range, some 1,800 kilometers above sea level. The city itself is between two "local" mountains, the Kohe Azama and the Kohe Sherdarwazah. A broad treelined avenue, the Maivand (paved, as were all of Kabul's main streets, by the Russians in 1953), cuts the city in half: it was at Maivand that the Afghans had defeated the British in 1880.

The Kabul River runs through the valley almost up to the border with Pakistan where it turns off into the Peshawar Valley. The valley will take you to the Khyber Pass some 90 miles away where, if you're lucky—or unlucky—you will see a strange mime performed in a few weeks—in February —when a high official of the United States will pose there for the cameras of the world aiming a Chinese machine gun at where you are now standing!

You had read in the press that you would find Kabul choked with Russian tanks and you were prepared to find them, but found none: except when, pushing through the tangled, uncontrolled traffic, you broke into Revolutionary Square, and there it was: that "minimal" Russian tank.

17

It stood, unquestionably Russian but already congealed in arrested time, slightly greening as though with a first wash—history had been in too much of a hurry to add age. It is the first tank that led the assault on the palace on April 27, 1978 which toppled Prince Daoud, and now stands perched on a pedestal waiting for History.

We shall explore Kabul more carefully later. At the moment we can give its tourist attractions no more than a passing glance.

Though clashes would break out later—especially in February—as far as we could see in the first days of January Kabul was quiet, and no houses danced. And yet, as we were aware, surface quiet was extraordinarily misleading. For though where we stood all was silence, around us the air was boiling with sound. We took to our transistors where we finally found the war we had been looking for.

It was a peculiar war. It was a war *for* a war. It was a war of words calling for a war of bullets. The U.N. was in session in New York that week, discussing what was happening in Kabul. It was part of the strangeness of the situation, even its eeriness, that so much talk should be going on in New York ostensibly about what we were looking at and not seeing. Carter was crying that what had happened here "was the most dangerous threat to peace since World War II"—* this very "invasion of Afghanistan" by Soviet troops which, though "massive," had shown itself to us only as a "minimal presence!"

We were watching a film whose sound was out of sync, not only with the lips of the performers but with the visible actions as well.

Men and women of over 150 nations at the U.N. were debating "facts" which, one would realize with growing clarity as time slipped by, had no tangibility. Afghanistan, the real Afghanistan of *fact*, of his old man on his burro coming into town to sell a bundle of firewood, did not exist. Something else had been created: a grotesque monster of the new Cold War, so recently disinterred from what had been hoped was its permanent grave, now superimposed over the reality. It was not so much Palmerston's "secret war" which he had managed to conduct out of sight of the British Parliament and the British people. This was something different—an ordered war, a war that was sent for and delivered. It was a war that started as fictional images on TV. A war that took place first in the imaginations of millions of Americans and so became a strange kind of fact after all. And only then did it become "real."

If there had been no intervention here by the West (i.e. the U.S.A.), there would have been no war at all.

---

* "For us, it is conventional wisdom that the President of the United States lies. That was unthinkable before the 60s." Rep. Gerry E. Stubbs (Dem. Mass), NYT, Apr. 5, 1982.

The Afghans have a fierce game called *Buzkhasi*. Mounted on their marvelous horses (so admired by Alexander the Great), they chase a headless calf like a polo ball, which the horses kick from rider to rider, until finally one rider manages to snatch it up and deposit it, bloody, battered and useless, in the winner's circle: food only for dogs.

Those correspondents who fell on Afghanistan that week in January and scourged the countryside in a desperate search to find the war that was already blazing in the newspaper headlines of the West were involved in a kind of fierce *Buzkhasi* of their own. But instead of a headless calf it was the battered and bloody truth which they deposited in the winner's circle: food only for dogs.

"You furnish the pictures and I'll furnish the war," the ghost of William Randolph Hearst inspired them all.

WAITING FOR KARMAL

We had been frisked by swift hands, sniffed at by a ticking metal-detector as we passed through a security check in the Foreign Office. There were about 200 of "us," foreign, mainly Western correspondents, representing all the "interested" countries of the world which had responded to the Karmal government's invitation to come and see.

Standing there among the crowd of correspondents, waiting to be frisked and marveling that I was there at all, I became conscious of another, purely Western element in the casual conversations that went on behind me. Three years in Moscow had almost made me forget this particular species of noisy, self-assured "sophisticated" prattle, which seemed to have been transported bodily from some New York, Paris or London cocktail lounge or cocktail party, complete with inside jokes and arcane references to a way of life I had happily put behind me. To this crowd, being here in Kabul seemed nothing more than a bothersome interruption to an otherwise self-absorbed life, inverted toward a center of Western power.

At certain points in Europe or places like Hong Kong, waiting there like firemen, small groups of American, British, French and West German TV and newsmen are kept on hold. They are waiting for the call from their home offices to move into action. World crises breaking determine their tomorrows. Once a crisis does break in some part of the world—a statesman, a Pope, a King or President assassinated—they scoop up their ever-ready overnight bags and are off by the soonest airplane.

Their assignment is to move fast, get to the scene before any others, take their pictures early so they can be processed without delay and appear on the night's TV screens all over the world. They know that the first image will be the controlling image for all that follows. But it must meet certain qualifications. It must be dramatic.

If, as so often happens, the dramatic event that brought them there in the first place can no longer be caught on film, some equivalent for the event must be found.

There is a name for them already: "crisis correspondents." They commute from crisis to crisis like ambulance chasers. So quickly do dramatic events break sometimes that such correspondents often have no time to familiarize themselves with the issues in any depth, or sort out all the players, or even precisely locate their destinations, and you can see them huddled in their seats on the plane poring over maps still crinkling from their newness, and picking each other's already overpicked brains.

The moment their planes set down at the airport whose name is often undecipherable in the native script (as Afghanistan's is), they make a dash for the embassy and there are quickly briefed by an officer who swears them to keeping his own identity secret but gives them carte blanche indulgence in the use of everything he's told them. They are free to quote but not to name the source.

By nightfall they already know all they need to know about the situation, who the main actors are, what the main elements of the crisis are—and where the nearest bar is.

For these journalists who had descended on Kabul that morning there was no month of grace reserved for them to make up their minds about Afghanistan. But they didn't need a month. For even as they were still fumbling with their maps to locate Afghanistan, they already knew what to think of it. Anti-Sovietism for them is an ever-reliable compass which always points north. It is a moveable feast. They had packed their opinions with their socks: they had come full tilt.

But by this time—as we waited—the metal snuffler had sniffed through our clothes as well, and finding nothing hidden inside our coats let us pass through with the weapons inside our minds undiscovered. We were ready to deal with Afghanistan, each in his own fashion.

Most of the foreign press was quartered in the deluxe Intercontinental Hotel on the hill overlooking the city. Mecca for tourists, it was equipped with all the modern necessities: cool bar and warm pool. We of the Western socialist press had been put into the Kabul Hotel in the center of town, within sight of the bazaars and well within sound of the muezzin calls to prayer from a nearby mosque (of which Kabul has 560). A loudspeaker played songs all day long which we were also obliged to hear. Nearby the Kabul River was so low one could walk across it. In this hotel, on the floor where I had a room, Ambassador Adolph Dubs had been held prisoner and perished in a hail of bullets on February 14, 1979, when Amin's men, disregarding advice to parley with the kidnappers, had stormed the rooms where he was being held.

Our first concern as correspondents was to locate the Telex office. We found it five minutes away from our hotel. It has been blown up by the "rebels," the newspapers had informed us, just days before. If so, it was operating now. There the group of young Afghan English-speaking medical students who had been assigned to us as guides and interpreters would take our copy to be telexed to New York, after first getting the censor's approval.

Most of the Western correspondents did not use this Telex, did not submit their copy to censorship. Supplied with diplomatic courier service by the American embassy (whose concern that the world learn the truth about Afghanistan was awe-inspiring) and other Western embassies, they sent their copy by plane every day to New Delhi from where it was filed to their home offices around the Western world. (The "West" is a flexible term and can include Japan and exclude Cuba.)

They had broken into Kabul like Hollywood cowboys on Saturday night —noisily, wildly, ready to shoot from the hip. They stormed into the hotels and stormed out again. They crowded the American embassy. They dickered with taxi drivers to take them "where the fighting was." One group of Americans, loaned a jeep by the ever-cooperative embassy staff, rode off into the countryside, without bothering to ask anybody's permission, looking for the Russians who had been announced as coming for so many years and yet had never quite arrived; and finally finding one halfway on the road to Damascus, shared a bowl of soup with him!

And so they found them at last: up on the hills, guarding the crossroads, scanning the horizon over which Pakistan was watching and waiting too to see which way the wind would blow. Nothing moved. There was no firing, no guns shooting. Occasionally one heard about sniper fire. A Russian soldier, laughing, showed you his bandaged hand and offered to exchange a Soviet cigarette for an American Winston.

This is how they caught Russia red-handed! Just in time for the evening news!

THE BATTLE FOR THE MIKE

Karmal's appearance in the room, accompanied by Sultan Ali Kesht-mand, vice-premier, was greeted by a flurry of applause from the socialist press but with a hostile silence, slightly modified with a glimmering of curiosity, from the bourgeois press.

At 51 (in 1980) Karmal is an intense, watchful man whose eloquent style of speaking seems to address itself not only to ears listening to him at the moment but to other ears unseen. As we looked him over he looked us over as well.

Behind him on the wall hung two portraits, one of Noor Mohammad Taraki, around whose death there still hung a great cloud of mystery, and the other of Mir Akbar Khybar, then unknown to most of the correspondents in the room. He was one of the founders of the People's Democratic Party of Afghanistan, a leading theoretician, and it was his murder by Daoud's police (acting, it would be charged, on orders from the Shah of Iran whose SAVAK, under American guidance, was already operating in Afghanistan) that had sparked the massive uprising in April 1978 that led directly to the overthrow of the Daoud government.

His black eyes flashing, his smile tilted at an ironic angle as he observed his enemies, Karmal launched on his press conference discarding all amenities. He lashed out:

> Friendly and unfriendly journalists!
> I thank the former on behalf of the PDPA*, the DRA**, the freedom-loving, valiant and independent people of Afghanistan! Likewise, I point out to the unfriendly journalists who have come here from the West, from imperialist nations and those attached to them, that when the CIA agent murdered the late Noor Mohammad Taraki, the first general secretary of the PDPA CC, the first president of the RC***, and the Prime Minister of the DRA in collusion with the CIA plot, and usurped the legitimate government in a conspiratorial manner, where were you journalists then?

* People's Democratic Party of Afghanistan.
** Democratic Republic of Afghanistan.
*** Revolutionary Council.

This was the first official allusion to Amin in which he was specifically charged with being a CIA agent. It was also the first time we were officially informed that Noor Mohammad Taraki, who had led the April (Saur) 1978 Revolution that overthrew Daoud, had been murdered on Amin's orders.

In September, hardly three months before, Taraki had returned from a meeting of the non-aligned countries in Havana, stopping in Moscow *en route*. Hardly did Taraki reach Kabul than the news came out that, after resigning all his positions in the Party and the government because of "health reasons," he had suddenly died in October.

Amin had taken over all other key posts (he was already Prime Minister and directly controlled the secret police force KAM and the army) and so emerged as the apparently unchallenged dictator of the country.

This is what we "knew"—most of it twisted.

Karmal went on:

> You unfriendly journalists, you so-called champions of the "Free World," led by Mr. Carter, where were you? Gentlemen, when the CIA agent (Hafizullah Amin) was savagely terrorizing our people and tens of thousands of our compatriots, including workers, peasants, honest clergy, the intelligentsia and men of learning, were chained, or groups of them sent to jails and chambers of horrors, or massacred, where were you?...
>
> Now please put your questions.

Well, that was more like throwing down the gauntlet for a battle than the opening to a press conference. True, the Western press for days had been noisy with the kind of hostile stories that would sound over the Western world in an even greater roar in the next few weeks. Their composite voice would rise higher and higher until it reached a kind of shrill peak— the "chorus" Carter had wanted so badly to be 'built". By this time at this press conference Karmal had obviously realized that he had let not objective witnesses into the country but, from his point of view, something more dubious, which probably accounted for his own bristly manner. And in the next hour he would realize it even better, as a fierce battle for the microphone broke out among the correspondents in the room—a battle that represented in microcosm the greater ideological battle raging everywhere in the world, and into which these correspondents, it became obvious, had been sent as shock troops, at "great expense."

Thus, from the moment the floor was opened for questions the Western correspondents leaped to the attack. According to the ground rules as explained by Rahim Rafat, editor of the *Kabul New Times,* who acted as monitor and interpreter both, one question only would be permitted each correspondent.

And they had questions! They had brought the questions with them, hot on the griddle. In a moment it became only too clear why Karmal was anticipating "unfriendly" journalists. They intended to be hampered by nobody's rules. For example, instead of asking one question (all that was allotted to them) they asked one question "in three parts." When the one question with three parts was answered—and that took up a great deal of time —they passed the microphone on to another Western correspondent—obviously there had been collusion here—who was primed, in his turn, to ask another question with three parts. And as this process lengthened the socialist correspondents waited with dwindling patience and growing consternation for the microphone to come their way.

They would have a long, long wait! As each question exploded and it became clear how things were going, the indignation (and then, finally, the panic) of the socialist press, including the socialist press from the capitalist countries, began to mount, and these correspondents belatedly realized that unless they got rid of their good manners they would be left, empty-handed and wordless, out in the cold. So finally, throwing aside those home-grown good manners and civilian restraint, they jumped feet first into what had already become a melee and now immediately broke into a brawl.

Shouting and yelling, pushing and shoving for the mike, the correspondents would in a moment have been at each other's throats. The room had become a bedlam. And at one point in the wild, swinging mass, as Rahim Rafat struggled to restore order, Karmal, calmly surveying the scene, remarked with evident irony: "Typical anarchism of the bourgeois."

The fact was that the world struggle had condensed into this moment. I found myself watching with a concentrated absorption, forgetting that I had a role to play. The man from ABC-TV, the mike gripped in his fist, asked Karmal sarcastically when Soviet troops would leave the country. Karmal replied that they would leave "whenever the aggressive policy of American imperialism, now in collusion with Peking leaders, and the provocation and plots of reactionary circles in Pakistan, Egypt, Saudi Arabia, etc., and the danger of aggression are eliminated—on that same day and that same moment the limited Soviet contingent will leave for home."

Abroad, Americans have to get used to being called "imperialists," not as just a curse word but as a self-evident description of their role in the world. They may boggle at it, but beyond the borders of myth they must deal with it or not deal at all. So he let the characterization pass, and handed the mike to the man from CBS.

The CBS man in his turn now launched into *his* three-tiered "question," and disregarding the answer—the point was to have the "question" recorded —he then passed the mike on to another Western correspondent as the socialist press fumed and cursed. It was something like the game adults tease children with—tossing a ball between two of them as the child vainly tries to reach up and, intercept it. Thus NBC, having run out of Americans, now passed the mike to BBC, its British "ally." Waiting in line were reporters from West Germany, Finland, India, Japan—all of them primed with questions with a slightly different inflection but still recognizable as the same goods from the same larder. They all spoke English and their questions all dovetailed with the others from the West.

When it came his turn, the man from BBC, in the silky, upper-class tones of the British landed gentry that had intimidated the British lower classes and countless fuzzy-wuzzies in the Empire for centuries, came up with this question:

> His excellency Brezhnev, in his congratulatory telegram, felicited you on the occasion of your election in a democratic manner as head of the Afghan government. My question is, on what basis were you democratically elected and under what conditions did this election take place? By the same token, had you been so elected, why did the Soviet forces help you to take power?

Coming from a British source whose empire had been brought into existence without the formality of peoples voting anywhere—including when the British were in Afghanistan itself—this "question" must have been particularly galling to Karmal. It was his answer that I would listen to again as it was replayed that evening as I sat with the workers at the Kabul Hotel before the television set, and which had brought out spontaneous cheers:

> You are the old face of British imperialism which invaded our country three times in the past and three times you got a bloody nose from the Afghans!
> I will answer your question in this way. If you recall, following the Saur (April) Revolution, I was vice-president of the Revolutionary Council, Deputy Prime Minister, and Secretary of the People's Democratic Party. After the plot hatched by the CIA and American imperialism represented by Amin and the Aminis, and the martyrdom of the late Noor Mohammad Taraki, the largest majority of the committed members of the PDPA CC and those of the RC together decided to destroy the CIA band represented by Hafizullah Amin.
> At that time, on the basis of principles followed by our Party and government, they nominated me as General Secretary of the PDPA CC, President of the RC and Prime Minister of the DRA.
> When I returned two months ago to my homeland through revolutionary routes and contacted the majority of the PDPA members and of the RC, we adopted all the necessary measures before American imperialism could implement their aggressive plan from the Pakistani borders.
> At that time, due to the wisdom and the awareness of the people of Afghanistan, a meeting was held which condemned the CIA agent, Hafizullah Amin, to execution, and decided to launch the second phase of the Saur Revolution.

Karmal could also have added that he had represented his Kabul constituency in Afghanistan's Parliament, to which he had been elected in 1965, re-elected in 1969, and was still serving when Parliament was abolished by Prince Daoud in the 1973 coup that overthrew King Zahir.

Karmal had been a student leader while still studying law at Kabul University, and at the age of 20 was already a revolutionary. He was arrested and spent five years in prison for his political activities. Released, he finished his law studies and worked in the Planning Ministry of the Daoud government from 1957 to 1965 when he became one of the founding members of the PDPA along with Noor Mohammad Taraki. He dates his conscious revolutionary activity as a Marxist since 1963.

But there was no time for his biography. A Finnish newswoman who had now gotten hold of the mike—as it passed me by—and noting, for openers, that "Afghan leaders had been killing each other," asked Karmal whether he too might not be murdered in his turn. Karmal, smiling slightly, replied with studied courtesy: "I can assure you, respected lady, that the last vestige of the plots of the murderous CIA will come to an end in Afghanistan..."

But hardly had she finished scribbling down Karmal's answer when a West German, to whom she had passed on the mike, was up "wondering if, with Soviet troops on Afghan territory, Afghanistan still considered itself to be non-aligned?"

Karmal said: "Yes."

An AP correspondent now wanted to know "if Western reports were right, that there are about 75,000 Soviet troops in Afghanistan. Or would that," he added, losing the courage of someone else's convictions, for he too had been led to believe he would see a Kabul choked with Soviet soldiers and had seen none, "be an exaggeration?"

The question of how many Soviet troops actually had come into the country—how large was the "limited contingent?"—had already become a bouncing ball that refused to settle on any one number.

The Soviets had never improved on their original statement of the "limited contingent" which had come into Afghanistan at the request of the legitimate Afghan government to help secure Afghan "borders" against outside aggression and, as Karmal had just stated, to remain as long as it was necessary to do that and no longer. But this formulation left the field wide open to speculation, and speculation rode the elevator ever upward.

The figures went, like Excelsior, ever onward and upward.* Then, suddenly, in Washington a few weeks later (Feb. 21), a kind of bombshell exploded: *The Washington Post* was reporting that the "Carter administration officials yesterday revised their estimates of the Soviet troop presence in Afghanistan, putting the total at 70,000 in contrast to the 90,000 or 100,000 issued by the State Department during recent weeks..."

---

* In 1983, they would—by American count—reach 110,000. But who did the counting and whether parts were counted for the whole nobody would tell.

Said the *Post:* "The high estimate, he ["an Administration official"] added, stemmed from counting *elements* of a division in Afghanistan as a *full* division.

"The purpose of issuing the refined estimate last night, Administration officials said, was to *undercut* any Soviet claims that they had begun a withdrawal from Afghanistan. Meanwhile, U.S. officials announced that a second flight of B-52 bombers had been sent over the Arabian sea and a third would be launched soon. . ." (All italics mine).

That the Carter Administration, as early as February, was worried that the Soviets might begin the withdrawal of troops from Afghanistan (which they actually did do in June) is perhaps a tip-off of how far ahead Administration strategists were thinking. The Administration was willing, in order to "undercut" any future Soviet moves to withdraw troops, to admit—to *insist*—that its early mathematics in estimating how many Soviet troops had actually come into Afghanistan was all cock-eyed. Counting *elements of* a division for a *full* division! No wonder 40,000 jumped to 90,000 in a week!

The aim of the Carter Administration, one soon began to suspect (and later would have confirmed), was not to get Soviet troops out of Afghanistan but to *keep* them in as long as possible. Carter was reaping too many political benefits from the situation to throw them all away in one gesture! Or so he thought. But this was all in the future. Meanwhile there was the question still hanging which the AP man had launched at Karmal. To him Karmal now replied: "Evidently these (figures) are an exaggeration. Aren't you familiar with the lie factories in the West?"

Ouch! The AP man didn't care for that. In any case, he retreated in favor of another questioner who wanted to know how many Soviet troops had been "wounded, killed, or taken prisoner"—figures that also would run the gamut, in the stories that followed, from "few hundreds" to "many thousands." To this question—with the Soviet troops as of January 10th in the country hardly more than three weeks—Karmal replied cryptically: "None of them."

It was a flat denial, and at that stage could very likely have been true. Up until that point I myself had heard of only one authenticated Soviet soldier casualty—and that was a hand wound by a sniper. In any case, no reliable figures of casualties would be forthcoming, for some time, from Soviet or from "rebel" sources.

It came to me with a jolt halfway through the press conference to realize suddenly that I was being included among the casualties there for we had been warned that Karmal's time was limited and he would soon be off, and the question I had nursed for flight all morning would die never having freed its wings.

As though propelled by no command from me, my hand suddenly shot out into the middle of the melee after that mike which the West German newsman, his "question" rebuffed, was passing on to a bourgeois newsman from India. Our hands met together on the mike and lo, for a grim moment we found ourselves engaged in real Indian handwrestling! As the unleashed American I now was I am sure I terrified him for, catching sight of my face, he let go almost instantly, and for a moment I looked at the prize I had won in sheer stupefaction: *I had it!*

And so I asked: "Why, in your opinion, did President Carter say that Amin was the only 'legitimate' president of Afghanistan? Why do you think Carter was so fond of Amin?"

You would have thought I had cursed the Holy Ghost in front of the Pope! The clamor that broke out in the ranks of the Western press honestly amazed me. I thought my question was a rather natural one. I had certainly not expected to arouse the press corps to such gibbering activity. In fact, they'd become so noisy that I missed most of Karmal's response. All I could see was his Cheshire smile, and I assumed from that that he had a ripe answer ready for me. It was a pity the exact words were run over by the press but I gathered from the words I did snatch in passing that he thought the reason Carter mourned the passing of Amin was because Amin was his bully boy!

That—at this stage in the game—was something of a shocker to me. But apparently not to the pressmen from the West, who were way ahead of me. At the moment they were busy asking each other who I was—who this interloper could be, this housebreaker who had somehow got past all the doorkeepers and guards and, inside the house, had blurted out the wrong question! Who had let him in?

Well, the revolution had let me in. I wasn't an AP, UPI or *Times* correspondent suddenly gone berserk or, worse, turned renegade. As far as I was concerned I was nothing more than the raggedy-assed boy I started out life as in Duquesne, Pennsylvania, son of a steelworker and Lithuanian immigrant mother, blown by the winds of our gusty times to Kabul right smack into this gilded palace.

It was, though he didn't know it, that peasant on his burro I had glimpsed that morning who had opened up these ormolu doors to let me in. It was the workers and peasants of Afghanistan, behind whom stood the organized working class of the world, who had given me space on which to stand from which I could ask the one question the entire press of the whole "free world" had found itself much too unfree to ask!

So that was all there was to it. I just wanted to know why. Why did Carter support Amin who killed Taraki?

IAGO TO THE REVOLUTION

That one may smile, and smile, and be a villain.
William Shakespeare, *Hamlet*

Who was this Amin?

Up until his overthrow the adjectives connected with the name Hafizullah Amin in the Western press, and particularly after the assassination of U.S. Ambassador Adolph Dubs, were "hard-core," "orthodox," "ruthless," "Moscow-aligned," but always "Communist."

When he replaced Taraki the same press opined that the change meant no change, for Amin was more slavishly pro-Soviet than Taraki had been. Hadn't he been Taraki's right-hand man? Hadn't he enforced policies on the country with a ruthless hand?

That was September. By December Amin had been overthrown and executed, and now it was President Carter who was defending his Communist integrity and the Soviets who were denouncing him.

What was behind this dramatic shift in attitude? What did it reflect? What role did Amin really play in Afghan events? And if indeed he was what Karmal who, after all, had been his rival for years, and whom Amin had exiled as ambassador to Czechoslovakia, called him now, "a bloody tyrant," why hadn't the Soviets seen this as well and refused to acknowledge him when he came to power over the body of Taraki?

And Taraki, what of him? What precisely was Amin's relationship to him and how much of the policy which had brought Afghanistan's revolution to the brink of disaster been Taraki's and how much Amin's? Failed tyrant, or betrayed victim?

And finally, would a man who was scheming to destroy the revolution from within—working in conjunction with the CIA toward that end—have called on the Soviet Union to send military forces to rescue it? If the aim of the betrayer was to betray the revolution, then by December 1979 Amin had certainly done his job well. From the point of view of counterrevolution the situation was all positive. Not only did counterrevolutionary forces occupy nearly half of the country's provinces. They operated out of "refugee" camps in Pakistan with total immunity—supplied with arms from the West, backed by the USA, and protected by Pakistan from "hot pursuit."

Not only that. The other wing of the Party, the Parcham wing, which had been the internal threat to Amin's power, had been in part destroyed by him. Thousands of Parcham members, with many of their leaders, were in prison, most of them slated for execution. In addition the army was almost demoralized after successive purges, after "untrustworthy" (to Amin) officers had been summarily removed.

The Party's program was almost in shambles—the land reform had stopped, commerce was crippled, the clergy were in opposition, thousands had fled the country.

The stage for a successful counterrevolution was set. And the question arises: if this is what Amin had schemed to do, then by December 1979 couldn't he say he had achieved his aim? With the removal of Taraki he now had total power in his own hands. Why then did he ask for the Soviets to send troops?

The answer to this and to other complicated questions will take us deep into the coiled springs that govern the workings of revolution and counterrevolution in our times.

Of the 27 intellectuals who had met at Taraki's home in Shah Mina district in Kabul on January 1, 1965, to organize a revolutionary party, whose object was to replace the monarchy with some juster form of government, not all of those present could be called conscious, let alone dedicated, Marxists.

The novelist and poet Noor Mohammad Taraki was chosen as the leader of the new party. This self-educated Pushtun, born of poor peasants, early showed a bent for poetry. Despite the fact that he never passed on to a higher school, he managed to acquire academic skills that made it possible for him to work as a clerk in Bombay and to take part in student affairs when he returned to Kabul. He edited various magazines during the 50s, already espousing a Left point of view. He was the editor for the six issues of *Khalq* (Masses) allowed to appear in April-May 1966.

Taraki had been a cultural attaché for the royal government in Washington, D.C., from 1952 to 1953, worked for the USAID (U.S. Agency for International Development) in Kabul from 1955 to 1958, and also as a translator for the U.S. embassy (and other foreign embassies) from May 1962 to September 1963. His novels depicting the oppression of the Afghan peasants and workers had made him famous in Afghan intellectual circles and established his authority as a spokesman for the Left. In any case, by January 1, 1965, he was chosen to lead it.

Hafizullah Amin was not among the 27 members present that day. Babrak Karmal was. So, too, was the only woman there who sat in the same room. Her name was Anahita Ratebzad. Amin joined the PDPA only in 1965 upon his return from the United States where he studied on a scholarship.

"When I was still a student," Karmal revealed, "he (Amin) was already recognized [as untrustworthy] by our movement. But what sort of power enabled him to continue his political career despite this? ... Amin was engaged in hatching plots with the CIA through his own network. Behind the mask of revolutionary phrases he slandered and smeared those who stood for real socialism. He used the Asian, Hitlerite and other methods of oppression, and with terrible demagogery, and with his secret connections to the CIA, he was planning to nullify all progressive principles and the democratic movement in Afghanistan. He carried out his policy with executions, lies, forgeries and torture...

"There are facts pointing to Hafizullah Amin's plans to liquidate half the population of Afghanistan, and he was to stay in power even if the country was cut to pieces...

"International reaction and imperialism are using their billions of dollars, which are the product of the sweat and blood of their own as well as of the world's working people, and through their vast organizations and complicated techniques and various other methods (they try) to place their agents in the revolutionary movement or even to the very top of the leadership..." (Press Conference, Kabul, Jan. 6, 1980.)

At the time Karmal made these terrible charges a tendency had already developed in the world, surfeited with stories of CIA manipulation, to pre-discount them to a certain degree, as I found myself involuntarily doing. It seemed to me that, devious and ruthless as the CIA undoubtedly (by its own admissions) was, still it couldn't control the world. Wasn't there too much of a temptation to lay one's own mistakes and defeats at its door?

Nevertheless, going into Amin's biography was like entering a maze of mirrors. This steadiness of purpose, this apparent ability to maintain his balance in the tumult and confusion of the times while others sank or got lost, could be understood on one of two hypotheses. Either the man was an extraordinarily single-minded and dedicated revolutionary whose integrity to the cause resolved all moral dilemmas and accounted for his courage and iron will—or the explanation lay elsewhere.

America's interest in Afghanistan was, historically speaking, fairly recent. The United States had recognized Afghanistan as a sovereign state only in 1934. The Soviet Union had recognized it in 1919. There was reason for the American delay. Emir Amanullah Khan had declared that Afghanistan was an independent nation—independent of Great Britain—and on May 6, 1919, the British launched an army of 300,000 men against it. It was a modern army—in fact, it was the army that had come out of World War I. And it had tanks and even planes to use. In fact, Kabul was bombed.

But this war—"the third bloody nose"—lasted only three months. It ended so abruptly not because the British suffered defeats in Afghanistan itself but because India (at its rear) had broken out in revolt, and their forces were needed more urgently there than in the mountains of Afghanistan. The British sued for peace, but a "peace" meant only to buy time, with Amanullah Khan. Peace, in fact, did reign in those valleys and hills for a time. But then, disguised as an airplane mechanic, a certain—later to be known as "Lawrence of Arabia"—British spy "working" at the Miranshah R.A.F. Station on the Afghan border, managed to provoke civil war in 1928-29, which put an end to Amanullah Khan's power altogether. After that, though an Afghan puppet reigned, it was the British who ruled.

While Britain was engaged in Afghanistan, the United States was obliged, in a gentleman's agreement, to keep hands off. This "hands off" included holding back recognition of Afghanistan's independence until President Roosevelt entered the White House in 1933 and, discarding the old deck in which previous administrations had dealt, broke out a new deck in which the cards were newly shuffled though the game was still the same.

Almost as soon as it began, American "aid" to Afghanistan was geared to the struggle against Soviet influence in that country, bending what Afghan powers were in control toward an anti-Soviet course.

American aid concentrated on those areas where that could best be done. Material projects tended to buttress the power of the class already in power. But even more important than buildings were men's minds. Not only would the Peace Corps arrive in Afghanistan in due course, but the Americans made a point of establishing close ties with the educational world. Much American (and some West European) aid centered on the educational system itself. Columbia Teachers College, for instance, was "affiliated" with Kabul University's Faculty of Education. Its "aid" included not only acting as a transmission belt for moneys through USAID but supplying instructors, and even American administrators who re-organized the entire educational system on American lines, "including a little-known but widely appreciated textbook program for primary and secondary schools" (*Afghanistan* by A. Arnold) and so decisively determined university policy as well.

It was into this educational setup that Amin entered at his appointed time. Amin "won" two scholarships to Columbia Teachers College—the first in 1957 and the second in 1963. Up until then he had been active, as a student, only in promoting the "cause" of the Pushtuns, who are the major minority in Afghanistan.

Amin's career, the more one examines it, comes up as nothing short of amazing. The very fact that he was able to rise to where he could secure a university education in a country where illiteracy is almost universal was in itself remarkable. His origins had been modest enough. Born allegedly of peasant stock in Paghman province, where his numerous relatives still live, he was able to attend elementary school, and from there higher school that led into Kabul University itself. After returning from Columbia Teachers in the late 50s he worked first as a principal at a school for boys of Pushtun origin, then later as a principal of Kabul's Teachers Training High School.

In 1963 he was back in New York. Hardly had he landed in New York this time and re-entered Columbia—and Wisconsin University—than he became head of the Afghan Students Association, assuming a position which *Ramparts* would later (April 1967) reveal had been previously occupied by Afghan students who had all worked for the CIA.

The history of this remarkable "association" is also an amazing one. It was founded in 1964 by the American Friends of the Middle East, later exposed as a CIA front and conduit. Included on its Board of Directors were a clutch of corporate officials, retired State Department careerists and, most notably, Kermit Roosevelt, who would later openly boast in his book *Countercoup: The Struggle for Control of Iran* (1979) how he and the CIA had overthrown Mossadeq of Iran and replaced him by Mohammad Riza Pahlevi, the ill-fated Shah who had earlier fled the country to save his neck. With the Shah returned to the throne Standard Oil also returned to (though it had never left) Iran, at least for the time being.

The CIA started out the Afghan Students Association with a million dollars, which was 90 percent of the ASA's entire income. In deciding how this money was to be disposed of, Amin (once he became president) obviously played a not unimportant part.

Ramparts, in April 1967, published an article by Abdul Latif Khotaki, charging that Mohammad Hashim Maiwandwal, Minister of Education and Prime Minister in the King's government, had actively encouraged recruiting Afghan students by the CIA. It was on his recommendation that students were chosen, in the first place, to go to the USA. In any case, the published story had explosive repercussions in Kabul and led eventually to the Prime Minister's resignation. But the fact that the CIA controlled the Afghan Students Association, including its officers which it hand-picked, and its membership which it kept under surveillance, had meanwhile been firmly established.

At the time that Amin was in the United States and headed the ASA, few knew then what the whole world would know in 1967: that it had been CIA policy for years to set up dummy "conduit" foundations, "education" and "philanthropic" organizations, unions, newspapers, political parties, etc. whose sole aim was to corrupt and subvert young people from foreign countries enjoying the overflowing hospitality of their American hosts.

Most foreign students were elite men and women chosen by their respective governments for special training abroad. They were destined for important positions at home—and often in fact rose to the very top of their newly independent, usually ex-colonial governments.

MORE ON AMIN

> The dialectics of history were such that the theoretical victory of Marxism compelled its enemies to *disguise themselves* as Marxists.
>
> V. I. Lenin

Ex-CIA man Marchetti would reveal in his heavily-censored book *The CIA and the Cult of Intelligence*:

> Its (the CIA's) basic mission was that of clandestine operations, particularly covert action—the secret intervention in the internal affairs of other nations. (New, revised edition, 1980.)

CIA documents would drive him to the conclusion that the organization devoted a great deal of its concern especially to students from the Third World, to countries like Afghanistan. Marchetti would write:

> The (CIA) operator does not always search for potential agents among those who are already working in positions of importance. He may take someone who in a few years may move into an important assignment (with or without a little help from the CIA). Students are considered particularly valuable targets in this regard, especially in Third World countries where university graduates often rise to high-level governmental positions only a few years after graduation. (*The CIA and the Cult of Intelligence.*)

A more handy instrument for the CIA's purposes than the Afghan Students Association, which it had founded and funded, can hardly be imagined. That so vain and obviously so ambitious a student as Amin would be overlooked by an organization which is always on the prowl for such types and can spot them through tons of "revolutionary" rhetoric, is hardly likely.

In any case, to become president of a CIA-financed organization one had to meet certain very specific qualifications. It is clear that Amin not only met them all but had quite a few left over. That he was a Pushtun nationalist, augmented later by his "conversion" to Marxism at Wisconsin University during the 60s student turmoils, was no mark against him. In fact, it was precisely his type of "revolutionary" that most appealed to the CIA, whose taste in young revolutionaries was catholic.

While Amin was president of the ASA not only did he control, at least ostensibly, its policies but he also—which is the same thing—had some power over deciding which students were to be accepted as exchange students from Afghanistan and which were not. The linkage between Columbia Teachers and Kabul University was quite close, as we've already indicated: in fact, it did not end at the University but extended into the Daoud government itself.

In his work Amin no doubt had the assistance of another "student," Zia Khan Nassery, CIA man par excellence, whose job it was to check on the political reliability—or unreliability—of Afghan students for the immigration service. It was up to Nassery to spot a real revolutionary, whose entrance to the USA would then be abruptly interrupted. And conversely.

Between 1950 and 1969 the American government allocated $10.3 million to bring 2,142 Afghan students to study in the USA. Although not all of them were successfully corrupted and recruited by the CIA, one must assume that the attempt was made to reach all of them who showed promise, and enough must have been indeed recruited to make the expenditure of government funds worthwhile.

Later, in his hour of peril, when Amin "at bay" needed help badly, names and addresses of old friends were close at hand. The only trouble was that he lacked the time to contact them properly.

In any event, in 1965 Amin returned to Afghanistan and immediately joined the revolutionary movement, that is, its semi-legal party, the People's Democratic Party of Afghanistan, newly established. Babrak Karmal, two other members of the PDPA and, more significantly, Anahita Ratebzad were already members of the *Wolusi Jirga,* the lower house of parliament, and represented a political position aimed at forming a coalition of all forces opposed to the monarchy, a United Democratic Front.

Hardly had Amin touched ground in Kabul and become a member of the revolutionary forces than "Amin became the organizing strongman of the Marxist group. Over the next four years he surrounded himself with young Pushtuns who had been radicalized by their school experiences and political ambitions. As a result, Amin developed a personal following within the organization and consequently considerable power. While he became a committed Marxist, his new career demonstrated that his primary interest lay in developing personal political power. Ideology came second for him." (*The Struggle for Afghanistan,* by Nancy and Richard Newell, Cornell University Press, 1981.)

Building a "personal following" among Pushtun students, Amin at the same time became a close collaborator of Taraki. At that time the Party was still a united Party. But the split that was to become so devastating to the future of the revolutionary movement in Afghanistan soon developed. Beginning "merely" as factions in the 60s, the split broke out most visibly soon after Amin's return to Afghanistan.

The *Khalq* (Masses), begun as a weekly on April 11, 1966, was suppressed by the government after only six issues, on May 23, 1966. *Parcham* (Flag) also began as a weekly on March 14, 1968, and it too was suppressed by the government in April 1970.

The first publication was edited by Noor Mohammad Taraki, and the second by Suleiman Laiyek (now Minister of Tribes and Nationalities) and later by Mir Akbar Khybar.

The full story of the inner-party struggle remains to be written. Part of it we know now. Differences in tactics between the two young, immature forces, which adopted the names of their two publications, already existed before Amin's appearance on the scene. He "merely" exploited the division in the Left ranks already there. This division had deep ideological roots, reflecting the economic and historical backwardness of the country and had dogged the Left almost from the very birth of revolutionary struggle.

At its first congress in 1965, the PDPA had agreed to a program calling for "an alliance of workers, peasants, progressive intellectuals, artisans, urban and rural smallholders and national bourgeoisie in one front."

When Karmal, Anahita Ratebzad and two other Party members were elected to the National Assembly in 1965, their position inside and outside the parliament was based on this same strategy of uniting all the diverse forces in Afghanistan whose interests coincided and could be fused into a national alliance directed against the monarchy and later against the Daoud regime. But this policy was fought not only outside but inside the ranks of the PDPA.

The forces around Karmal recognized that the urgent task of any revolution in a feudal society was to carry out the democratic changes, long delayed, which had been holding back Afghanistan's progress. To move directly into socialism, imposed by the "dictatorship of the proletariat"—ready or not!—was dangerously reckless and considerably premature.

But one can see how this "militancy"—calling for immediate socialism—could be demagogically contrasted to the "conservatism", or "revisionism" of those who contended that the road to socialism ran through stages, each one of which had to be fully explored (though not deified) before the question of socialism itself could be confronted. Amin was a "hard-liner" of the first water. His "leftism" appealed to the immature, and it was this "militancy" that opened up the path of power to him, especially after the successful revolt against Daoud in April 1978.

In July, 1977, the split between the two factions had been healed in a meeting which elected a Central Committee evenly divided between both factions. At that meeting Taraki was elected General Secretary of the Central Committee and Karmal was also elected to the secretariat of the new party.

It was a united party, therefore, which led the assault a year later resulting in the overthrow of Daoud. But two months after the revolution, Nur Ahmad Nur, a member of the Political Bureau of the PDPA, has stated, "ominous events set in. The Party's unity weakened and it virtually began to fall apart. Reprisals were showered on Karmal and his associates. A terrific blow was struck at professional party cadres. Some had to emigrate or to go underground, others were arrested and some even paid with their lives." (Quoted by Pavel Demchenko, *Kommunist,* No. 5, 1980.)

In power, and wrapping himself in the enormous prestige which victory had brought to him, Amin moved now with accelerated speed to get rid of his oponents and with their going to get rid of the policy now apparently discredited by the form taken by the revolution—a palace assault, an act of will. Amin had no patience for alliances with "peasants, progressive intellectuals, artisans," and especially "urban and rural smallholders and national bourgeoisie." He put into operation a "hard-line" approach to the implementation of the Party's program. What followed was a laboratory example of how a positive policy can be wrecked by crude and arrogant administration. A "proletarian dictatorship" was forthwith imposed on a land of nomads, who wandered like clouds from country to country, of peasants whose brains were darkened with superstition and illiteracy, a country of Moslems whose Islamic beliefs were central to their history and wholly colored their consciousness. The handling of power in such country like Afghanistan needed caution, therefore. But caution was the last thing in Amin's mind. The assault on Daoud's palace had proven that the *will* of an organized, determined group of revolutionaries could prevail. There was no reason to believe that, now that he was in power, he could not enforce that will even more readily: arbitrarily, gratuitously, and by force.

On this "way of doing thing" the two sides split once again. As those whose policies of a united, broad front had not proven victorious, Karmal and his supporters were sent into exile, or into the provinces. When, soon after, Amin's methods began to arouse widespread opposition among the people, some taking to arms, some fleeing to Pakistan, opposition to his policies began to assert itself within the Party's ranks as well. And it was this opposition which aroused Amin and drove him on, ever more recklessly, to actions which ended in his death.

The part the CIA plays in such a situation is not, in most cases, to originate policy, but to attach itself to a policy already gone wrong. The interplay between wrong policy "sincerely" arrived at and the machinations of treacherous leaders and sectarian practices constitutes the nature of the diabolical complications. The villain Amin needed the honorable Taraki. Conscious villainy fed on naiveté and subjective blindness.

Later developments and circumstances—among others—argue strongly that Amin was not just an ideological fellow-traveler of the CIA. Ideological differences provided the background and the motivating forces which turned him into a conscious, ever-more-willing and probably recruited agent of the CIA (American imperialism). Absolute proof of this is of course in the hands of the CIA itself, which is not likely to be of too much documentary help in any case.

"Devil," Karmal would call him: "devil incarnate." That Amin was Iago to Taraki is now beyond dispute. In the end, just as Iago maneuvered Othello to his own destruction, so, too, did Amin maneuver Taraki to his exploiting his virtues as weaknesses.*

But the question remains: why did Amin snare Taraki's "mind and body?" To what purpose, since he was supposedly not only his firmest supporter, as he never tired of declaring—and in the most fulsome terms—but also his "friend," as Taraki was his "beloved teacher?"

In a pamphlet written, by all the signs, under Amin's direct tutelage if, in fact, not literally by him, published by the Political Department of the People's Democratic Party of Afghanistan in the Armed Forces of Afghanistan, May 22, 1978, we find this passage: "However, on the one hand, Comrade Taraki's revolutionary personality, political virtue, moral strength, high prestige among the masses, political consciousness and mastery of scientific socialism proved highly effective, as far as the assimilation of patriotic officers in the Party were concerned, as his stature, among the working class, on the other hand, the miraculous impact of the epoch-making, working-class ideology, and the strong stand taken and the high prestige enjoyed by the Party among the masses contributed to its further strengthening. Comrade Amin, as Comrade Taraki's most loyal colleague and follower... Under the prudent guidance of Comrade Taraki, Comrade Amin, with his proletarian courage, bravery..." and so on, all of this coming scarcely a year before Amin, as Taraki's most "loyal colleague and follower," put his "teacher" to death. This removal of Taraki was not done openly, in a political trial that would have exposed Taraki's errors to the people. It was done covertly, and it was lied about. Amin killed Taraki because he feared that he himself would be called to account for policies that had objectively merged with counterrevolution.

The question was: were they intended to? Was Amin following a conscious counterrevolutionary line? Was he no more than a misguided but ardent revolutionary? Or was he a criminal? Did anyone inside of the country, and the Party, have any suspicions about this all-too-eager young man, so much in a hurry? Karmal says, yes. In fact, he insists, suspicions about Amin had existed since his student days. But in 1977, after more than a decade of intense factional struggle and bitter division of the Party into two separate

---

* "Curse on his virtues! they've undone his country."—*Cato*, by Joseph Addison.

groupings, which Amin had done much to bring about, the Party was finally reunited, the factions were dissolved and "a decision was taken to investigate Amin's divisive, factional activities. As a result of the inquiry, exactly one month before the Saur Revolution (April 1978), the Central Committee of the unified PDPA passed a decision, in accordance with the Party Constitution, to punish Amin and to remove him from the Central Committee. But implementation of this decision was delayed by some invisible hand and slackness of the Central Committee. And then, on Saur 7, our glorious revolution was accomplished." (WMR, April 1980).

The removal from the Central Committee would have led, as the investigation turned up more damning facts, to Amin's expulsion from the Party itself. But an "invisible hand" interfered. Whose was it? "From the start," Karmal notes, "they [reaction and imperialism] took steps to infiltrate their agents into this movement and into our Party." *(Ibid.)* In saying this Karmal was only echoing what Lenin had already said in 1920: "In many countries, including the most advanced, the bourgeoisie are undoubtedly sending *agent provocateurs* into the Communist parties and will continue to do so. A skillful combining of illegal and legal work is one of the ways to combat this danger." (*"Left-Wing" Communism—an Infantile Disorder,* by V. I. Lenin.)

But *skillfully* combining legal with illegal work was precisely what the newly-born party was least able to do. It had to function with a more or less fragile legality. Almost from the beginning it was penetrated by the police, who made no bones about admitting to the American Louis Dupree, who had an abnormal interest in such matters, that the activity of the PDPA was closely monitored and dossiers on all leading members were kept up to date. When Daoud inherited the King's secret service (*estehbarat*) and the know-how of the Shah's SAVAK which, in turn, had been trained (and continued to be led) by the CIA, the process of zeroing in on all key revolutionaries within the Party's ranks speeded up and grew more sophisticated. But if the government nevertheless displayed a certain complacency about the potential such revolutionaries represented, this was due not only to the fact that it felt the police had the situation well in hand but to a further, even better, reason. Their man was in the top councils of the Party. They had reason to look forward to achieving the maximum which every police dreams of: gaining complete power over a revolutionary party. Nor was this a delusion. Such police successes had already been registered in various parts of the world, including over the Cambodian Communist Party, and perhaps the Chinese.

If Karmal is correct (and he was in a position to know), then Amin was aware, as early as 1977, that he was under dark suspicion by his comrades and that his days in the Party leadership were numbered. In fact, the decision to remove him had already been made. An "invisible hand" had saved him and then, in April, he was "saved" by the revolution itself in which he played a "significant" role. Nevertheless, the revolution, which he had some part in bringing into being, would turn out to be a tiger on whose back he had leaped, certain he could ride it to absolute power and thus safety. At a certain point however he would find it impossible to hold on and equally impossible to let go.

Karmal, who referred to himself as "to some extent ... an expert" on Amin, having known him from student days, characterized him thusly:

> An agent of the CIA and a Machiavellian schemer, Amin wanted to drive a wedge between the population and its conscious and staunch revolutionary representatives. He destroyed thousands of proven revolutionaries, subjecting them to savage tortures, incarcerating or expelling them from the country, fanned national, religious and inter-tribal discord, and, in effect, steered a course towards knocking the ground from under the feet of the Party, the government and the army. (WMR, April 1980).

He goes on:

> The criminal acts of Amin and his henchmen inflicted enormous harm on the revolution. Our people's traditions, religious beliefs, and way of life were ignored by the manner in which socio-economic reforms were put into effect. Subjectivism and leftist extremes undermined such important projects as the agrarian reform and the campaign to eradicate illiteracy among the adult population, among women in particular. Little wonder the people began to militate against the barbarous methods used by the Amin gang to "enforce" these reforms. In response, the population was subjected to the most brutal repressions. Towns and villages were bombed and shelled, and thousands of innocent people were killed. These criminal acts, the gross infractions of revolutionary legality, the arrests, the tortures, and the executions without trial or investigation confused and sowed widespread confusion. (Ibid.)

WHAT HAPPENED IN DECEMBER

I pray you, in your letters,
When you shall these unlucky deeds relate,
Speak of me as I am; nothing extenuate,
Nor set down aught in malice: then, must you speak
Of one that lov'd not wisely but too well.

William Shakespeare, *Othello*

In a press conference on January 6 (1980), Babrak Karmal charged that the date for the underground uprising against Amin, which had been set for the end of the month of December (1979) had been brought forward to December 27th because the Party had learned that Amin was planning a preemptive coup on the 29th.

The groundwork for the coup had already been laid, Karmal charged. Having removed Taraki from Party and governmental leadership in September, Amin had launched a wide-ranging assault on the opposition, which was mainly gathered around the underground Central Committee of the Party now organizing resistance to him. Karmal arrived secretly in Afghanistan in October and had contacted this committee and had taken charge of the political preparation for the uprising.

Amin's repeated purges and high-handed treatment of the army officer corps had alienated, as it partially demoralized, a significant section of the army. But his measures had convinced a more important corps within the army leadership that Amin was aiming for total Napoleonic power. By October he held all top positions within the Party and the State being the head of the Revolutionary Council, General Secretary of the PDPA and Acting Minister for Defense. When Karmal made contact with the army, he found it ready to move. That it was now so overwhelmingly anti-Amin was testimony to Amin's reckless policies toward the military, whose leadership he was trying to replace with relatives and henchmen.

But why was a preemptive coup considered necessary for a man who already had complete power? Amin had long been aware that a strong opposition had organized underground, and his secret police, headed by his nephew Asadullah, had been frantically hunting for its leaders, offering rewards of 20 million afghanis to anyone who would give them that information. They subjected suspected members to torture, including one of the leaders of the women's movement, Soroya. Some 2,000 members of the Parcham

42

faction, which had now set up a rival organization, had been arrested, and many of them, after harsh torture, were now in Pule-Charhi prison some 10 kilometers outside of Kabul, awaiting execution. At least 500 were in fact executed there before Amin was overthrown. Among those prisoners awaiting execution was Taraki's widow. As for Karmal, he had been denounced by Amin as a traitor months before and attempts had been made to have him returned from Czechoslovakia to Kabul to "stand trial."

Since Taraki had returned to Kabul in September, Amin was aware that serious opposition was now being organized against him. It is known that at the first meeting of the Central Committee the question of removing Amin from leadership had been raised. But Amin was also prepared. He had seen to it that *his* Central Committee was behind him: he had coopted members into it. Instead of Amin resigning, therefore, it was Taraki who was forced to resign. Taraki was officially declared to have been stricken with an illness, and then his death was announced. Actually, he had been murdered.

While we were still in Kabul in January, an investigation into the death of Taraki revealed the following. Two of the three men directly involved in his murder had been caught. One had managed to escape. The main testimony came from Captain A. Voddud, who had been in charge of carrying out the assignment. Here, as TASS recorded it, is what he said:

> I was appoined chief of KAM, and on October 8 I was on duty in the Guards. In the evening I was summoned by Commander of the Guards, Djandad, and told that on the orders of the Party and the Revolutionary Council I was to kill Noor Mohammad Taraki. I asked him, how I was to do that, and Djandad answered that everything had already been prepared, including the tomb and the shroud. He also said that taking part in the murder would be Ruzi and Egbal.

> I came off duty and met with Ruzi and Egbal in Djandad's office. Djandad ... once again said that the Party had decided to put him (Taraki) to death ... we left the office, got into a white landrover and went to Kote Bakhchi [the palace where Taraki was staying]. After arriving there, we left the car at the entrance, entered the building and went upstairs to the second floor, where Taraki was...

> After following Ruzi, we went into the room, where Taraki was. Ruzi told him: "We must take you to another place." Taraki gave Ruzi his Party membership card with the request that he should turn it over to Amin. He gave Ruzi also a black bag with money and some adornments asking that it be turned over to his wife, if she was alive. After which we all went downstairs.

> Ruzi took Taraki into a room ... and told us to bring a glass of water as he wanted to drink. But he immediately changed his mind and said that neither myself nor Egbal should go for the water. Nevertheless, I ran out of the room. I didn't find a glass for water, and when I came back I saw that Ruzi and Egbal had already tied Taraki's hands and forced him on the bed. Ruzi began strangling Taraki by pressing a cushion over his mouth, while Egbal held his feet. Ruzi also ordered me to hold

Taraki by the feet, but I couldn't. Fifteen minutes later Taraki was dead. We put his body in a shroud and took him out of the building...

It was now 23 hours and 30 minutes. We put Taraki's body in a car, which was waiting for us at the entrance... On our way we were stopped by Djandad and Ruzi was given a small walkie-talkie and ordered to keep in contact with him, Djandad. We arrived at the cemetery and saw that the tomb had already been prepared for Taraki...

After Taraki had been buried, Ruzi communicated by radio with the Guards Commander and reported that the job was done. Then we all went to the Guards to see Djandad (who) ordered food for us. We declined supper, as we were still very agitated. Djandad reassured us by saying that we were not responsible, as we were fulfilling the order and decision of the Party...

So much for murder. In any case, though Taraki was out of the way, things did not improve for Amin. In fact, they got worse. Only a month later the AP correspondent would report: "Senior diplomats who knew Mr. Amin personally said that by mid-November he was acting like a man at bay." (Feb. 7, 1980.)

At bay by mid-November?

All the chickens had come home to roost! The economic situation had meanwhile worsened drastically with the sowing cut by 9 percent and a subsequent drop in grain production by 10 percent. Industrial crop production had gone down even further—by 20 to 30 percent. Per capita income had dropped to a new low—about $ 139 annually.

Counterrevolutionaries were spreading havoc in 18 of 26 provinces.

Having murdered Taraki, Amin was well aware that he was simultaneously signaling to all sides concerned what his intentions really were. They were listening in Moscow to those signals as well. But they were also listening just as intently in Washington. So, too, were the underground forces inside and outside Afghanistan. These last forces read the death of Taraki as a certain sign that Amin planned now to take over dictatorial control and that the hour to save the situation had grown late. Amin indeed set about swiftly to consolidate his power, to destroy the opposition, of which he was well aware, and to make a preemptive move in December (Dec. 29th, in fact) that would announce a new organization of the Party, of the state and of the country's political direction. Time now crowded everything together into one place, one decision. It came down to a question of who would strike first. The underground revolutionary forces led by Babrak struck first.

On February 13, 1980, some weeks after the December 27th uprising, Kuldip Nayar, writing in the *Indian Express,* revealed that "He (Amin) approached Islamabad in early December. General Zia told me that Amin sent him frantic messages for an immediate meeting. He said, 'For obvious reasons, I could not have gone to meet him. I asked Mr. Agha Shahi [General Zia ul-Haq's advisor on foreign affairs] to go but the day he was to fly to Kabul the airstrip was under snow and later it was too late because the Russians had arrived.' "

"*The Indian Express* article also suggests that Amin sensed something was 'in the offing,' that is, while he depended on Soviet assistance to stay in power, he knew that the Soviet government and large sections of the PDPA disagreed with his regime. Facing this opposition, Amin had to search for other allies to maintain his position. Apparently he tried to play two cards simultaneously: he called for additional Soviet assistance including the deployment of troops on Dec. 15 to help him stave off immediate military opposition, and, at the same time, attempted to develop closer ties with Pakistan, and possibly even some factions of the 'rebel' movement in an effort to reduce his dependence on the Soviet Union which, in his view, had become an 'unreliable ally.' " ("CIA Intervention in Afghanistan", by Konrad Ege, *Counterspy*, Spring 1980.)

The Russians meanwhile, answering one more urgent request of the government, and the last one (of four) from Amin personally (instructed to do so by the Revolutionary Council), had begun to arrive.

The first technical contingents were already on the scene by December 8, and the Americans were well aware of it. Others soon followed. "According to the State Department official, who did not permit use of his name, the equivalent of three combat-equipped Soviet battalions arrived at Bargham Air Base north of Kabul, the Afghan capital, within the past two weeks," *The Washington Post* reported out of its deep throat. (WP, Dec. 23, 1979.) At that time the response of the American government was moderate: "There was no charge that the Russians had invaded Afghanistan." (*Ibid.*) In fact, the *Washington Evening Star* saw this entry of Soviet troops not as a blow *against* Amin but as help *to* him in his efforts "to stamp out a stubborn rebellion." And the *Post* would say, "The troops apparently were invited by the pro-Soviet regime of Hafizullah Amin." (Dec. 23, 1979.)

What changed this fairly moderate attitude on the part of the American government? "Officials said yesterday, as they have in the past, that no direct link is evident between the Soviet moves in Afghanistan and the crisis between the United States and Iran." (*Ibid.*) But though' this had to be a great relief to Washington, which feared a tie-up between the Soviets and the revolution in Iran, "some other officials have found it paradoxical that the United States is under intense criticism in part of the Islamic world for its pressure on Iran in the hostage crisis, while the Soviet Union's military role in crushing a rebellion by Moslem tribesmen in Afghanistan had been little noted ["remote from the reach of U.S. Power"—Brzezinski in April] and *relatively uncontroversial.*" (*Ibid.* My italics.)

Too "remote," "uncontroversial," "little noted," what changed all that? *The Washington Post,* observing in December the presence of "5,000-plus advisers" and some 1,500 Soviet "combat-equipped" troops in Afghanistan, took Carter to task for his slowness in responding to the Soviet move. Conceding that the Administration was "trying to draw international attention to the Soviet moves," which, before December 27th, still fell into the category of moderate aid, by "emphasizing its anti-Islamic content and contrasting it with the United States' own benevolent attitudes toward Islam," the *Post* felt that Carter should now come out of his corner with both fists swinging. (WP, Dec. 26, 1979, published in IHT, Dec. 27.)

Stories reflecting opinion in the White House and the State Department underlined the dilemma: with Iran "lost' to an Islamic crusade, and indeed all of the Arabic world ready to rally around its defense, American oil interests in Southern Asia stood in considerable jeopardy, or so it was interpreted. The Soviet moves into Afghanistan, considered to be "essentially local" up until then, had taken on far greater significance with the catastrophe in Iran. The "loss" of Iran was seen practically as the loss of Texas. World opinion—and particularly Islamic opinion—had condemned America's attempts to bring down Khomenei's Islamic Republic. But, "paradoxically," the Soviets' activity in Afghanistan, also a Moslem state, "had been little noted and (was) relatively uncontroversial."

This would never do. The trouble was that the Soviets had been helping Afghanistan for more than 60 years—ever since 1919 when, on Lenin's instructions, both financial (1 million gold rubles) and military (guns, airplanes, ammunitions) aid was extended to the then-struggling and newly-independent government under the Emir, and continued under the King and President Daoud. There is a solid historical foundation behind the Afghan-Soviet mutual political as well as military cooperation. And it should be borne in mind for objective analyses of what happened in December 1979. Here is a bit of the past.

In 1919, Lenin had, in fact, sent a message to the Peace Conference in Paris specifically asking for a guarantee from Lloyd George and Woodrow Wilson of Afghanistan's independence by agreeing to "a mutual undertaking by all states not to use force for overthrowing the government of Afghanistan." Even earlier, on March 3, 1918, as the Russians dickered with the Germans at Brest-Litovsk on terms for ending the war between them, the proposed Treaty included a clause calling for "respect for the political and economic independence and territorial integrity of Persia und Afghanistan."

Instead of granting any guarantee of Afghanistan's independence, the British began their third war against the newly-born and anxious to be independent country, and though they received another "bloody nose" and were forced to sign a kind of peace treaty, they signed this one, as they had all previous ones, with their fingers crossed behind their backs. They would never give up their intrigues in Afghanistan. In their effort to overthrow Amanullah Khan, the British were not averse to employing all means that came to hand. While the British upper class played out the game of civilization at home—as Henry James would watch them—they had no hesitation about using the most uncivilized means abroad to ensure that they could go on playing the game serenely at home. Marx had summed it up with Great Britain in mind that the "profound hypocrisy and inherent barbarism of bourgeois civilization lay unveiled before our eyes, turning from its homes, where it had assumed respectable forms, to the colonies, where it went naked."

It was a fact that the newly-born Afghan state owed much of its independence to the aid of the equally new-born Soviet state. Lenin accompanied his prompt recognition of Afghanistan as a sovereign state on March 27, 1919, with a message to Amanullah Khan: "The establishment of permanent diplomatic relations between the two great peoples opens up an extensive possibility of mutual assistance against any encroachment on the side of foreign predators on other people's freedom and other people's wealth."

This policy declaration was then followed up by a series of cultural and economic treaties and continued down the years. They included agreements which rendered crucial assistance to the Afghans at critical moments in their early history, as when the Soviets allowed the Afghans to move their products, duty-free, over Soviet land when Pakistan, in June 1955, probably prodded by Dulles, closed its borders with Afghanistan, thus denying passage to her goods through Pakistan to the Indian Ocean. It was an attempt to strangle the young country economically and force her to fall in with Dulles' grand design to outflank the U.S.S.R. with hostile states.

In 1932, the Soviets helped Afghanistan to withstand the worst of the world depression by further extending commercial relations on a favorable basis. This aid had followed the signing of the Soviet-Afghan Treaty of Neutrality and Non-Aggression on June 24, 1931. This treaty, which stressed coexistence between states with differing social and economic systems, was based on the already-elaborated Leninist concept that commercial and cultural relations between socialist and capitalist states (or feudal or any other kind of state) could continue peacefully and with mutual benefit.

Soviet aid to Afghanistan always included experts and teachers, and military advisers. It was, therefore, with such a history, no struggle for any Afghan patriot to understand that the very existence of his country as an independent country owed much to the Russian revolution and the socialist power it gave birth to. To most Afghans, therefore, the Bear from the North, now that it came with hammer and sickle, was no menace.

Karmal would say: "Soviet moral and material aid, including military assistance, is not something new in this country. It has been completely legitimate... At the Grand National Assembly, 'Loya Jirga' of 1334 (1945), under Sadar Mohammad Daoud premiership, due to the differences existing between Afghanistan and Pakistan, our people, including the Afghan clergy, endorsed in the traditional manner, that in order to preserve its independence, territorial integrity and settle its national problems, Afghanistan was entitled to ask for military help from any country it wanted to... So the Soviet military aid to Afghanistan is not a new matter. In the reign of the deposed King Mohammad Zahir, Afghanistan used to receive military assistance from the Soviet Union and there were Soviet military advisers in Afghanistan." (*Kabul New Times,* Jan. 8, 1980.)

In fact, Afghanistan's foreign policy was based, from the very start, on a continued friendship with the U.S.S.R. and, from that positive beginning, the U.S.S.R. had maintained a friendly relationship with every subsequent Afghan government. In World War II, though "neutral," the Afghan government not only resisted the blandishments (and threats) of the Nazis to allow Hitler to use Afghanistan as a base from which to attack the U.S.S.R. as well as India, but booted the Nazis out altogether at the request of the Soviet Union and Great Britain.

There is no evidence available from any source whatsoever to indicate that the Soviets were not satisfied to accept Afghanistan permanently on their southern flank as a friendly, neutral, though not socialist (much as Finland later became) neighbor, whose independence (from Great Britain, then the U.S.A.) it would honor as long as the Afghans themselves honored it. This friendly policy remained in effect for 60 years. (It was the Soviet Union which backed Afghanistan's entry into the U.N. in 1946.

But the development of Pakistan into a tool of now-hostile China (backed up by an even more hostile U.S.A.) aiming at disturbing the equilibrium in that part of the world by turning Afghanistan from a neutral to a pro-imperialist (and anti-Soviet) role changed everything. The discontented mélange of Afghan ousted landlords, usurers, medieval obscurantists could have been easily contained in their efforts to win back their past power if Pakistan, under Zia ul-Haq, had refused to give them aid and comfort.

Undoubtedly, the revolts they spawned domestically would have been short-lived if American power had not stepped in to support and refuel them and turned Afghanistan's internal troubles from a "conflict as essentially local in nature and implication" to one with international consequences.

Thus, the Soviet presence in Afghanistan was not new, nor arbitrary. The complication here is one of timing. The Soviet entry into Afghanistan, at Amin's request, took place at the same time, more or less, that the Karmal forces rose to overthrow Amin.

48

Was this move a mere coincidence? The Soviets say yes. So do the Karmal forces. The Soviets claimed then and claim now that their entry, at Amin's bidding, was legal and the timing was Amin's. The fighting that broke out was conducted by the Afghan regular army, and the Soviet forces remained apart, though perhaps not entirely uninterested, as Amin now "at bay" fought for his life with his handful of loyal (mostly family) followers.

Does this "coincidence" claim hold water? Not to everyone. "To argue," the late Jack Woddis, the British Marxist, wrote, "that Amin's pursuit of a sectarian, dogmatic course, especially toward those of Moslem belief, and his harsh repression of political opponents had alienated popular support and left his government in a weak and isolated position is one thing.

"But to charge him with being a U.S. agent is another. It is not credible that a man who is accused of having plotted with the U.S. to betray his country should have 'repeatedly requested' Soviet military aid." (London *Morning Star,* Jan. 15, 1980.)

The Spanish and the Italian and Japanese Communist parties would not only repeat these charges but go further and deny that a revolution had been endangered by Amin, and even if it was, Karmal had no moral right to replace him by force, nor did the Soviets have a right to enter the country and—as they charge—give military support to Karmal. Others made similar charges, rushing in to render judgment, it might be noted, long before all the relevant facts could possibly have been clear, making one wonder whether the judgment was based on the facts themselves or on past already formed—what were now—prejudices. The Woddis statement, published on January 15 (1980), stood on an interpretation of the event that lacked, if nothing else, time—the time-to-come: perspective.

AMIN LOOKS FOR AN ESCAPE

> Revolutions are not made to order.
>
> V. I. Lenin
>
> *A horse! a horse! my kingdom for a horse!*
>
> William Shakespeare.
> *King Richard III*

On January 13, 1980, there appeared an article on the Op-Ed page of *The New York Times* written by Selig Harrison, described as a "senior associate of the Carnegie Endowment for International Peace," and also as the author of the book on the "impact of Communist Afghanistan on Pakistan and Iran." Harrison writes (this is now just weeks after Karmal has come to power):

> It should be remembered that Amin, not the Russians, took the initiative in organizing the Soviet-assisted communist coup of April, 1978. Elbowing aside Moscow's favorite, Bobrak Karmal, Amin moved quietly to consolidate his personal power in the military and in the secret police.

As we have already seen, this "ruthless Marxist" had his price. By November he was openly in the market looking for the most likely bidder. In New York, in 1978, ostensibly to attend the opening session of the U.N., Amin, wearing a bullet-proof vest, met secretly with the Americans, and though Harrison maintains his offers (not characterizing what they were) were "ignored" by the Americans, there is every reason to believe that the opposite is true. In fact, it's inconceivable that anyone in the American government, which was up to its ears in anti-revolutionary schemes in Afghanistan (not to speak of Iran and Pakistan), would "ignore" such a remarkable chance to get in on the inside—to bargain with a man ready to sell. After all, the whole point of foreign policy was to capture the leadership of a revolutionary party by the CIA and millions of dollars were spent, both legally and illegally, to make it possible to do so.

It is also important to note that Amin's message of condolence to the American government—to Carter personally—at the death of Adolph "Spike" Dubs, the American ambassador to Afghanistan who had been assassinated on February 14, 1979, is interpreted here as a "direct signal" to the Americans of his "anti-Soviet feelings."

But how could that be? The circumstances leading up to and surrounding the assassination of Dubs (which occurred in the hotel I was now staying in) had been extremely murky.

Abducted by four Moslem youth described as "fanatics" of the fundamentalist Shia group, who found the Ambassador unaccountably accessible without any kind of bodyguard, Dubs was taken to the Kabul Hotel to the second floor, where two of the four Moslems barricaded themselves. There they began to parley. They demanded the release of various Moslems Amin had thrown into prison, and to make known to the world that Moslems were being persecuted by the Amin regime. But in abducting Dubs they had an additional aim. They wanted to prove, through his lips, that Amin had direct connections with the American government and that both were working hand-in-glove in suppressing Moslems.

True or false? We will probably not soon know. For ignoring advice of the Soviets and others to continue parleying with the abductors of Dubs (and Dubs' own appeals), Amin ordered the police to storm the barricaded rooms, and in the exchange of fire that followed Dubs and two of his abductors were killed outright. But two others had earlier been taken alive—only to die in police hands soon after.

Mystery surrounded every aspect of the incident. At one point it was charged that a political officer of the U.S. Embassy in Kabul who was on the scene, Bruce Flatin, had refused to shout to Dubs in German (which Dubs understood but not the Moslems) to hide in the bathroom as the guards opened fire. This might have saved Dubs' life. But no explanation as to why Flatin had refused (if the facts are correct) was ever advanced, other than that Flatin was afraid the abductors also knew German. In any case, Dubs paid for the mistake, if mistake it was, with his life.

The American government raised a considerable fuss at the time, denouncing Taraki and refusing to replace Dubs with another ambassador.* The Soviets were denounced as well, and under this cover of calculated confusion those actually guilty of the affair made good their escape. But one point was made unmistakably clear—the Taraki regime was declared beyond the civilized pale as far as Washington was concerned.

That being so, those who had followed events were a bit taken aback to learn that Amin's later "regret" over the death of Dubs was interpreted as a message to the Carter Administration which, spelled out, read more like this: "I appreciate your placing the blame for Dubs' murder on the Russians." The acceptance of this "message" meant, in effect, that the Americans were willing to trade one dead Ambassador Dubs for one live Premier Amin. As they say, a fair exchange is no robbery.

On January 16, 1980, W. A. Watanjar, member of the Central Commit-

---

* To this day. Only a *chargé d'affaires* sits in Kabul.

tee of the PDPA, member of the presidium of the Revolutionary Council, told Bakhtar (Afghan news agency):

> Evidence is mounting day after day to the effect that Hafizullah Amin was an agent of U.S. imperialism, an agent of the U.S. Central Intelligence Agency. All of his practical activities were aimed at undermining the revolutionary movement in Afghanistan, discrediting the April Revolution, creating a situation of terror in the country and undermining the foundation of the people's power.

Continued W. A. Watanjar:

> We are in a position today (to say) precisely where and with which career CIA agents Amin met in 1973-78, receiving from them assignments to bring about a collapse of our party.
> It is now established beyond doubt that Amin continued to collaborate with U.S. imperialism in the period following the April Revolution... In September 1979, Amin began preparing the ground for a rapprochement with the United States. He conducted confidential meetings with U.S. officials, sent emissaries to the United States, conveyed his personal oral messages to President Carter. All this is well-known to the present *chargé d'affaires* in the Democratic Republic of Afghanistan who had a talk with Amin on October 15, 1979.

On January 21 (1980), Sayid Gulabzoi, Minister of the Interior, and himself a key figure in the 1978 revolt that toppled Daoud, charged in a press conference in Kabul that Amin had been planning to stage a coup on December 29th and, working hand-in-hand with the Hez-Islami Party, one of the counterrevolutionary forces stationed in Pakistan, install a new government with himself as dictator.

Sayid Gulabzoi was no newcomer on the scene. He had been in charge of contacting revolutionaries of the air force in April 1978—in fact, he had worked under Amin's direction then, according to Amin's own account. Later, he had come under suspicion and had gone underground only to emerge as one of the leaders of the revolt which destroyed Amin. That he could not trust all his "friends" and corevolutionaries, even those who were Khalq members like himself, was a canker in Amin's soul which accounted for the frenzy with which he had his secret police, under the direction of his nephew Asadullah, search for conspirators everywhere, even within his own ranks. Since they were so hidden, the only sure method of extracting information on who and where they were was the method most sanctioned, if not mellowed by tradition: torture. Many accounts of the most brutal torture would be forthcoming from survivors. Millions of afghanis were also offered as rewards to anyone who led Amin's police to the headquarters of the underground Central Committee, which Amin knew, and could see, existed and was functioning.

Gulabzoi charged at that press conference that after Taraki's murder

Amin had moved quickly to establish and re-establish contacts with domestic and foreign counterrevolution. In September (1979), he charged, one of Amin's emissaries had met secretly with Gulbuddin Hekmatyar, the leader of the Islamic Party of Afghanistan, the Americans' most favored counterrevolutionary instrument, though they neglected none. At this meeting, not only of persons but of minds, agreement was reached on matters of strategy and tactics which was hoped would bring the war to an end and the Islamic Party some portion of power. (It must be remembered that fierce rivalry existed among the various counterrevolutionary groupings, and which one would emerge, assuming Karmal was overthrown, as supreme beneficiary over the others depended on various factors, not least of which was behind whom the U.S.A. would throw its full support.)

Gulabzoi further charged that on October 4, 1979, Amin actually secretly met with envoys of the Islamic Party and worked out practical plans for a *coup d'état*. A *coup d'état* was necessary for, until it was proclaimed, the Party activists, the army and all those who were involved in the struggle to defend the country and its revolution would have assumed that Amin was continuing Taraki's policies as he was sworn to do. It was planned that after he had made his bid for supreme power Amin was to issue a statement that the previous program of the Party had proved to be unworkable—in fact, had brought the country to the brink of ruin (as indeed it had) and in the name of the survival of the nation he now repudiated it. The blame for its failure would be laid at the door of Taraki, thus also providing the rationale, post-factum, for his removal, even his execution. The new state would model itself more closely to Western acceptable patterns, perhaps like Pakistan, ostensibly as a true Islamic republic. Amin would be declared president, Gulbuddin Hekmatyar would be prime minister, and room would also be made for Amin's huge family—his brother Abdullah first of all, who already was being quoted in the Western press as saying that the time had come to put an "end to the game of revolution."

In December 1979, a personal representative of Amin flew to Paris, Rome and Karachi, and in those cities met with agents of the U.S. special services whom he briefed on Amin's plans. Amin sent a special messenger to Peshawar in Pakistan on December 22-24, presumably, if the published story is correct, to let Zia, already closely monitoring the situation, as he himself has admitted, know what was happening and to ask for help as well as to invite him to visit Kabul personally. It was charged by Gulabzoi that by the time Amin had already received assurances from Washington that Washington would support the coup politically, materially and, if necessary, militarily. Amin was charged with dealing directly with the CIA through Richard Elliott, then under Richard Helms' direction in Kabul itself.

So, according to Gulabzoi, the stage was all set for December 29th. But on December 27th that same army, which Amin had purged so often that it should by then have been reduced to an impotent and wholly demoralized force, struck first. Even the 4th tank division, stationed in Kabul itself —and considered to be Amin's protection—and in which the revolutionaries had no contacts, joined the revolt. The air force, headed by Colonel Abdul Kadir (though in prison), was anti-Amin to a man.

Calling for Soviet aid remains an apparently imperfect piece in this puzzle, but only if we ignore certain facts. One of these is that Amin could not afford to be toppled by counterrevolution, thus losing all bargaining power. If Kabul fell, he fell with it. The Soviets could be used to act as a buffer. He had already confided to Selig Harrison (and no doubt others) that he knew how to "use" the Russians. Also, as Karmal points out, there were members of the Revolutionary Council, as well as others of Amin's faction of the Party, who were *sincere,* who believed that the ultra-Left Amin really did represent the best interests of the revolution, and who would have turned against him if he had exposed himself prematurely. Taraki had already asked the Russians for help. In fact, when Amin made the request that was granted it was the 15th of such requests, four of which he made personally with mounting urgency, all the preceding ones having been turned down by the Soviets who held that the Afghans could still rely on their own resources.

There was also another element in the picture. And that was a matter of calculation—judgment. Was Amin aware of the estimate of American "State Department specialists on the Soviet Union" who, in June, had come to a decision on what "the Kremlin's likely reaction to the escalation of fighting inside one of its most important bordering client states" would be?

Was there any reason why Amin should have believed that if Moscow had refused help in June to its trusted friend, Taraki, it would grant him that help in December, though he must have known, or more than suspected by then, that the Soviets had not bought his version of events that led to Taraki's death?

But there was also reason, with the Revolutionary Council pressing him to take a chance. And even if the request for aid was granted by the Soviets—and first contingents arrived in Kabul as early as December 8—it would be he, Amin, who would decide how this aid was to be used—certainly not against him. In fact, when the main body of Soviet troops actually did arrive in Kabul on the 25th, the *Washington Evening Star* at least thought it was "to help ... Amin stamp out a stubborn rebellion..." We know now that even as he was asking the Soviets for aid, as of December 15, Amin was also feverishly trying to make contact with Zia ul-Haq and others as he worked to activate his options in every direction.

54

Still, what proof existed that the Soviets, who had refused 14 previous requests, would honor the 15th? In any case, Amin felt he had no choice but to make the requests: the conspiracy to turn the country over to counterrevolution was not a *mass* movement. It existed only within a small circle of trusted fellow-conspirators, largely made up of his family members (in a feudal society like Afghanistan blood ties play a decisive role). Whatever one might say of the political acumen of the Khalq members, one could not accuse them of consciously conspiring to bring on counterrevolution. Amin had to conceal his real aims from his fellow Khalq members as well. If they had gotten a whiff of them, it would have been all over with him much earlier.

Then there was the other fact: Amin planned to take over absolute power on the 29th. He would confront the Russians (and his own followers) with a *fait accompli*. He controlled the secret police and (as he thought) the army. The opposition, if there was any, could do little in such circumstances. If the leadership of the country *legitimately in power* (as Carter would declare that Amin was) elected to place restraints on Soviet "behavior," or even later demanded their withdrawal altogether, à la Sadat, the Soviets could put up very little resistance to world opinion, "orchestrated" by the Americans. As Amin had already been assured, the Americans would back him up in every way, including militarily. Then there were the Chinese ready to make a contribution of their own.

In any case, time for negotiations would be won, even with—or even because—the Russians were on the territory, *while* they were on the territory. If the *Washington Evening Star*, which had its pipelines to the White House and Langley Field, believed that Amin intended to use the Soviet army to put down a "stubborn rebellion," why not use the Red Army's authority behind him as a bargaining power—acting from their strength? If the counterrevolution succeeded in overrunning the country, taking power by its own efforts, why would Amin be needed then? Hekmatyar would be enough! Why would a triumphant Hekmatyar need a deposed Amin?

And to sum it up here is Karmal's view of the December events:

> After Amin seized power (September 1979), the external danger loomed larger as a result of his actions, of which I spoke above. It was then—and I emphasize this—that the dedicated patriotic forces on the Revolutionary Council, the nation's supreme state organ, and the PDPA Central Committee, again demanded that he ask the U.S.S.R. for military assistance. A refusal to do so would have meant self-exposure, dropping his mask, something he could not afford to do at that time... (WMR, April 1980.)

He goes on to add:

> There is no doubt that in appealing to the Soviet Union for assistance Amin also had his own mercenary aims in view. Being engaged at that time in

a savage purge of the Party and the army and the destruction of all the revolutionary forces loyal to the revolution, he feared that he would not have enough time to complete his dirty work before the people he had aroused rebelled. Obviously, in that situation foreign mercenaries would have overrun the country, meeting no resistance from the Afghan army already disorganized by Amin. But Amin meant to use the presence of the Soviet troops to whip up nationalistic feeling and thereby incite the people against our friend, the Soviet Union, and then to accomplish a volle-face such as Sadat brought about in Egypt, turning to the United States and China for assistance, and inviting Gulbuddin Hekmatyar, the rebel beader, to take over as Prime Minister. *(Ibid.)*

When the revolutionary forces struck on December 27th, upsetting the timetable of treachery, Amin had nobody to defend him except a handful of his palace guards and the No. 4 tank unit which, however, joined the rebels during the uprise. When word came that he had been executed, there was dancing in the streets of Kabul.

In Washington, D.C., there was a loser in the White House who heard the news of Amin's execution with consternation and read it as a premonition that his own trilateral house of cards would fly apart the moment anybody opened the door.

Whatever social reasons lay at the root of the division of opinion within the Party, Amin saw in this mutual hostility his opportunity. In any case, Noor Mohammad Taraki found himself with no more fervent supporter than the ex-student who had graduated from Columbia University and was on good terms with some very important Americans!

The relationship which then developed between Taraki and Amin, in the depth of perfidy to which one sank and the magnitude of the tragedy which overtook the other, needed, to describe it adequately, as Karmal would later note, "a Shakespeare." And indeed, Shakespeare had already described it. Its name was *Othello*. At the close of this monumental tragedy Othello would cry, as Taraki well might have:

> *Will you, I pray, demand that demi-devil*
> *Why he hath thus ensnar'd my soul and body?*

To which the Iago-Amin answered:

> *Demand me nothing: what you know, you know:*
> *From this time forth I never will speak word.*

Today, we know why, or at least we can give an educated guess as to why, Amin wanted the Soviets to come, *sincerely* wanted them. Their coming would save his neck.

But why did the Soviets *choose* to come? They knew that their entry into Afghanistan would stir up a hornet's nest of charges against them as "imperialist", as "invaders", with even some Communist Party leaders joining in. They knew, also, or at least surmised, that with Carter looking for an excuse to torpedo detente (he had already placed the SALT-2 treaty he had signed with Brezhnev in Vienna on the "back burner"), this act would be a political plum apparently dropped into their laps.

Why then?

If counterrevolution triumphed, the consequences were incalculable, not least of which would have been that the southern flank of the U.S.S.R. would be exposed: an aim that the Americans had inherited from the British and which had been the *leitmotif* of Dulles' machinations in that part of the world in the 50s and had been taken up and refined by Brzezinski, et al.

But there was another, an overriding reason to act. What had happened in Indonesia was fresh in everyone's mind. Hundreds of thousands of Indonesian peasants who wanted no more than to live more decent lives have been massacred and the struggle for freedom was set back for a generation at least. But Indonesia is far from Moscow and Kabul is near.

Officially the Soviet Union justified the entry of its troops— a limited contingent—into Afghanistan on the basis of the Soviet-Afghan Treaty, which Taraki had signed in Moscow, on December 5, 1978, and of Article 51 of the U.N. Charter which clearly defined aggression, explicitly stating that "Nothing in the present Charter shall impair the inherent right of individual or collective self-defense if an armed attack occurs against a Member of the United Nations. . ."

This clause was further buttressed by a Security Council Resolution 387 (passed March 31, 1979) stating that the Security Council reaffirmed "the inherent and lawful right of every state in the exercise of its sovereignty to request assistance from any other state or a group of states."

In 1974 the U.N. had passed a resolution in which the General Assembly found that a State would be considered guilty of committing "aggression" for, among other things, ". . .allowing its territory, which it has placed at the disposal of another State, to be used by that other State for perpetrating an act of aggression against a third State; the sending by or on behalf of a State of armed bands, groups, irregulars or mercenaries which carry out acts of armed force against another State. . ."

The Soviet-Afghan Treaty of Friendship, Good-Neighborliness and Cooperation in addition to providing for economic and cultural relations, also contained the following clauses:

> Acting in the spirit of the traditions of friendship and good-neighborliness as well as the United Nations Charter, the parties to the Treaty will be consulting each other and with mutual consent will be taking appropriate measures to ensure the security, independence and territorial integrity of both countries.

In the interest of reinforcing defense potentials of the parties, they will continue developing *cooperation in the military sphere* (my italics).

With these documents to refer to, it would seem the Soviets could make a substantial *prima facie* case for their entry into Afghanistan.

Was the Soviet entry into Afghanistan a surprise to Washington? Earlier in June *The Washington Post* was reporting from Washington (June 8, 1979) that "Mr. Taraki's rule may be crumbling." The report added *(in June, 1979,* it must be remembered) that "The insurgency is spearheaded by a group of 10,000 to 20,000 guerrillas operating in Afghanistan *out of refugee camps in Pakistan"* (my italics). The position of the Soviets was as follows:

> The unceasing armed intervention, the well-advanced plot by external forces of reaction created a real threat that Afghanistan would lose its independence and turn into an imperialist military bridgehead on our country's Southern border. In other words, the time came when we could no longer put off responding to the request of the government of friendly Afghanistan. To have acted otherwise would have meant leaving Afghanistan a prey to imperialism, allowing the aggressive forces to repeat in that country what they had succeeded in doing, for instance, in Chile where the people's freedom was drowned in blood. (Leonid Brezhnev, *Answers to Questions by a "Pravda" Correspondent,* Jan. 13, 1980.)

REASONS

They are the enemies of hope, my beloved,
the enemies of running water,
of the fruit-laden tree,
of a growing and improving life.

Nazim Hikmet, "The Enemies"

CIA activity, the "third option"*, against the revolutionary movement in Afghanistan, did not begin with the appearance of Karmal on the scene. It had started long before—even before April, 1978, and continued when Karmal came to power. One American official, using the pseudonym, "Abel Baker", put the date of the CIA's direct intervention in Afghanistan's internal affairs as early as the regime of Daoud himself, which began in 1973.

In *The New York Times* (July 9, 1980), "Abel Baker" wrote, under the heading, "A Needed 'White Paper' "**, that, among other things, what was critically needed to understand events in Afghanistan was "in greater detail, a description and exploration of official *and unofficial* U.S. policies and the activities of its allies in the area toward the 'left-leaning' Mohammad Daoud regime between 1973 and 1978. Particular attention must be paid to the charge that pressure on Mr. Daoud from the Iranian SAVAK (allegedly with CIA encouragement) to move to the right may in fact have provoked the revolution of Noor Mohammad Taraki and coup." (Italics mine.)

According to Konrad Ege, a CIA-watcher, even before the 1978 revolution—in 1977, in fact—the CIA, under the then leadership of Robert Lessard, had transferred its attention wholly to Afghanistan, establishing headquarters in Pakistan from which to operate more easily in Afghanistan (not to speak of Pakistan itself and nearby India). Lessard had been active in Iran, under the wide tolerance of the Shah, for at least 10 years before, since in fact the CIA's overthrow of Mossadeq had put the Shah back on the throne. The CIA had had a free hand in Iran from that point forward, molding the SAVAK in its own image. When one speaks of puppets, incidentally, one can do no better than to refer to the Shah. ("CIA Intervention in Afghanistan," by Konrad Ege, *Counterspy,* Spring 1980).

---

* *The Third Option: An American View of Counterinsurgency Operations,* by CIA-man Theodore Shackley, Readers Digest Press.
** We are still waiting for it.

But there was even better confirmation of CIA activity in Afghanistan before 1978. This testimony comes from Anthony Arnold, described on the cover of his book, *Afghanistan, the Soviet Invasion in Perspective* (1981), as having "served as an intelligence analyst (shy way of saying spy) in Afghanistan . . . specializing in Soviet relations. . ."

Writes this CIA alumnus "in perspective":

> The only counterforce that could have thwarted the PDPA was Daoud himself. *If* we did have the information (and we should have had it), and *if* we did assess it correctly (as we should have), some way should have been found to put it in Daoud's hands without compromising the means by which it was acquired. [That is, the "means" used was a plant in the PDPA itself, perhaps the top man himself?] Had that been done, it is likely that the coup of April 27, 1978, would not have occurred.

Arnold goes on to consider the alternatives for aiding the counterrevolutionaries today. (This is before Reagan had come into power when the options were still being worked out. They have been settled since.):

> Rather than go into details, we will confine ourselves to the recommendation that aid be afforded to the Afghans with neither confirmation nor denial that it originated in the United States. The corollary recommendation holds that if it comes to a conflict between secrecy and efficiency, efficiency should prevail. Security considerations should neither unduly limit nor significantly delay arms aid. (In this regard it is to be hoped that the U.S. officials can regain their right and courage to respond to probing journalists [which journalists with what probing questions does he have in mind?] with a simple 'no comment' answer when appropriate—a capability that seems to have been largely lost in recent years.)

Activity against the revolution stepped up dramatically after April, 1978. The venerable British historian, author and past editor of *Labour Monthly*, Andrew Rothstein, composed a calendar of events prior to December 1979 that proves, with almost schematic precision, not only that counterrevolution was well launched by that date but that its strategy had already been worked out in considerable detail as well. Rothstein indicates what had become clear enough by the middle of 1980, that another fiasco (like Amin's plans to stage a coup) propelled America's policy-makers to the point of hysteria where all caution was thrown to the winds. This fiasco, of course, was the well-known April extravaganza when Carter, following an all-too-obvious Hollywood script, had tried to overthrow Iran's Khomenei under the guise of rescuing the American Embassy hostages. This whole adventure had collapsed in a gust of unplanned desert sand on April 24-25. Carter had hoped to catapult into the presidency for a second term on the success of this mission. But he had also hoped to confront Afghanistan with another hostile neighbor—to place her between the pincers of Pakistan and an Iran without Khomenei (who, though hostile to the Afghan revolution, was not hospitable to all its enemies either).

Taking the year 1979 from January through December, Rothstein ticks off stories culled from the British and French press that add up to a portrait of counterrevolution that is so clear that one can hardly think of what more is needed to make it more convincing.

In January (1979) "fiercely anti-Communist Moslem guerrilla insurgents" were already telling correspondents (this one from *The Daily Telegraph*) that they had control of "about one-third of Kunar province ... bordering on Pakistan." They were already complaining that they lacked sufficient weapons. *Agence France-Presse* would confirm that the rebels were waging a "real war," which, it pointed out, had led "to the creation of military camps for the training of rebels on the territory of neighboring Pakistan." The French correspondent would write that he had visited one such training camp quite near to the Afghan border, where 300 rebels were training in Pakistan army barracks and were guarded by Pakistan soldiers.

In view of the fact that Zia ul-Haq would later blandly claim that no such camps used to train counterrevolutionaries existed in Pakistan, only camps for refugees which he had compassionately put at their disposal as a humanitarian duty (as he simultaneously threw thousands of Pakistanis into prison for opposing his dictatorship), such early charges that military camps training counterrevolutionaries already existed are important to note.

In fact, various European and some Asian correspondents repeatedly made the point that camps for training counterrevolutionaries for military action not only existed in Pakistan before 1978 but had the active support of Bhutto, then still in the good graces of the American CIA. Such evidence came from correspondents for *Le Figaro, The Daily Telegraph,* the *Economist,* the French *Libération, Le Point,* the *Times of India* and others. They noted American activity in Pakistan with an unimplicated eye, and in due course the activity of the Chinese as well as the Israeli, Egyptian and other secret—and not so secret—services. Perhaps inadvertently, or even unwillingly—and some willingly—they spilled the beans on what was going on before December 27th, 1979, which Carter would declare to be the day when the "greatest threat to peace since World War II" had been struck by the Russians. (See "Afghanistan: A Short Calendar of Counterrevolution," by Andrew Rothstein, in *Political Affairs,* July 1980.)

Working under the cover of the Lahore Narcotics Control Authority, a whole bevy of CIA men, like CIA's Louis Adams, spent the bulk of their time hopefully coordinating the various counterrevolutionary insurgent groups into one united group (a dream that never came true), and the time left over, if any, to "controlling" the drug traffic that was so rife and so profitable. Placing such a man in charge of a drug-control program was a classic case of placing the fox in charge of the chickens. For if the CIA had, in fact, managed to "control" the enormously profitable drug traffic (which directly serviced the U.S.A. drug underworld), it would have ended their cover (and income for the "holy warriors"), and where would they have found a new one as good?

In August 1981, Carl Bernstein who, as a reporter for *The Washington Post,* had been instrumental, along with Bob Woodward, in blowing the cover of other CIA conspirators resulting in the now historical Watergate expose, charged in an article in the *San Francisco Examiner and Chronicle,* that "The Central Intelligence Agency is coordinating a complex, far-flung program involving five countries and more than $100 million to provide the Afghan resistance with the weaponry of modern guerrilla warfare."

CIA interference in Afghan internal affairs had been "personally ordered by President Carter and carried out under the direct supervision of National Security Adviser Zbigniew Brzezinski and CIA Director Stansfield Turner" —a fact which *Newsweek* had already reported in 1979.

Bernstein went on to charge, in that and in other places, that Carter had cautioned the CIA to do nothing "to disturb the impression that the Afghan struggle is an Islamic struggle"—exactly what Iran's Khomenei, no friend of Carter's, would also claim. Two minds here met as one, but with a small difference. For the struggle for Islam in Iran, which saw America as the prime devil, did not seem as appealing a struggle to the members of the National Security Council as did the struggle for Islam in Afghanistan where the Russians could be cast as the devil.

The possibility that the Moslems might become such fierce *Mujahiddin* as to burn all of the infidel Marxists, root, branch and school-books, converted most of the Security Council into Moslems overnight, including the born-again Baptist Carter and the (as far as is known) only once-born Catholic, Brzezinski.

At a press conference in Paris in March 1980, Michael Barry, described as representing the International Federation of Human Rights* and author

---

* Mr. Barry, a "Socialist" in Rome one year turns up another year as the protegé of the ultra-reactionary "Freedom House" in New York. Somehow, this "candidate for a PhD degree in Islamic affairs" at McGill University in Canada, who "lives in Paris and does occasional work for the People's Tribunal" (NYT, Jan. 28, 1982), manages to cross into Afghanistan apparently at will, moved to do so presumably only in the pursuit of his elusive PhD.

The "Afghan Relief Committee", which footed the bill for Barry's extravaganza, describes itself as a "private American group that assists Afghan refugees in Pakistan," which—as any tyro in the business can tell you—is nothing but code language for a front group with more than brotherly ties to the CIA. It is true, however, that the CIA had been solicitous about Afghanistan's welfare long before the Soviets entered that country.

of *Afghanistan* (1974), which had been awarded France's *Prix des Voyager,* had this to say, as reported by the *Herald Tribune:*

> Since the Communist takeover two years ago (1978), he (Michael Barry) said executions at the main prison near Kabul have been "carried out in a manner reminiscent of Auschwitz..."

But those executions, which nobody disputes, were carried out under the direction of Amin (twice-blessed by President Carter and the CIA) and the secret police headed by his nephew. Barry went on to cite as his source "about 100 refugees" he had questioned in Peshawar. "Since the 1978 Communist takeover, Mr. Barry said, persons have been imprisoned without trial and tortured at the Interior Ministry by such means as electrical shock, beatings or by being hung from the ceiling for as much as 15 hours at a time.

"He said another method of executions was live burial in a field near the prison. 'Prisoners were carried off every night by truck,' he said. 'The people were unloaded from the truck, their eyes were bound, trenches were dug, the prisoners were cast in and the trenches were filled by bulldozers.' "

I would personally verify similar stories, speaking to the victims who survived, and visiting the prison where some were tortured and from which almost nightly selected groups were taken out and shot. Other cases were reported in the press, like that of Ali Mohammad Zahma, who had spent 25 years as a Professor at Kabul University but had been arrested by Amin's police earlier that year (1979) and been saved from death by torture and neglect by the December 27th uprising. At the moment (in January 1980), he was in the Jamhoriate Hospital. His crime was—that he was a professor at Kabul University. After his release (when Amin was toppled) he said: "I have no connection with any political group, but like every other patriot I take an interest in the fate of my nation and its people and I think about them." He added: "It is natural that I wished to return to my family and see my children after months of torture and imprisonment—of insult, humiliation, desperation and sickness. But this was not my only feeling. The moment I was released I thought of thousands of my missing compatriots and thousands of afflicted people of my homeland who had suffered much from the tyranny and cruelty of the hangmen of Amin's regime. We must resolve to build our country and heal the wounds of our people." (Interviewed in *Kabul New Times,* Jan. 6, 1980.)

Munawar Ahmad Zeyar, a Pushtun scholar and writer on linguistics, was asked why he had been jailed by Amin's police: "I was imprisoned following the glorious Saur Revolution at the order of the cruel American spy, Hafizullah Amin, because I made efforts with a group of patriots to contribute to the ending of feudal and pre-feudal production relations, because I deemed it my duty after 20 years of studies, to repay my people in this manner."

He went on: "My offense was obvious. I participated in a very active way in the progressive movement to change our medieval society in a revolutionary manner according to objective laws of social evolution, and make some contribution to the victory of the epoch-making working-class ideology. Further, I strongly believed in Party unity, and this ran counter to the wishes of those who claimed preferential treatment because they served Amin as his yes-men."

He had been arrested by KAM (the secret police) and sent to the holding prison in Kabul where political prisoners were first interrogated. "Actually, every victim of Amin's internal machine was subjected to tortures at KAM. And after surviving all the excruciating torments, they were sent to Pule-Charhi Bastille or to some other smaller but secret jail...

"December 27, 1979 is the most important event in our nation's history after the glorious Saur Revolution. The national-democratic uprising staged by our people on April 17, 1978, was really re-directed and safeguarded under the united PDPA. Under the fascist regime of Amin and due to the mismanagement of the country by his band of assassins, the country was on the verge of being entirely overrun by rebel groups. Meanwhile, the public treasury was almost empty owing to the squandering of funds by those in power.*

"Amin's diabolical machine was bent on liquidating at least one million of our people who were under suspicion. I don't know what they had in store for the others. Maybe not much better." (*Kabul New Times*, Jan. 5, 1980.)

Mr. Barry, meanwhile, quoted by the UPI, apparently with the notion that Amin's crimes could be transferred bodily to Karmal, since both were "Communists," went on to reveal a bit more in his interview with the press in March 1980:

> Mr. Barry said refugees quoted the warden [of the prison "near Kabul"] as saying "One million Afghans are sufficient in order for us to build socialism. All others are infected with the old thoughts and must no longer live. As for your traitors in prison, none will ever find out about the fate you so richly deserve..."

For those with ears to hear, these words, which I take to be authentic, can detect in their funereal toll, echoes of the very same words

---

* How much the far-sighted Amin had squirreled away in foreign banks has still not been cleared up. But nothing was left in the treasury when Karmal came in. All had been stolen.

that have been attributed to Pol Pot of Kampuchea, who is quoted as saying, "We need only one million Kampucheans to build a new society," itself an echo of Mao Tse-tung's infamous statement, quoted in the pamphlet, "Long Live Leninism!", made hardly ten years earlier, that no revolutionary should fear an atomic war because, though two-thirds of mankind might perish, a "greater civilization" could be built by the surviving one-third on the ruins.

In fact, the further one probed into the reality of Amin, the stronger grew the smell of Pol Pot. Then, of his master not much further back: Mao Tse-tung. At a reception which Mao Tse-tung gave to Pol Pot and Ieng Sary in Peking in celebration of their "victory" in clearing the cities of people by driving them into the countryside where they died by the thousands, herded in "communes" run on the most primitive of communal principles, not only pre-capitalist but even pre-feudal, he is quoted as saying: "Comrades, you have scored a splendid victory. Just a single blow and no more classes! The rural communes with poor and middle-class peasants of the inferior layers all over Kampuchea will constitute our future."

The "single blow" had eliminated about 3 million Kampucheans, the entire leadership of the Cambodian Communist Party, and all other loyal members of the Party as well as intellectuals and the educated. When I was in Kampuchea I would learn first-hand what this meant as I stood among heaps of bleached skulls of one-time university students, unable to tell by looking at those empty sockets which was a student of French, which of English.

Hatred for both "revolution" and "Communism" was inevitable as a result of Amin's crimes. Many Afghan villagers *did* go off to Pakistan and some *did* join the rebellion in a holy war, and nobody, least of all Karmal himself, blamed them for it. The question arises: was stirring up a hatred for revolution and Communism Amin's aim? And if so, isn't this proof enough that he acted not as a Communist, which he never was except in the costume he wore, but as an imperialist agent?

In Afghanistan there would be people who, while fighting to save their homes from the *Mujahiddin,* the "holy warriors" out of Pakistan, "hated the Communists," though they liked Karmal and his policies which, contrasting so dramatically with Amin's, in their eyes were therefore not "Communist." To them Communism was what Amin taught them it was.

Thus, as the evidence accumulated, Amin's treachery became more and more credible. The rationale for such treachery, and even the name for it, had already been invented by Mao Tse-tung. It was he who originated the formula, materialized in the demonic so-called "Cultural Revolution," where youthful, ignorant and half-baked petty-bourgeois forces, much like the American Weathermen groups and the Italian, German and Japanese "Red Brigades" terrorists, laid waste the entire revolutionary tradition by their extremism, whose real purpose was not to promote the revolutionary cause of the oppressed but to discredit genuine revolutionaries. But from the "Left!"* Mao's elevation of the peasantry to revolutionary sainthood was cited as the moral basis for killing intellectuals, not only in China but in Kampuchea, where mere residence in the cities before 1978 was proof of "counterrevolutionary" guilt from which there was no appeal. Absolutizing the poor peasants of the countryside as the decisive revolutionary force in the liberation of Kampuchea was the justification for Pol Pot's destruction of Pnom Penh. Hatred of cities as centers of corruption, a primitive throwback to a purely feudal concept, a kind of anachronistic Ludditeism, has nothing of course in common with Marxism which builds its ideological concepts on the modern working class which developed precisely in the cities.

So the model for "revolutionary counterrevolution" already existed. The rationale was at hand. The "theory" (the three-world idea; the country versus the city; the notion of uninterrupted "commotion under heaven," etc.) was bruited about as "new," as a "deeper" development of Marxism, as a revolutionary restoration of the ideas of Marxism corrupted by the "revisionists," headed by the Soviets.

The theory, therefore, and the means for carrying it out, existed ready-made. It had behind it, to give it authority, the enormous prestige of a successful revolutionary, already deified. To "revolutionaries" in a peasant country with a backward productive system, which lacked a substantial working class, therefore, such ideas were almost irresistible. To such "revolutionaries" it seemed plausible that the "revolution" should be a peasant one—they themselves were peasants. It seemed equally logical to accept a distortion of Marxism in the name of acclimating the ideas of Marx, which arose out of the conditions of 19th-century Europe, to their own backward peasant countries where workers and the working class existed at most in embryo. In fact, adaptation of Marx's propositions *was* necessary when applied to a backward peasant country. Karmal himself raised the question: "What could be the role of a party that has adopted the ideology of the working class, of scientific socialism, in a backward peasant country?"

But Lenin had solved that problem long before. Karmal continued: "Let us recall that Lenin, addressing the revolutionaries of the East, said: wherever such parties might emerge, they would have to work among the mass

---

* Alexander Haig has tried to equate such "terrorists" (most likely penetrated and even directed by the CIA) with Communists, and more precisely with Soviet Communists, and so, in the name of "fighting terrorism," torpedo detente. But no Communist anywhere has anything in common with such provocateurs and counterrevolutionaries.

of the peasants and take into account their way of thinking and traditions, including religious traditions. The peasant of the East, Lenin said, is a typical member of the *working* mass. But even in such countries, he added, the parties taking the working-class stand could give a lead to the national movement and develop in the peasant mass the capacity for independent political thinking and for independent political activity... At the same time, considering the general uniformities of revolution, including national-democratic revolutions, we are absolutely sure that the forces loyal to the ideology of the working class can carry out such revolution even in a country where the working class is not strong enough. But for that, I repeat, the national, tribal and religious traditions, and the people's immediate demands must be taken scrupulously into account. However, all these principles were trampled by Amin and his henchmen." (WMR, April 1980. Emphasis in the original.)

HOW TO RECOGNIZE A REAL REVOLUTION

> Whoever expects a "pure" social revolution will *never* live to see it.
>
> V. I. Lenin

And yet, let this all be so—Amin proven to be a traitor, the CIA proven to have masterminded a takeover of Afghanistan—*still,* it is argued in some quarters, what happened in Afghanistan is not a real revolution but an imposed one: revolution was brought to Afghanistan on the bayonets of the Soviet Army. At most, domestically, it is asserted, it amounted to a military *putsch* engineered by a handful of disaffected officers of the Afghan army supported by members of a rival faction of the Party. All that happened was that one set of factionalists was replaced by another set in what was no more than a struggle for power.

The charge that the uprising of April 1978, which overthrew Daoud, did not have popular support rests on the assertion that the *form* which this uprising took—an attack led by the military—was a palace coup: Daoud really was in his palace and he was really attacked by the army.

Here we resort to Lenin. He pointed out that the test of a real revolution was the passing of state power from one class to another. He went on to amplify that it was the first, the principal, the basic sign of a revolution, both in the strictly scientific and in the practical political meaning of the term.

It is true that Karmal did not claim that the December 27th events that overthrew Amin marked a revolution; they marked the beginning of the "second phase" of the revolution, of the wounded but still breathing revolution which had already taken place in April 1978, and in fact, as some bourgeois observers would note, "to their surprise," entirely without Soviet support. What December did was to counteract an internal *counterrevolution* combined with external aggression—and this, too, is a revolutionary act.

The Afghan peasant who was issued free land, which had been confiscated, "expropriated," from the feudal landlords, couldn't care less about the esthetics of the transfer of power which brought this land to him. If the devil himself had brought it, it would have induced him to change his opinion about the devil. That the Soviet army had come to protect him in the possession of what the Afghan revolution had brought to his hand could not offend him. The test of whether a foreign army is an army of occupation or of friendship is also to be determined by whose class interests that army is serving. When the Soviet soldiers come out into the fields to help the Afghan peasant plant his crop, they are not acting like occupiers but like friends.

In this connection, one of our young Afghan interpreters—a medical student from Kabul University—told me, in those first days of January when all was still in confusion, that he had been approached by a bourgeois correspondent (they were everywhere) who posed him this question: "How do you feel about foreign troops—*any* foreign troops—being in your country?"

The question was a trap. Nobody is happy about having *any* foreign troops in his country, as a general concept, and if our student had innocently responded to this abstract proposition "abstractly," the correspondent would have immediately filled it with concrete substance. He would have quoted "an Afghan university student" as having told him that he objected to *Soviet* troops in his country and, from a Jesuitical point of view, he would not have been lying. But he had picked the wrong student in our friend Moneer, who, at 19, had already been in the revolutionary movement for four years, having joined a youth group.

He countered: "I cannot eat what you offer me on your spoon with my eyes closed. What troops? Friendly troops or enemy troops?"

It was the wrong answer from the point of view of the correspondent and would never find a place in his dispatch to the folks back home. But it was the right answer from a true patriot's point of view. It made all the difference in the world to Moneer—and to his people—whether the troops that came into Afghanistan were friendly, like the Soviet, or unfriendly—like those who came out of Pakistan.

It must not be forgotten either that, aside from the hairsplitting in which some people indulged in trying to determine how pure the revolution was, for thousands of people, especially before the December 27th uprising, such moralizing was literally Jesuitical weighing of their life and death. In the first weeks of January some 15,000 of Amin's prisoners were freed. These included not only Party members but also non-Party intellectuals, clergymen, small merchants, small landholders, etc. Many of them were slated for execution. Many before them had already been executed. If the December 27th uprising had done nothing more than to save their lives it would have been an act of tremendous humanitarian significance in itself.*

Afghanistan was one of the poorest countries in the world with an aver-

* Which Amnesty International at the time actually did acknowledge.

age per capita income of less than $200 a year. In a country with 800 doctors and 75 medical establishments, the death rate of children was 50 percent. Life expectancy was 40 years. The illiteracy rate was 90 percent with that of women closer to 99 percent. Only 28.8 percent of school-age children went to the 4,200 schools, 70 percent of which were hovels, unfit for humans to be in.

Suffice it to say that the U.N. in an overall survey of world health and literacy conditions, listed Afghanistan (1978-79) as 127th in public education and 119th in the adequacy of health care. For some 15-18 million people there were only 71 hospitals with 3,600 beds, mostly concentrated in the biggest cities. Of 1,027 doctors 84 percent lived and worked in Kabul.

A country whose population has been variously put at 15 to 18 million was dominated mainly by landlords, three percent of whom owned over 70 percent of the land. Along with landlordism came a feudal religion—Islam. Most of the Moslems were Sunnite (80 percent), while the minority (about 20 percent) were Shiite. Although the Pushtuns are the major national group, there are 22 other national minorities as well, divided into tribes and clans. The principal languages are Pushtu and Dari, in both of which the national business is conducted. But since Karmal came to power efforts to give all the languages in the country, in addition to Dari and Pushtu, which are the two official languages, an equal dignity have been vigorously pushed.

The first actions of the new government in 1978, headed by Taraki, included expropriating the huge tracts of land from the big landlords—40,000 of them—making instant "refugees" and "holy warriors" who turned to the "free world," where public education and health care had existed for generations, to help them get their lands back, and the illiteracy and diseases that went with them.

In the first six months after the April 1978 Revolution, 300,000 peasants received expropriated land. A maximum of 30 *jeribs* (one *jerib* equals one-half acre) was allotted to each. This was a daring, revolutionary act which cut broadly but—as it would later be admitted—not too discriminately. Nor did it mean that once the peasant had a legal right to the land he forthwith assumed psychological ownership of it and tilled it as really his own. It was, in fact, for many a peasant too shocking a fact to digest: that from landless, deepest poverty and ignorance he should become a landowner overnight, *as a gift!* His sense of dependency on the landlord for everything, his generations' inbred conviction that he was nothing in the sight of Allah and his landlord (who seemed to go together), his superstition that life for him was predestined to toil and deprivation: these were profoundly rooted psychological obstacles which no mere proclamation from Kabul could overcome. Some dead counterrevolutionaries were discovered with land deeds still in their pockets—deeds presented to them by the Taraki government but which they had not dared to believe. They died fighting to restore land that could have been theirs—to Allah and their landlords!

Many also feared that the power which donated the land to them was not strong enough to protect them in their posession of it. Deep was the fear of the landowner, buttressed by the fear of the wrath of Allah, instilled in the peasant by thousands of *mullahs,* some of whom were themselves landowners. Taking over real ownership of the land, therefore, proceeded slowly. In addition, counterrevolutionaries came out of Pakistan at night and burned the peasant's field, his home, his wife and children, and himself. In the beginning not only did Amin, whose responsibility it was to protect him, fail to do so, it seemed as time wore on that it was deliberate policy to fail to do so. In any case, by 1980 only 180,000 families had joined the cooperatives and were farming their lands in this mutual-aid form—a higher level of consciousness beyond individual farming. With the entry of Karmal on the scene new measures were taken to reassure the peasants that the land belonged to them and that they would be protected in holding it.

Another of the early acts taken by the Taraki government after coming to power was the truly revolutionary one of abolishing usury, which was done in July 1978, as Decree No. 6. As an almost pure feudal society, usury flourished in Afghanistan as it had (and does) in all feudal societies. The peasant was literally bound to the usurer whose high interest rates on his primary loan (which was often nominal)—amounting to 45 percent annually—could never be paid. Debt mounted on debt, and if the peasant had no property that could be sold, he sold his children. He himself literally worked to death.

Canceling the peasants' debt to usury literally lifted a burden of 33,000,000 afghanis from the backs of 80 percent of the population, which meant liberating about 11 million individuals. Some 160,000 families of peasants had their fines for tax delinquency of payments, amounting to 822,000,000 afghanis, canceled. These acts no doubt impoverished thousands of usurers who could not have looked upon the Taraki government more kindly therefore. They, too, became instant *Mujahiddin,* "holy warriors" so beloved of the editorial writers of the *Times* and *Post* and State Department poets.

The status of women was even more typically feudal. That is, women had fewer rights than some animals who were more necessary to survival. They were not only slaves in society, but inside the home they were doubly, even triply slaves to their husbands and to the male children. They could be and were sold into marriage as children, were forced to wear the *chadri* from the age of 13 until the night of their wedding—usually the first time they saw the face—and age—of their new husbands. If they were fortunate enough to be married to a rich man they very likely had to share his bed and board with other wives. It was legal to have four wives, and 10 percent of Afghan men had more than one wife (and concubines).

It hardly has to be added that they were kept illiterate, profoundly religious, backward in every respect except in those skills and talents needed to serve their husbands. While the husband was free to indulge himself in every luxury and vice (according to his wealth and taste), punishment of the straying wife (and of the single woman) was merciless. As late as 1970, Kabul's *mullahs* had held a month's demonstration against women wearing mini-skirts, and had attacked some of the liberated women with acid. And in Saudi Arabia, a "model" feudal society still, where Brzezinski's "arc" held fast, as late as 1982 religious police *(mutawwa)* went about the city cracking the knees of women in short skirts with their clubs (NYT, Feb. 7, 1982). As for Pakistan, erring wives could be and were stoned to death, while in Iran the walls held slogans calling for "Death to women whose heads are uncovered" (NYT, Apr. 21, 1982).

After coming to power the Taraki government launched immediately an extensive campaign to abolish illiteracy, and though this campaign suffered from the same distortions that every other aspect of his policies did, and for reasons both "natural" and "unnatural," still the distortions did not affect the basic validity and need for the programs. People *needed* to become literate. That dreadful mistakes were made in applying the policy does not affect the need for the policy itself.

In fact, when Karmal came to power he did not criticize the Taraki government's program in principle but only in administration. The problems were many, the time was short, the cadres for carrying out the program were untrained and, in addition, among them were conscious and unconscious saboteurs. But it was necessary to improve the health of the population, teach the children, liberate the women, break up the feudal landholdings, eliminate usury, build homes and promote industry. That they should bungle some of these tasks would have been inevitable even under the most favorable conditions. But the conditions under which they tried to drag the 12th century into the 20th—almost literally by the hair—were anything but favorable.

It is noteworthy that the "Western" powers had been more than complacent about Afghanistan's backwardness for years under kings and feudal lords. It was taken for granted that 50 percent of the children should die and that women should be slaves. But the moment the people themselves began to take power into their own hands, and started to refashion their society, *then*—and then only—did the hounds of hell leap out of their London and Washington lairs and start baying to the world that tyranny had fallen upon that benighted land!

Plans to destabilize the revolution did not begin, as we have seen, in April 1978. One can date them even much earlier—during the entire 19th century when, as Kim in Kipling's book of the same name, enlisting as a spy for the British, noted that the "Great Game" had already been going on for years in that part of the world and would always go on.

The fact is that neither the April 1978 Revolution, which overthrew Sardar Daoud, nor the December 27th, 1979 uprising, which overthrew Amin, was the work of a mere handful of adventurists without popular support. Nor is the revolution in Afghanistan to be encompassed in the concept of the "great game" which allegedly went on forever between the great powers —between imperial Britain and imperial Russia in the 19th century and between capitalist America and socialist Russia in the 20th: a change with no change, as the French say.

There *was* a change—a real one. By 1978 there were between 343,000 (Central Statistical Office) and a million (PDPA estimate) unemployed in Afghanistan. Social conditions had worsened dramatically. As for the popular backing for the revolution, Mahmood Baryalai, a member of the Central Committee of the PDPA and of the Revolutionary Council, and editor-in-chief of the Party paper, *Haqiqate Engqelabe Saur,* would tell us in July that the Party's membership at the time of the April 1978 revolt was 50,000.*

The April uprising was sparked by the police-inspired assassination of Mir Akdar Khybar, one of the founding members of the PDPA, an immensely popular leader. His murder was followed by a roundup of Party members, headed by Taraki (but excluding Amin), who was slated for execution.

The funeral of Mir Akbar Khybar became a mass protest demonstration which brought thousands of people into the streets of Kabul and led directly to the uprising itself a short while later. But the thousands who had poured out into the streets of Kabul to follow their leader to his resting place were an unmistakable "vote" on how they felt, and when the revolutionary officers and soldiers went into action against Daoud they found no opposition among the people and very little from Daoud's soldiers as well, most of whom deserted to join the rebellion.

And yet, impressive as the proof of Amin's betrayal and of the popular support for the revolution, and for the Karmal government that came into power to save the revolution, all of it based on objective evidence, as it

* Another figure is quoted in the *New Age* (India) of Sept. 9-23, 1979, as "less than 10,000." By July 1982 the Party membership was 70,000. The earlier 50,000 figure presumably included both factions. Since 1979, 90 percent of the new Party members are workers or peasants. The rest are intellectuals, civil servants, or soldiers. By mid-1983, the membership of the PDPA had reached 90,000.

undoubtedly is, there is still one more bit of proof which, in its way, is unique, not to say exotic, without any exact precedent in history but which, because of its very nature, is all the more convincing.

I had hardly expected to have my qualities as a film critic called upon to help form a judgment of Amin's personality. After all, Amin was not an actor, as Trotsky had once been, and as Mao's wife had once been. Or was he?

In Kabul that January we saw a documentary film, a co-production of the (Soviet) Uzbek Popular Science and Documentary Studios and the Afghan-Film Studios, called "Afghanistan: the Revolution Continues."

It was a routine film, though interesting, in all respects but one. And the part that made it of absorbing interest was not the contribution of either film studio. It was the contribution of Amin himself.

The film began familiarly enough by reviewing the beginning of the revolution, giving us scenes of happy peasants receiving land, of liberated women taking off the veil, of children trooping to school, and so on. All true, all predictable.

But then came a bizarre episode. At this point it was as though the producers of the film had just turned their documentary over to Amin himself to do with as he chose. Actually, they had found this unedited film in the studio, still in the can; Amin had come to his end too soon to edit it, let alone to show it.

Amin had "written" the script, directed it and acted it. Earlier footage of the official newsreel had shown Taraki on his arrival at Kabul airport from Havana (having stopped in Moscow) in September. A welcoming delegation was there carrying flowers. Heading the delegation we see—Hafizullah Amin. He moves toward his "Father" and "teacher," bends slightly and, grasping Taraki's hand, kisses it. This tableau is the very picture of the loyal and devoted son showing his loyalty and devotion to his esteemed father and leader of the country.

Later film sequences, still of the official newsreel, show him standing poker-faced in the margin of the scenes where Taraki is featured, silently and modestly playing second fiddle to the man whom he had already planned —or soon would plan—to murder.

Knowing more about his psychology as it developed later, we can be sure that enduring his role of loyal second-in-command must have been an enormous strain on this headstrong and imperious plotter, and incalculably galling to his enormous ego and monumental vanity. For only some weeks stood between that kiss of Judas and the command from those same lips that choked out Taraki's life.

But there is more. At a certain point in the documentary, as we've already noted, the movie is turned over to Amin himself. This footage, not having been edited, is shown raw, just as it came out of the can.

In order to educate the people—most of whom are illiterate—about the role he played in the revolution, Amin decided to re-enact on film (much in the style of CBS' Dan Rather later on) the heroic events leading up to the triumph of April 1978.

It seems incredible to me now that what I then saw—or thought I saw—was actually what I did see. For this film shows Amin himself—an untypically outsized Afghan, ebullient, handsome, bursting with elan, masculine in the way we now call *macho,* with self-confidence oozing out of every pore—in the process of making a movie. This section shows (because it is unedited) several retakes of scenes which he had found fault with, and we are treated to numbered clapboard mug shots introducing each new take, where we see Amin posed immobile for the identifying shot, passive, frozen-faced (almost unrecognizable), until the command, "Roll the camera!" must have been issued, because his face "suddenly" comes to life the way an actor's does, and he becomes a miraculously "charismatic leader" whose visage had begun to bloom on the walls of the government offices throughout the land.

We now see him, in the next uncut, unedited scene, roused from "sleep" in his bedroom (though we could see he was only feigning "sleep" the way children do) by his son, Abdullah Amin Raman, and our credulity is strained by this fakery from the very outset. His son tells him that the police are at the door. In an instant Amin the actor is out of bed, has bounded to the cupboard to get hold of the plan for the uprising, placed in his care by Taraki, which is wrapped in his wife's shawl.

But the actor-police are on him before he can swallow it all. They take books and other material which they pile into a sack and then tote it away. Surprisingly, they don't arrest Amin, though they had already arrested Taraki. Instead, Amin is put under "house arrest," but so casual is this "arrest" that he can conduct the entire subsequent uprising from its unguarded portals.

He sends his son out to contact the key revolutionaries (one of whom is Gulabzoi) to tell them that the date of the uprising had been brought forward (because the previously set date was now known to the police). In all these comings and goings his children, including another grown son, Abdur Rahwan, were never molested nor was his wife, though Taraki's most certainly was.

Amin is so free of any surveillance by the police that even two of his American admirers, Nancy Peabody Newell and Richard S. Newell, in their book, *The Struggle for Afghanistan,* find it "remarkable," and wonder about "collusion" between Amin and the police (i.e. Daoud, now working hand-in-glove with the CIA through SAVAK and the Shah of Iran).

The fact that "during the time between his arrest and his removal to prison the police suffered a lapse so remarkable as to invite speculation about 'collusion'" is an interesting admission from writers who would also admit that "Amin was not their [the Soviets'] man; he had seized power against their wishes." *(Ibid.)*

In any case, while Taraki, whose wife was slightly wounded by an arresting soldier's bayonet, was in prison (where Karmal already was), Amin was free—and just free long enough—to set the insurrection into motion. He dictates the entire new plan for the uprising to one of his lieutenants, who was to pass it on to Sayid Gulabzoi,* in direct charge of the uprising, a plan that contained dozens of names and innumerable details and precise instructions (and would have taken hours to do) with no help but his memory—an incredible feat indeed.

Then, just hours before the uprising itself, but not before he had tidied up all the details and with everything in shipshape working order, is he also arrested and taken to prison, from which he will quickly emerge as hero and triumphant leader of the revolution—and we shall see all this in the film as he re-enacts that day, now as an actor, riding on a tank waving his hands still wearing the handcuffs he presumably was too busy to take off.

Since he is the actor acting himself, he presents us with a double view of the man (as we critically see him) and of the man (as he wants us to see him). What he wants to tell *us* tells everything about *himself*. Since we, as viewers, know the real ending of this film, we can see in its given sequences how he had intended it to end in life and by what means. The means were fraudulent, the end was as fraudulent as the means. That he could not endure the idea of a professional actor performing his role speaks volumes of the man's vanity and need to have absolute control over everything the people should know. He wanted to have power not only over the events themselves but over the fictional depiction of those events. If there was to be a crack between art and reality he wanted to fill it with himself!

You found yourself watching this charade in disbelief. This ham actor—for you are watching a *ham* actor—not only murdered the leader of his country but was now literally trying to reconstruct the past to fit his version of events. *He* was the actor—that is, he remained as consistent before the cameras "acting" himself as he was before the cameras that caught him at the airport kissing Taraki's hand—acting still. In his mind the distinction between history and art had disappeared—all was theater.

Nevertheless, villain or just ham actor, or both, having asked the Soviets to come, and being off guard quite possibly when they *did* come, this Amin

---

* Now (1983) Minister of the Interior, directing the internal police force. Stuart Auerbach had him arrested and ousted from office in July 1980.

still had one hope to save himself—the man in the White House who had also to some degree confused cinema with life.

But cinema is not life, and when he needed him most the man in the White House was shelling peanuts. Still, at the U.N. it was possible to cast a vote for his ghost in the guise of voting for a principle which Amin had violated ever since he understood the convenient difference between truth and fiction and how to manipulate one against the other.

Taraki's Iago had signaled his intention to sell his country to the American paymaster long before he had the actual power to do so. Nevertheless, it was precisely toward this end that the CIA, in funding his leadership of the Afghan Students Association, had been heading him. Amin would confide that he had been "converted" to Marxism at a student meeting in Wisconsin in 1963—hardly a source one might expect to produce working-class revolutionaries of much depth. The "New Left" of the American 60s later proved to be a rich source for anti-progressive forces even as it thinned down into a frail reed on which the "Establishment," much abused by them, learned to lean.

As is fairly clear now, the CIA had staked its best money on this newly-minted American-brand, New Left Afghan revolutionary and maintained a constant, more than avuncular interest in this man who was "by nature a cruel person. His isolation made him the Pol Pot of Afghanistan." (Inbisat Ahmad Alui, *Arabia,* April 1982.)

Nevertheless, in New York, when the time came to vote, the figures would read 104 countries calling for an exit of "all military forces" from Afghanistan (but not from Pakistan), with 10 voting against and 30 hiding in the men's rooms.

True, James Reston of the *Times* would caution readers soon after that they should not read the vote too literally. He noted in his column (Jan. 19, 1980), after canvassing some of those at the U.N. who had voted for the U.N. resolution, that though America's allies were supporting Carter's sanctions against Iran and the Soviet Union, "we shouldn't be misled. What they are saying in public and what they are saying in private are quite different."

In addition, Carter's precipitate action in declaring a boycott of the U.S.S.R., along with other moves and melodramatic denunciations which could only be justified as preliminary to a declaration of war, had appalled West European opinion. George Ball, former U.S. Secretary of State, would tell reporters in London: "This has caused some criticism of the United States and had some rather disturbing repercussions on our relations with them." Significantly, he was speaking at a meeting of the Trilateral Commission, which had godfathered Carter into the presidency. (UP, Mar. 24, 1979.)

SHOPPING ON CHICKEN STREET

I fear thee and thy glittering eye,
And thy skinny hand so brown.

Samuel Taylor Coleridge,
The Ancient Mariner

But what did Kabul look like six months after Karmal had come to power? In a July 8 (1980) dispatch from New Delhi, Stuart Auerbach would tell the readers of *The Washington Post* that "Afghan rebel groups based in Pakistan have expanded their influence into the *heart of Kabul* [my emphasis], where pictures of their leaders are pasted up and their proclamations are circulated, *travelers* [again my emphasis] and *Western diplomats [sic!]* report here." And he states flatly: "There is no doubt, however, of an increased rebel presence in Kabul in the past month."

That was July 8. Surely those "pictures of their leaders" would still be visible in "the heart of Kabul" two days later when I arrived again? Surely, if there was actually an "increased rebel presence" which could be seen all the way from New Delhi, it wouldn't become so dim by the time I arrived that its "increased presence" became actually invisible to my eyes though my hotel was in the "very heart" of Kabul and I often visited the bazaars?

Kabul in July was hot: 30°C. We made a run on the good Czechoslovak Pilsener the hotel featured. Beggars and the homeless now could be seen lying on the streets. But we had seen housing going up in Parwan Maina near Kabul—a whole complex, in fact, complete with mosques, kindergartens, three primary schools, one market, one cinema, clubs, health offices, etc., a total of 4,230 apartments with a waiting list for many more. Similar projects were on the way or being planned. The Soviets had donated a prefabricated housing construction factory earlier. New housing was badly needed in a city where the average Afghan lives in less than three meters of space and where out of 70,000 dwellings only 30,000 are considered fit for human habitation.

The famous bazaars, where rumors sold more quickly than their goods (many of which came from as suspicious sources as the rumors), were crowded, but real commerce, like the Kabul River, had almost dried up. But we could, and did, go there unaccompanied, despite horrendous stories of unwary Russian shoppers leaving behind not only their money but their heads. In the shops lining the streets we could smell dust and time, and though we saw all kinds of things, from garnet necklaces to lapis lazuli rings, from tiger skins (with the bullet hole that brought it to this shop) to karakul, we never saw a picture of any "leaders" on any walls. It obviously would have been highly risky to have hung them there. In any case, after the failed *putsch* of February such pictures had been consigned to the moth balls. The merchants had decided Karmal was here to stay, and nobody was threatening their businesses.

The city is full of merchants, big and little: 30,000 of them (more in other cities). You come across them everywhere with names painted in Pushtu and English: Maria Beauty Salon, Kabul Hairdressing Salon, Antique Boutique, Candlelight Restaurant, New Snack Bar, Marco Polo Restaurant, and windows advertizing Toni hair coloring ("only your hairdresser knows for sure").

Everywhere you go you come up against people who want to sell something—boys offering Winston and Marlboro cigarettes, garnet necklaces and cigarette holders made of alabaster. Lapis lazuli, bluer than the sky, is a street hawker's common ware. Merchants stand in their doorways and lure the customers in with ingratiating smiles and promises of unbelievable bargains.

Hawkers, bargainers, buyers and sellers: nevertheless, these are not the developed businessmen of the West. They still smell of camels and donkey dung. They are pre-capitalist. Their forte is cunning, not *Realpolitik*. They have no power—they are not General Motors or ITT or Bechtel. They rub hands and salaam. They don't command.

These student guides of ours from Kabul University (who shoo away little giggling child-beggars who tug at our coasts and turn up "pathetic" eyes at us) carry textbooks with them and cram for the coming exams. Even a revolutionary upsurge has not really interrupted their studies. Some had already passed their major tests and, like our Moneer, served us (me) almost all his time.

He wears (in January, when we first met him) a Russian-styled fur hat and a thin topcoat, both of which he keeps on when eating. He has the narrow face of an ascetic and the eyes of a sleepy cat. His passions are still to be aroused. When I asked him if he, at 19, had a girlfriend (in the innocuous American sense), he misunderstood me and assumed I had asked whether he had a mistress (in the Afghan sense), and answered: "No, it is immoral." He meant "immoral" as a revolutionary, not as an Afghan male.

He and his brother Bashir* had learned their English at the American

---

* I had learned that they were brothers by accident. When I asked them what their family name was they surprised—and puzzled—me by telling me that they had none—that family names were not used by Afghans. The names they bore—Moneer

Center, which had been financed by Asia House, the CIA front, though they were hardly aware of it at the time. Still, they took some ironic satisfaction in pointing out the Center to us as we passed it, and waited patiently as we read the notice (in English) which the departed Americans had pinned up in December:

> The English language program and the Library of American Center will be closed temporarily. The American Center regrets the inconvenience. Students and library patrons check again after the New Year.

Alas for optimism! Checking "after the New Year" still found the Center closed, the "inconvenience" supposed to be "temporary" well on its way to being permanent. Nevertheless, here was where Moneer and his brother (and some others) had learned their English (he was also now studying Russian) and had picked up bits of American history so that he could match what he knew of Lincoln with what I knew.

In any case, the Americans of Asia House, tax-exempt in New York City, had never figured that they were training Afghan youth to service the "inconvenient" revolution which expelled them. Asia House, still functioning in January, was no longer functioning in July, or at least not in the same way. Both Afghanistan and the U.S.A. still considered it politic not to break off diplomatic relations entirely (as was true with Pakistan, which maintained a consulate here as well).

Between press conferences and meetings our students took us shopping in those areas much favored by tourists, mainly on Chicken Street. Going in and out of the shops, sidestepping street vendors, haggling over prices of souvenirs, we were hardly aware in the midst of this desultory bargaining (our minds were not on it, we were not genuine tourists) that we were in the middle of a raging war as it came to us over BBC and VOA.

We did meet an occasional important looking Russian who was accompanied by a friend carrying a submachine gun. Presumably some people

---

and Bashir—they had given themselves or, more probably, some more important member of the family had given it to them. At most, they were "the son of" their father who, in turn, was the son of his father. But they shared no family name. However, it had become the practice (in the 20s), at least for intellectuals, to give themselves a second name, and they told me I could add "shah" to their names if I had to have a second name. Both had learned their English at the American Center and Moneer, who was given the assignment of finding interpreters for us, included his brother among those he chose. Moneer had important Party duties and was "more political" than his brother Bashir, though he was younger. When they told me their father, a retired army officer, had two wives and two sets of children—14 in all—I was taken, as they say, somewhat aback and wanted to know how two wives, one husband and 14 children all managed to get along. Fine, they assured me. I reserved my doubts.

needed such protection. But we had none, and no danger seemed possible from the shopkeepers who welcomed us hopefully into their shops.

They stood, these shopkeepers, in their doorways, or even came out and sat in the winter sun, talking. Curious about them, I asked Moneer what, in his opinion, they were thinking of "right now?"

He threw them a contemptuous glance. "Right now?"

There had been a revolt only days before and the government had changed hands. The world was up in indignant arms at what the Soviets were allegedly doing here. "Yes, what are they thinking of right now?"

"How to make money!" he snapped. "How to buy or sell something. How to get you inside their shop to cheat you. They don't care what else is happening in the world."

His ascetic student revolutionary's soul was offended by them. He had the contempt of an aristocrat for a tradesman: that a nation should shape its policies on their need to trade seemed grotesque to him.

He warned us that they were very shrewd and would certainly clip us if we weren't careful, and though he detested the chore agreed to do our bargaining for us—but only to protect us from being cheated. He would take it on as his revolutionary assignment.

As for support of the revolution—obviously, one did not look for revolutionaries among the proprietors of the Kabul Hairdressing Salon or the Antique Boutique! In February, when these shopkeepers went "on strike," this action did not so much surprise Moneer as deeply offend him. Shopkeepers on strike! It was an obscenity...

Later, I asked a young shopkeeper who was fussing around me trying to fit my feet into a pair of Afghan slippers (which I had decided to buy in order to engage him in conversation) what he thought of the Russians being in his country. I told him I was an American journalist, which I imagined would open up the sluices of indignation in him, which it did. I gathered from the flow—he spoke English—that burst out of him that he didn't like the Russians, but whether it was because their presence aroused his latent patriotism or that the ruble had very little standing in the money markets in the world I couldn't quite decide.

It had already amazed me how professionally even the boy hawkers on the street could quote you to the decimal point where the world's monies stood in relation to each other—and all to the afghani—at any set moment. When I asked one of them how much the garnet necklace he was touting was worth, his mind's little tumblers could be seen racing to search out exactly how many afghanis came out of how many dollars (24 afghanis to the dollar legally but much more on the Black Market, which seemed to be the only Market functioning). Rubles were not exchangeable and the Russians, who had access to a limited quotient of afghanis, were not good customers, therefore. This, I think, and not the "invasion," was the real atrocity, in their heart of hearts, the merchants charged against them.

The shopkeeper who sold me the slippers confided to me that he hoped the Americans would come, and I had no doubt that in February he needed no prodding to close the doors of his shop. Incidentally, the "bargain" I got from him at a "special low price" turned out not to be such a bargain after all when I tested it back in Moscow. I, too, have an account to settle with one merchant in Kabul!

From him, I move on down the street. A boy of no more than twelve jumps out of his shop and takes me by the hand. *"Davai! Davai!"* he urges me, mistaking me for a Russian, but immediately adding: "Come, come!" His eyes are fixed on me.

"Why?" I ask him, wanting to explore this moment.

"I have good products!"

"But I don't want any."

He takes this for an opening ploy—steps away and, adopting a bargaining pose, cries, holding up two fingers. "Two minutes! Two minutes!"

He's so urgent, so insistent, so *promising* that, having dallied for a moment, I now felt somehow committed. And then, how could anyone refuse the least of mortals on this earth at least two minutes? Karmal had promised a new social system. This boy was promising me something more rewarding close at hand, asking of me only a moment of my time! There was a tug in him, there was a seduction in his voice as he waited to see if he had awakened the strongest emotion he understood in a human being: avarice.

Laughing as I went, I let him pull me into his shop. I knew I was a fraud. I knew I was going to disappoint him. But I wanted to see how this mite of a man, so old at twelve in the ways of bluster and barter, would play me. The shop was filled with carpets, sheepskin coats, gowns and leather suitcases. He spread his hands expansively toward them, jutted out his chin and demanded sternly: "Your maximum!"

What was the most—that is, the least—I was willing to pay for these goods? What was my "maximum?" How could I let him know that my "maximum" had nothing to do with what he had to offer in his shop? My "maximum" would have sent him out of there into school, though it was obvious he had already picked up bits and pieces of at least four languages without benefit of classroom instruction. His English had surprised me. His Russian, more. I saw that the drive for profit was a powerful instructor!

Still, I watched in amazement as this midget merchant performed an extraordinary dance for me, a kind of wooing ritual, weaving back and forth on his nimble feet as he held me with his calculating eyes. His face, slightly swollen with his passion to sell—to snare me—verged on obscenity, and was saved from that by the fact that, though the intent was to show me a merchant wise in the ways of commerce, the actual effect was a child's parody of a merchant's cunning. He was too young to have mastered the style of a procurer. The child beneath lingered visibly.

This distortion of childhood came vividly home to me only now in this encounter—for if I had met this dancing merchant in Paris or London or New York I would have shrugged him aside without a word. But the revolution had provided a moral backdrop for everything. And suddenly, children being turned into obscene little hagglers who hoped to deceive you about their goods, and all for your omnipotent dollar, was no longer the exotic thing in an exotic setting tourists are amused to see and photograph, but the ugly, immoral thing it really was.

It was not enough to have learned the English, French and German for *how much, give me your maximum,* and *here's bargain.* There was much more to English, French and German than that. And more to Russian than *"Davai!"* (Give). And there was more to arithmetic than the skill of short-changing the visiting stranger who couldn't remember what the exchange rate between the afghani and the dollar was that morning.

Still, he wouldn't let me go even though I kept spreading out my hands and pantomiming my poverty. A Westerner without cash? He assumed the fault lay in him: he wasn't communicating. He nailed me to the floor with a sharp command and ran next door to get his father. His father came running, shot one sharp, calculating glance at me, sized me up instantly (every hair of me) and ran back to where other customers were more promising. The poor boy stood there stunned. The last look he threw at me now was filled not merely with disappointment but—yes, something else: hate, I think.

To have found this passion for profit functioning so vividly, so autonomously here in this city among merchants while the greater passions of revolution and counterrevolution drove over their heads touching them only like shadows—like clouds—sobered and depressed me. I could see that it would take more than resolutions adopted by a new government to change things on Chicken Street!

We kept on moving. And as we passed from shop to shop we became conscious of the fact that at one point a shadow had quietly attached itself to us, waiting on the sidewalk for us to leave each shop, following us to the next one. We could see she was a woman, but of no particular age. She made no demands but was there, our other self, part of the gathering darkness of the late afternoon.

Once, when I hurried out of the shop where I had bought a pair of slippers I bumped into her where she stood, a mute, now vaguely accusing figure connected to me in some unspoken complicity. I mumbled something. She said nothing. Made no attempt to touch me, to hold me, to barter.

Others were there offering necklaces of lapis lazuli. She just held out her hand.

We'd grown tired of beggars. They had tried to hold you, force you to look at them. She had tried none of these tricks. But this time, because I had actually touched her, I looked up to see who was confronting me with an unspoken accusation here on Chicken Street, and recoiled with horror. There was no face there! Just a mask. The rest had rotted away, and where her nose should have been were two dark holes. As she caught my horrified reaction her eyes glittered with a distant and malicious amusement, as though she had expected to see this, had seen it often. I quickly dropped a coin into her hand and hurried from her as though I was running from feudal Afghanistan itself, with all its misery and disease brought down from the rotted past, diseases unknown to the rest of the world for decades, even centuries—scourges, plagues, afflictions that ate off parts of one's body and seemed like a cancer voraciously alive, devouring what meagre flesh was there still wrapped inside the rags of poverty and misery.

These two images—of the boy merchant and the silent ghost who followed us so relentlessly—remain the living prototypes of Afghanistan's past and what was wrong with Afghanistan's present, and nothing the bourgeois press would say later about how the Kabul merchants, groaning under the "heel of the Russian oppressors," had risen to strike a blow for liberty, would impress me.

"Give me your maximum!" that twelve-year-old merchant had demanded.

"Look at me—*dare* to look at me!" the woman beggar had said to me without a word, seeing in my white face and Western ways the source of her torment.

RAMADAN

> *The revolution cast off the yoke forever,*
> *Our ancient land is young again,*
> *Over its villages and towns*
> *Floats the banner of the republic!*
> *Arise, land of our fathers,*
> *The dark night is receding—arise!*

Suleiman Laiyek,
"Rise, Native Land"

In the long week (Jan. 30 through February 17th) I spent in Kabul, when the iron was glowing hot on the anvil, and later, the week I spent in July (10th to the 18th), when the hammer had begun to shape the red-hot iron, I would meet with an impressive succession of the Afghan revolutionary leadership, beginning with Babrak Karmal himself, whom I interviewed twice (along with other journalists).

Most of my time was spent in Kabul and its environs. Aware that some might consider this a crippling limitation, distorting my view of the whole phenomenon, I made sure that I met and interviewed people from all over Afghanistan, including those who had been on the "front" lines.

Not necessarily in the order in which they were interviewed—and aware that some changes have since been made—is the list of Party and government officials whom we questioned (checking what they said in January with what we ourselves saw in July): Rahim Rafat, editor of the *Kabul New Times,* who often translated for Karmal at press conferences; Mohammad Khan Jalalar, Minister of Commerce, who had held that post through three governments starting with Daoud, and who was not a Party member; Abdul Aziz Sadegh, President of the Religious Scholarship Association, as well as various *mullahs,* who was on the counterrevolutionary death list; Shah Mohammad Dost, Foreign Minister; Burhan Ghiasi, First Secretary of the Democratic Youth Organization; Lt. Col. Mohammad Rafi, the young Minister of Defense, who had been awaiting execution in Pule-Charhi prison and was saved at the last moment by the uprising which disposed of Amin; Sattar Purdely, Chairman of the Trade Unions of Afghanistan; Faroug Karmand, President of the Social Sciences Institute, which trained activists for ideological work in the countryside and elsewhere; Allam Hamidi, Director of Handicrafts Production, which accounted for a good proportion of Afghanistan's foreign trade; Nizamuddin Tahzib, Chief Justice of the Supreme Court; Mahmood Baryalai, Head of the International Department of the PDPA, and editor of the Party's paper, *Haqiqate Engqelabe Saur,* also "reported" in the Western press as having been assassinated; Zahir Moafar, Azam Karigar, members of the Kabul City Council; Zohor Ramjo, Kabul Party Secretary; Zoyar, Natiba Notaki, Sorya, Palvasha Jamil, members of the Central Committee of the Women's Democratic Association; Nimat Kudus, Party Secretary of a region 30 kilometers outside of Kabul; the head of Kabul University, Ahmad Assis Bagtash; students, waiters, taxicab drivers, shopkeepers, prison guards, ex-prisoners, boy cigarette vendors, and other assorted and unassorted witnesses and non-witnesses to turbulent events who crossed our path. To Sultan Ali Keshtmand, Deputy Prime Minister in January, and Anahita Ratebzad, Minister of Education, we shall devote special attention.

Between the snows of January and the heat of July much had changed in Kabul. If in January, with the new phase of the Saur (April) Revolution only two weeks old, a feeling of uncertainty, of hanging in mid-air characterized Kabul while the new leadership, in a sense, was introducing itself to the people, who were taking their time to look them over, by July all this had noticeably changed.

By then the first period of uncertainty was behind them. Counterrevolutionary thrusts (most notably in February) had been contained. Hidden enemies had been rooted out. Even the merchants, who had been cowed into neutrality, or even into cooperation with the counterrevolutionaries in February, now had developed a new confidence—or resignation—that the regime would hold. Students, who had been tempted into gestures of their own brand of criticism, had seen how these gestures, so innocent and well-meant, had been picked up by the sinister forces of counterrevolution and carried into the streets with bombs and fire.

Much had been learned by everybody in a few months. More remained to be learned. By July the new program initiated by Karmal had been published and scanned. But not much more. Time was needed—and tranquility, it hardly has to be said—for the new plan to bear fruit. Meanwhile, of one thing the people were certain: the days of indiscriminate arrests were over.

Karmal's declaration of general amnesty, made on the first day of his resurgence as the leader of the revolution, that freed thousands of prisoners from Amin's jails, and not just political prisoners, Parchamite members, but all prisoners of Amin, was taken to mean that he was a man of his word. That same crucial week, on January 11, Friday, Karmal who had designated the day as a "Day of Mourning" had led the entire Party and government leadership to the mosques where they mourned with the people for those whom Amin had put to death. In coming to the mosques Karmal was simultaneously proving to the people that his proclamation that Islam was the "sacred" religion of Afghanistan was to be taken seriously and the faithful could be at peace.

Soon after, a decision was taken on replacing the present state flag (a red one, which the Taraki government had introduced in 1978) with a flag that would express the national character, its "independence and freedom." By April 1980 a new flag, red, black and green, with the image of a mosque clearly emblazoned on it, had been officially adopted, and the red flag was reserved for the Party only and flown at Party convocations. This move was widely accepted as further proof that the new government represented all the people and not just revolutionaries.

These, and other acts of a similar character, developed a sense of security among the people of Kabul, a feeling which was further reinforced when the militia and people's forces proved that they could control and even defeat the assassins and arsonists. Almost every day the newspapers and TV would show arrested criminals standing, hangdog and betrayed, in the midst of the piles of arms and pamphlets that had been dug out of their homes, with the text of their sullen confessions of criminal complicity running alongside their pictures.

In addition, a housing program, which had been initiated by Taraki, was vigorously pursued by Karmal.* Health services were expanded. Classes to eliminate illiteracy were resumed on a new voluntary basis. No measures were taken against those merchants who had participated passively in the February events.

There were changes, yes. But centuries of habit, custom, reinforced by religious law cannot be overcome in one, two (or quite possibly) 50 years.

Nevertheless, it was the eve of Ramadan (which returns each year 13 days earlier) and the BBC assured us that on the beginning of that holy lunar month as the sun, marking its first day, rose over the mountain, and a white thread could be clearly distinguished from a black one, a new uprising was due to break forth in Kabul.

Any "uprising" is something to look forward to. But this one interested us particularly, and we studied our white and black threads with more than routine concern as the time approached.

But as we waited for the merchants, the bargainers in the bazaars, the hidden (but still visible) "rebel groups" to rise again and strike a shatter-

---

* No proposal which seems simple and sensible to the Western mind is ever that in the East. Who could have foreseen, for example, that one of the reasons why some people opposed new housing was because, in those 12-story buildings, it was quite possible that the man living on the 11th would have a woman in the 12th standing over his head—and no woman was allowed by the Koran to stand over a man!

ing blow for freedom, registered only, as it turned out, in New Delhi and London and Washington and the editorial offices of *The New York Times* and *The Washington Post,* we had time to visit and interview government and Party officials who, as we plied them with questions, hospitably offered us drinks of Coca Cola and Fanta but refrained from drinking any themselves since they were bound to abstinence by the holy laws of Ramadan.

And "under cover of departing day, slunk hunger-stricken Ramadan away"—but no uprising, thus once again undermining our faith in the integrity of the BBC and VOA.

Meanwhile, we had work to do. I shall include interviews here I did in January along with those I did in July, and since the statistics of January and July 1980 are outdated today, I shall concentrate more on underlying factors, which do not change as rapidly.

SELF-CRITICISM

> The attitude of a political party toward its own mistakes is one of the most important and surest ways of judging how earnest the party is and how it *in practice* fulfills its obligations toward its *class* and the toiling *masses*. Frankly admitting a mistake, ascertaining the reason for it, analyzing the conditions which led to it, and thoroughly discussing the means of correcting it—that is the way it should perform its duties, that is the way it should educate and train the *class* and then the *masses*.
>
> V. I. Lenin

The problems which the new phase of the revolution confronted, at the same time that the invaders from Pakistan had to be repulsed, were formidable. All the active members of the Party and the government had just survived an experience that had brought the nation to the edge of catastrophe. They knew on their bodies what the payment for mistakes consisted of. They were in no mood for sentimentality, for either despair or mindless optimism.

But neither in January nor in July did I feel the slightest weakening or even momentary slackening of revolutionary élan in the attitudes of the men and women we met and with whom we ranged over the entire spectrum of problems—present, past and in the future. In January they struck me as slightly dazed with success. In July they were more soberly settled down. As a group they seemed to me to be competent and dedicated and morally, compared to the pigmies of the counterrevolutionary "leaders" invented by the American CIA and puffed up by the press, they were giants; however they laughed at such characterizations.

So confident had Karmal grown in the stability of his government that on July 12 he surprised the world (and the hostile press to which he supplied "sensational" copy) by announcing a national conference in which every department of his administration would be subjected to withering criticism, and his own work as well.

The Western press had labored hard to fix the image of Karmal as an incompetent, blundering puppet, politically subsisting off the grudging crumbs thrown to him from the Kremlin table. His history as a revolutionary from his youth, which included time in prison, and always accompanied by threats to his life, was kept secret from American readers. That he was a considerable theoretician, a practical politician as well (having served in the Afghan parliament to which he was elected twice), and thus hardly anyone's valet, did not suit his detractors. That he was, in fact, the instrument by which Amin's treachery was exposed and Amin (and his U.S. backers) eliminated, understandably did not endear him to the West.

Here is how the bourgeois press pictured Karmal up to this point:

> Islamabad, June 20 (1980), UPI—Radio Kabul said several members of the Afghan Cabinet were touring Afghanistan to appeal to the people not to listen to rumors. The tours follow reports that Mr. Karmal attempted suicide in his official residence last Friday, but was disarmed by his Soviet advisers. The reports said the 53-year-old president could not leave his palace without Soviet permission.

Stated as a *fact,* with "corroborative detail, intended to give artistic verisimilitude to an otherwise bald and unconvincing narrative," as Gilbert and Sullivan's Poo Bah would put it, this tale out from whole cloth was not intended to be believed, for Karmal not only "survived" but continued to work as usual, as anyone soon saw. It was intended to construct the permanent context in which the newspapers wanted the readers always to see Afghan leaders: a context of violence, mutual suspicion, abject dependence on the Russian masters, who had reduced them to such impotence that they couldn't even commit suicide successfully! (What competence does it take to bring a pistol to your head?)

After the first denials of such stories the Afghan leadership ignored them. France's Claude Gatignon of *Revolution,* who had interviewed Karmal in July, would write: "Babrak Karmal is a staunch fighter. I remind him of the reports on his alleged suicide. He laughs, and says that what is needed in our time is to wage a struggle, not suicide." (*Revolution,* France, July 18-24, 1980.)

In any case, in July, hale and hearty, we would see him on television delivering the main report of the conference and saying:

> Despite the new phase of the Saur Revolution, we have not been able, so far, to put the government machinery entirely at the service of the people. One must regretfully admit, in the way of self-criticism—and have the courage to do so—that despite the power being wielded by the working-class party ... our government machinery still does not fully respond to the needs of the people. (*Kabul New Times,* July 14, 1980.)

There were reasons for this, he went on: lack of experience, the underdevelopment of social relations, the tradition of nepotism in government, the omnipresent *bakhshish,* bribery, as a way of Oriental life, traditional lethargy and passivity inherited from centuries of feudalism in which nothing improved, nothing worsened.

This was the past. But Karmal was not looking to the past for alibis for the failures of the present. He went on to say:

> However, the Party leadership is determined to rectify, with all its power and energy, this obsolete machinery which has assumed bureaucratic and partly militarist character.
>
> The Party must put the government machinery in Afghanistan into the service of the people in a given period and in the real sense of the word. In case the PDPA leadership is unable to discharge this formidable and heavy historic duty, it must admit before the people that it lacks the required efficiency and consequently tender its resignation. (*Ibid.*)

Quite a statement! When has a leader of an Islamic country (or of a Western country) ever made such a serious and candid appraisal of his party's character and its duties?

This was neither a dictator nor a puppet speaking. Nor were these "admissions" of errors torn out of unwilling lips, as they have to be out of the lips of politicians in all bourgeois countries. They were part and parcel of the new, revolutionary style of his administration, which he embodied in his own person and whose character he detailed in the same speech:

> The PDPA CC and the DRA Council of Ministers have reaffirmed the importance of further developing the democratic principles concerning activities of party, government, economic organs and mass organizations—free and constructive criticism and self-criticism, strongly condemning the postponement of complicated problems, hushing up the urgent issues concerning the people, the existing shortcomings, drawbacks and difficulties and fear of free discussion of the pressing issues of social life.

And he then presented the conference with two immediate goals: 1) the reorganization of the various ministries and departments of the government to prepare them to carry out the proposed economic and social plans; and 2) "work on the preparation of an effective socio-economic plan for the year 1360 (1981) must begin right now."

This plan was largely the work of its Planning Minister (the already-assassinated Sultan Ali Keshtmand!) At the same conference at which Karmal spoke, looking imperturbably alive, Keshtmand outlined in more detail just what the problems facing the country actually were.

He was speaking, as Karmal was speaking, to the basic of the Party *actives*, and therefore concentrated not on poetry but on facts.

Keshtmand began by admitting that the First Five-Year Plan, which had been inaugurated under Taraki in 1978, "was not successfully implemented." He then listed its failures. "For instance, only 86.8 percent of the plan was achieved in production."

How did those failures come about? "Due to the shortcomings and errors in connection with the land reform and subversion by counterrevolutionary elements in rural areas, part of the arable land was left untilled. Likewise, more cattle were slaughtered than necessary."

But when all was said and done, that was the past. No matter whose fault the past was, the present was all theirs, and it was up to them to make a success of it. A new plan had been drawn up, "taking into account the real performances of the 1358 (1979) plan, and the social situation in the country." Though difficult, the new "plan ... is entirely realistic and practical." What is necessary for success is for the various ministries to organize themselves in more efficient ways and to carefully put the new plan into operation and stay with it. This meant that "priority" was to be given to agriculture for the coming (1981) year, when production was to rise 4.4 percent over the previous year.

To ensure that there would in fact be an increase in agricultural production, the government would see to it that the peasants, who now owned their own land, were provided with improved varieties of seed (6,000 tons of high-grade seed for grain-growing would be supplied for the 1982 sowing campaign), more fertilizer and water where needed. Loans at small or no interest would be advanced and three years of delinquent taxes would be cancelled. Prices paid to them for their products, set by the government to avoid speculation and the vagaries of the market, were fair. In fact, to stimulate production, prices on some products were set to favor the peasant. Meanwhile, prices to the consumer were also set—as the wages of workers were raised—and controlled by the government, which took up the slack between what it paid to the peasant and what it received from the consumer by subsidy.

To forestall the sabotage of "thieves, criminals and highwaymen," whose raids on the peasants' holdings Keshtmand conceded had caused a certain amount of damage to crops and farms and had terrorized a number of peasants so that they either abandoned their farms or didn't plant as much as they could have, they would organize self-protection units among the peasants in every village. Experts would be sent to the countryside to introduce scientific methods of farming. The formation of cooperatives would be encouraged on a volunteer basis, making certain that the old, Amini methods of coercion were strictly prohibited. Those farms abandoned by their rich feudal landlords (now sending mercenaries, often their own previously bound peasant-serfs, into Afghanistan from Pakistan to burn and pillage) and not yet parceled out to the peasants, would be turned into state farms where the most advanced techniques in grain-growing would be applied, and where the workers worked for wages. Tractor stations, located strategically throughout the countryside, would soon supply the farms with modern technical aid in plowing and sowing as well as in reaping. Irrigation projects, like the huge complex already being built to service the area around Jalalabad, would be extended into the water-hungry deserts.

This plan of the Karmal government was very ambitious, perhaps too ambitious. But that didn't matter. For our purposes what is important is not whether it was carried out to the decimal point but that it existed at all. Even allowing for some distance between the "reach and the grasp," and even granting in advance (though I have no authority for doing so) that not all the goals would be achieved, the important thing to register is not that their reach might exceed their immediate grasp but that it was possible to reach (plan) at all!*

No genuine Marxists have ever advocated the slogan: "Bomb the Past!" Nor have they ever defined the past as a "blank page" on which they could write "anything" at will. This was Mao Tse-tung's approach, echoed by Pol Pot. Arbitrary change is worse than no change at all. But when change is overdue, *then* one's past weighs on one like the lid on a coffin. Mongolia, before its revolution in the 20s, had become a stagnant, socially frozen society. It had not moved forward for centuries. It was sealed in the ice of a feudal theocracy that had no need of change, except that the whole people had begun to slip into oblivion in a kind of social entropy. Mongolia was rotting into its own social grave. Revolution saved it from extinction.

One has to have been in a colonial country, African or Asian, if one wants to get a hint of how heavy the burden of the past rests on the minds of the people, of the enormous inertia that that past generates, a kind of leaden historical gravity that pins people into their ruts with a power so great that only a gigantic explosion (a revolution) equal in its energy, or more than equal, to the passive energy of inertia, can wrench them free.

But the commonsense wisdom of the people, built drop by drop over the centuries of pain and blood, like a stalactite in their souls, argues against sudden change—against hope in change, against liberation. The people instinctively wish to preserve what their vast experience has given to them, and not to jeopardize what is known to the unknown.

Far more deadly to the new government than the depredations of the hired cutthroats sent in from Pakistan with their bought-and-paid-for bazookas and last-word-in-sophistication plastic mines undetectable by the usual means (for these could be eliminated in time) was the influence of the hostile *mullahs* (more than two hundred thousand of them) who had spun a web of ignorance, fear and superstition for centuries around the minds of the people. They had a stake in this ignorance. They supported the counterrevolution.

---

* In fact, the Gross National Product grew by 2.4 percent in 1981-82, and national income by 3.4 percent in the year 1360, ending March 20, 1982.

But not all had gone over to the counterrevolution. Not all were land-lords or the retainers of landlords, and those who had broken with their masters were marked men. Yet many had.

The fight on the battlefield with guns was reflected in all fields, including religion. Within Islam itself two sides emerged—one that declared "holy war" against the infidels in the name of Allah, which meant the preservation of all previous social relations; and the other, which taught that Islam was not only conformable to the humane objectives of socialism but in fact was a religious expression of socialist principles. *Mullahs* of this persuasion would tell us that Islamic teachings did not support poverty and ignorance.

In March 1981, the elders of the Pushtun tribe of Ahmadzai adopted a resolution which read: "We have seen with our own eyes that not a single mosque has been destroyed, no one is forbidden to pray and people freely attend mosques. Thus we declare that we have been misinformed."

More than one captured Afghan "rebel" revealed under questioning that what had set him against the revolution was the fact that by promising to educate his children and free his wife (from *him*!) the revolution, particularly as Amin presented it to them, threatened to erode the very minimal basis upon which he was able to confront life at all.

In this ostensibly conservative form which his beliefs took there is nevertheless a positive kernel which it was the job of the Marxists to extract. They had to convince him, and not only him but the women as well, that their sense of being, painfully accrued over the years, would not be destroyed by some arbitrary, therefore brutal, change, replacing what they had known with what they knew nothing of.

It was this consciousness that change must not be imposed dramatically from without that impelled the PDPA, in April 1980, to issue its statement of Fundamental Principles in which it pledged itself to protect and preserve the traditional Afghan family and the Afghan way of life, and that the historical continuity which traced its roots thousands of years in the past would not be violently and abruptly broken, leaving a nation an orphan in history.

None of the officials and Party members I would interview in the weeks of January and July denied this declaration of principle. Many were Moslems themselves.

But these same revolutionaries, so young and some so callow in the struggle, knew that the machinations of the feudal landlords to bring back the old times, implemented by American dum-dum bullets, gas grenades and poison pellets dropped into the drinking water of schoolchildren—as happened in May and on June 6, 1980—was not the way to teach their own or any children how to read and write.

UNBINDING MINDS

> "Perhaps it is foolish to expect people to read newspapers
> with rabbinical or juridical care to sift out the fair from
> the unfair or the justified from the unjustified inferences
> that can be drawn from a collection of words..." *The
> Washington Post* apologizing to Jimmy Carter who had
> sued the *Post*—millions of dollars worth—for slander. (Oct.
> 11, 1981.)

We had seen Sultan Ali Keshtmand on TV. But that's not enough now-
adays. There's such a thing as tape. It's important that we see him in the
flesh—touch him, ask him questions, for we had read the following dispatch
in *The New York Times* of February 24, 1980, from Peshawar, Pakistan
and under the name of James P. Sterba:

> Meanwhile, Afghan sources in New Delhi [from New Delhi via Peshawar
> about Kabul to New York and the world!] said that Vice-President Sul-
> tan Ali Keshtmand of Afghanistan who had been reported wounded in a
> shooting incident Feb. 7, died after unsuccessful medical treatment in
> Moscow.

In response to this, TASS said:

> Moscow, Feb. 25—The Reuters Agency transmitted from Islamabad on
> Sunday a "sensational story" that turned out to be a total invention. With
> reference to "trustworthy sources," it reported the death of Afghanistan's
> Deputy Prime Minister Sultan Ali Keshtmand and with detective-story de-
> tails at that.
>
> It was contended that he (Keshtmand) was wounded three weeks ago dur-
> ing a shootout at a meeting of the revolutionary council in Kabul and sent
> to Moscow, where he died. The Agency even mentioned persons who pur-
> portedly saw the coffin with his remains that was brought to the Afghan
> capital from the Soviet Union.
>
> The other Western news agencies immediately circulated this "sensation"
> through their channels.
>
> The Afghan embassy in Moscow categorically refuted these inventions of
> the Western news service as obvious slander.

Bakhtar News Agency (Afghan) would say that Keshtmand had indeed
gone to Moscow for medical treatment. He, too, had spent months in
Amin's prison after enduring torture. He had gone to Moscow to repair

the damage to his stomach caused by his stay in prison. Other members of the government would go to Moscow from time to time also for medical care, and usually for the same reason.

So, this being the case, it was important to see Keshtmand in the flesh, not because *we* doubted that it was really him we saw on TV, but because there is nothing like the pressing of flesh to rid one's self of ghosts. The fact that Keshtmand, so high in the government, was a Hazara, a minority mercilessly persecuted in the past, was of more than passing significance.

And we did meet him again. And we did see that he was alive and now well. And we pressed flesh. And so, again, the "Western press" (which included not only Reuters but Agence France-Presse, BBC, Voice of America, Deutsche Welles, Peshawar Radio, AP, *The New York Times, Time* magazine, *Newsweek,* etc.) was caught in a lie, and the Soviet press, which Americans had been taught to distrust from infancy, had told the truth. What was going on here?

At least, being in his office, seeing and speaking to Keshtmand, we were in the real world. (Keshtmand had been elected in June, meanwhile, to chairmanship of the Council of Ministers.) He looked not only unwounded but most definitely unburied and, like Karmal in a similar case, was ironical about reports of his death.

A busy man has little time for such stuff. You smile and shrug it off. It's obvious that the Western press would like Afghan ministers to spend their time denying the stories which it could set up faster than the Afghan ministers could knock down. It was also increasingly obvious that such stories, so easily refutable, were not just mistakes: there was method in that kind of "mistake." The idea was to draw a picture of internal dissention among the top leaders of the Afghan Party and government that one saw "subliminally" as operating like Chicago gangsters, which is the only way puppets dangling from the Moscow string could be expected to operate. It didn't matter that the particular stories were refuted. The general impression could be counted on to remain.

Keshtmand made some remarks about the economy we were already familiar with. But he went into other fields as well. He said that progress toward establishing the National Fatherland Front—a national coalition of various progressive and non-party organizations, also called the Patriotic Front—was fast developing, and he hoped to see it established before the end of the year. (By the end of the year, in December in fact, it was established. By August 1982 Karmal would announce that the NFF had "15 collectives and hundreds of thousands of individual members ... committees ... in 23 provinces, 15 districts and three cities ... 78 in Kabul...")

He had things to say about the PDPA, the state of the army, relations between Afghanistan and the U.S.S.R., commercial relations with other countries, though he emphasized that the U.S.S.R. remained Afghanistan's leading trading partner.

"We have," Keshtmand explained, "commercial relations with all countries, including the USA. There has been no reduction in foreign trade. As for diplomatic recognition, which some of you have asked about, we don't need it: we already have it. No country has broken off diplomatic relations with us, including the USA. Some credits have been stopped, but that's had no real effect on our economy. We get 80 percent of our credit from the USSR, and on favorable and long-lasting terms. We get economic aid from other socialist countries as well.

"Of course, there's been some economic damage from sabotage of the counter-revolutionaries, the mercenaries. But it hasn't crippled us. We will make it all up. Our larger projects have in no way been affected by counter-revolutionary sabotage—hydroelectric stations, irrigation systems, dams, etc.

"The attempt of the USA, through the CIA and other counter-revolutionary groups, to topple the revolutionary government of Afghanistan has failed. We are not a second Chile. We have major internal support. Just a few days ago, a conference of religious leaders came out in support of our revolution.

"You know, the burning of schools and mosques—whatever the aim was—did not arouse support among the people for counter-revolution. It did the opposite. People are most indignant at such acts. Instead of supporting the counter-revolution, people have come out in support of the revolution more firmly—they cooperate with us more closely, tell us where the counter-revolutionaries are hiding, what they're scheming. They don't see in them their saviors, and resorting to violence, like the criminal poisoning of schoolchildren, further alienates them. Such acts in any case show that the other side has lost hope of politically influencing the people. It's proof of their impotence.

"The guarantee which we would accept for the withdrawal of Soviet troops from our country remains what we said of that in our May 14th proposal—we want all foreign bases in Pakistan dismantled; an end put to counter-revolutionary activity; and an end put to interference in our internal affairs.

"Capitalism," he said, "was not fully developed in Afghanistan when the revolution took place. Resistance today comes not from capitalists. They are too weak. It comes from feudal landlords mainly, from the backward clergy, and those influenced by them.

"Sixty percent of our foreign trade remains in private hands, and we intend to leave it that way. We don't plan to interfere with private trade, which has a future in our country.

"As to our working class, we should consider not only its size but the quality of its growth. Workers of Afghanistan have been in the leadership of the people. Small though it is, the working class will inevitably grow and develop further. Implementing our long-range program for the development of industry will also bring into existence a larger and better-trained working class. Incidentally, the counter-revolutionaries get nowhere with our workers, as for example when they made their thrust in February, and prefer to steer clear of the factories where the workers are organized into self-defense units."

Keshtmand's style, informal, confident, moving from facts to theory and back again, was typical of most of the officials we were to interview. They were all young—still mostly in their 30s. They had not been in power long enough to acquire bureaucratic habits. Keshtmand had said the day before: "It is our duty to create a new-type government machine to be able to carry out the urgent tasks before us in an appropriate manner with initiative. We will carry out these tasks with firm determination."

Dr. Anahita Ratebzad, member of the Political Bureau of the PDPA CC, Minister of Education (later replaced as Minister of Education by Dr. Faqir Mahammad Yaqubi), President of the Democratic Organization of Women which she founded years before and which had been outlawed by Amin, though it continued its underground existence, and President of the Union of Friendship Societies of Afghanistan with Foreign Countries, is a woman with a great deal on her mind, as we would discover when we interviewed her in January.

But, as with Keshtmand, Karmal, Gulabzoi and others, we must first check whether she's alive or not. For, some months after we interviewed her in January 1980, we would read in the July 23rd issue of *The New York Times:*

> Afghan Education Minister Anahita Ratebzad, the only woman in the government [this "only" sounds like a fault when in fact it's a historic breakthrough] was shot to death Monday in Kabul, Radio Pakistan said today. The Associated Press reported that the broadcast monitored in New Delhi, said the vice-minister of internal affairs, who was not named, also was shot and killed Monday in Kabul.

The story was written by Stuart Auerbach, whose talent for imaginative fiction we will have reason to enjoy more than once. It would have upset me considerably to learn that this extraordinary woman whom I had talked to in January—and who "liked" Americans—had since been killed, if I hadn't already gone through the same comedy with reports about Keshtmand and others, all of whom seemed to have the extraordinary ability to rise unscathed from their tombs, a trick hitherto confined to a certain obscure Nazarene.

She made clear, in our meeting with her, that her most important immediate job was to correct the distortions of Amin in the field of education and women's rights. The full liberation of Afghanistan's women, she emphasized, however, depended on the economic factor. Until they could earn their own wages at their own jobs there was no practical way in which women could liberate themselves from what was no mere phrase—their slavery.

But, as we would learn more concretely from the head of the Afghan trade unions, Sattar Purdely, the industrial level of Afghanistan was still so low that jobs for women remained at a premium.

"The April Revolution opened up great prospects for all the working people of Afghanistan to get an education. Hundreds of schools were built. Hundreds of groups for eliminating illiteracy were set up everywhere and attended by about a million workers, peasants and soldiers. However, some errors, in particular the *compulsory* education of women, were made by the Amin group. However, the record was not all dark. Over 800 schools had been opened since 1978, and at the moment there were 40,000 teachers, though this was far from sufficient.

"Today, we still fight illiteracy but we've developed a plan setting up a system of general education, based on modern and progressive teaching principles. We are restructuring all the existing types of mass education—but not touching those schools directly under the supervision of Moslem clergymen. We will have a single study plan, syllabuses, teaching principles. The process of creating a school system to meet pressing needs will take 10 years to complete."

The U.N., in a world survey of educational levels, had placed Afghanistan 127th. Illiteracy was almost total, and among women, where the exceptions were so rare, one could say that it was total. The Taraki and Karmal governments both were keenly aware that central to the success of the revolution was education. So, too, were the counterrevolutionaries, and teachers and schools were constant targets for murder and sabotage.

There are parents, particularly in the outlying districts, who still refuse to let their children go to school, and others who will not allow their girls to sit in the same room with boys, even when they allow the girls to go at all. In fact, the attitude of the revolution toward women was often the spark that turned many peasants against it.

Some of them were also opposed to the revolutionary government's law that forbade the marriage of males before 18 and of females before 16, and fixed the bride-price, paid to her father by the bridegroom, at a maximum of 100 afghanis, or a little over $6.

Even after two years of the revolution only one girl could be enrolled in primary school to seven boys. The ratio was even smaller at the university level, as we would learn first-hand.

"We are confident that the path we have chosen is correct and that we can build a new society in our country," Anahita Ratebzad wrote on Lenin's 110th birthday. "No one can put out the torch of liberation, which the great Lenin ignited."

She became involved early in student groups organized by the young Karmal, already politically active, and became one of the founders of the People's Democratic Party of Afghanistan.

She was even a representative of the Party—though parties as such were not legal—in the following elections (in 1965) to parliament and won a seat (one of four women to do so). She was elected to the Central Committee of the PDPA in 1977, when the two factions (she belonged to the Parcham) of the Party amalgamated. Amin recognized an enemy in her and sent her out of the country as ambassador to Yugoslavia in 1978.

Now (1980) she is Minister of Education, whose job it is to bring somehow—by enticing, luring, charming—millions of women out of their slavery, out from behind the veil into the sunlight of real freedom for the first time literally in centuries of feudal imprisonment.

But legal emancipation, she would tell us herself, was merely the first step in the long and difficult process which was what *emancipation* really meant. It was one thing to wipe out legal restrictions. That could be done with a stroke of the pen. It was quite another thing to wipe out the "restrictions" that had sunk deep into the psychology of women over the centuries. One can drop the veil hiding one's face. But there is also a veil hiding one's soul even from one's self, and that is much harder to remove.*

Amin had tried to do it by force. Anahita Ratebzad would use other methods—*time* she needed badly, and peace. But time and peace are exactly what counterrevolution, with U.S. backing, struggled every day to deny her. But meanwhile, even under the most adverse of conditions, Anahita Ratebzad explains that the road to liberation for Afghan women runs through economic independence first of all. The speed with which Afghan women can be fully liberated depends on the speed with which Afghanistan can be industrialized, and helping in this is the Soviet Union and other socialist countries. Hindering it are the ultra-reactionary states headed by the U.S.A.

And yet she had no ill will toward the American people, and when I

---

* For instance. While we were in Kabul, the newspapers published an item about a man who had sued to divorce three of his wives in order to marry a younger one but the three wives fought his divorce action. Didn't they want to be free? No. For if they were "freed" (divorced), who would then support them? They would become beggars. If, however, jobs were immediately available it would have been a different story, no doubt.

identified myself as an American correspondent she smiled and said that she'd enjoyed her time in the United States (in 1949) where she studied nursing and "liked the American people."

Counterrevolutionaries attacked schools and teachers first of all, realizing that in the liberation of the peasant's mind lay their greatest danger. In June 1982, Sayid Mohammad Gulabzoi, Minister of the Interior, would report that, since the step-up of counterrevolutionary activity in 1980, "they have murdered hundreds of teachers and reduced 1,700 schools to ruins. They have attacked educational establishments 32 times in the last two months alone... In Herat on April 25, the counter-revolutionaries fired on a local high school building with grenade dischargers and submachine guns. In the Lagman Province, a school bus was attacked: 11 schoolchildren were killed and 16 wounded. Five other children were blown up by a guerrilla-planted mine near the school in Mazar-i-Sharif. A time-bomb made in West Germany was found quite recently in a Kabul University building. Two other such bombs were defused in the courtyard of an Ibn Sina school..." (*Moscow News*, June 27, 1980.)

Teachers were not just—you might say—humanely shot. They were subjected (along with Party activists, who were often the same person) to the most gruesome tortures. Torture, incidentally, is not expressly forbidden by the Koran (as these *Mujahiddin* interpreted that holy book) and, in fact, torture is considered to be an art in the East (in feudal times, that is), with its own skills and techniques developed to a refined point. Those who are good at it are eager to show off their skills and often embarrassed (if they didn't shock) Western reporters who were extended the privilege of watching them perform. Zia ul-Haq would reprimand Western correspondents who recoiled from the idea of flogging as a just punishment for criminals by pointing out that flogging was administered in the prisons with "style"; as indeed was flaying as well. Mrs. Kirkpatrick, too, could have seen the show if her time denouncing Soviet "atrocities" hadn't been filled up.

One of their "favorite" tortures, as *The Washington Post* (May 11, 1979) would report without apparent disapproval, was the one in which they featured "cutting off their captured 'Communist' schoolteachers' noses, ears and genitals, then removing one slice of skin after another."

Here is a closer look at such a *"mujahid"* fighter:

> Sarapul means "a place near the bridge." It is a small district in the northern province of Jawzjan. The district was terrorized by a gang led by a man called Saifuddin. The bandits attacked and seized villages and small towns there, hanging and shooting Party and local government activists and all "suspects." Saifuddin, the gang leader, tried to make the district center, Sarapul, his residence. Addressing the townsfolk ordered to gather in the town square, Saifuddin boasted that he would "do away with all Commu-

nists" in Sarapul in two weeks, then capture the provincial center Shibergan and go from there to Amu Darya and then Moscow itself.

Saifuddin is not a new man for the local residents. Before proclaiming himself a gang leader, he was a notorious bandit, robber and rapist. He has a long jail record. . .

Saifuddin, the "freedom fighter," kept a traveling harem of 40 to 50 girls forcefully taken away from their parents in the districts terrorized by the gang. Saifuddin's cutthroats left villages burnt to the ground and brutally maimed corpses behind them where they were not given "a warm welcome." The gang had its own executioner, Kasob ("cutthroat"). He killed his victims by first piercing their eyes and then dismembering them in front of their terrified fellow villagers. (*Sovetskaya Rossiya*, Apr. 25, 1981.)

This story turned out happily (or unhappily, depending on one's point of view): "Bakhtar news agency has an epilog to this story. The armed forces and units of the defenders of the revolution surrounded and eliminated the remnants of the several counterrevolutionary gangs. Gang leader Saifuddin and his right-hand man [a certain "grey cardinal" and "ideologist" with links to the CIA, Alemi, an ex-*mullah*] and a number of other gang leaders were taken prisoner." (The Afghan army *did* take prisoners.)

Terror-torture is effective only against other terrorists. Against a cause which is morally and historically superior to its own, terror by the other side can exercize only a temporarily "inhibitive" effect. Torture in the name of Islam, with the promise of a return to pre-revolutionary feudal social relations, aroused fear no doubt. But it also aroused hatred, especially when it was used against schoolchildren as was the case in Kabul in May 1980 when the children's drinking water was poisoned.

When terror become a major—practically the sole—weapon in the service of reaction, at a certain point it loses the power even to inhibit because it is sterile. Massive terror was used against the Soviet population by the Nazis in World War II and it failed—and those who used it, and those who apologized for it finally had their day to explain at Nuremberg. As for those Afghan children whose schools were burnt down and whose teachers were murdered (often in front of their eyes), no doubt they were terrified. But they were not *persuaded* that illiteracy was preferable to literacy. And in this fact lay the eventual total defeat of counterrevolution.

Meanwhile, those schools that were burnt down (1,470 since December, 1979) were rebuilt (600 in 1980-81) and those that took too much time to rebuild were substituted for in other ways. Teachers were killed but new ones were trained to replace them. Since the beginning of the revolution (April 1978) 15,185 teachers were trained to teach in primary schools alone. The government announced plans for a "blossoming" of education in Afghanistan, and predicted that illiteracy would be eliminated altogether from Afghanistan in 10 years and from the cities in seven.

So the struggle went on. A first congress of teachers was held in Kabul on April 10-12 (1980). A seminar "of the leading officials of the provincial departments" of all Afghanistan took place in Kabul in December 1980, in which "representatives of all provinces discussed questions of further development of the educational system, change-over to a new program more consistent with the present time, problems of the earliest elimination of illiteracy, especially in the provinces." (TASS, Dec. 19, 1980.)

They mourned that they had been able to publish only 3 million textbooks (plus 300,000 books on supplementary subjects) at a cost of 110 million afghanis to this date, but millions more textbooks were needed, not only in Pushtu and Dari (the main languages) but in the minority languages as well—Uzbek, Turkmen, Baluchi and Nuristani.

And yet, for the year beginning on March 22, 1981, a spokesman for the Minister of Education could report that 80 percent of all children aged 7 would be enrolled in schools, which was an increase of 10 percent over the preceding year. Twenty-five special schools for children who had never been to school, or had dropped out before though they were now in their teens, were set up in Kabul. Some 400 elementary and six lycee (high) schools "will be newly established in the current Afghan year in the cold (northern) regions of the country alone. Another 30 elementary schools will be promoted to the secondary schools and one secondary school will be upgraded to a lycee." Cost: 12 million afghanis. Some 12,273 students were also enrolled in 30 vocational schools, and eight new ones were scheduled to be opened for the following year.

As for the campaign against adult illiteracy, it was reported that over 600,000 people planned to enroll (voluntarily) in classes for the year beginning March 22, 1981, and that this was 50,000 more than the previous year. In no pre-revolutionary year did more than 5,000 adults enroll in classes aimed at teaching them how to read and write. To carry this campaign out, 19,000 teachers (of whom 3,000 were volunteers) took over.

The hunger for learning ran deep. In this struggle to bring learning to people—a bitter, often bloody struggle—the issues dividing the people from their "liberators" could hardly be more starkly defined. Characteristically, in the name of the children of Horace Mann and free public education, the American government lined itself up on the side of dark ignorance. Should Americans then complain that among the first words an Afghan child (and his father) learned were words that declared that revolution was the force that brought them to light and that Communism was its name?

Tired of having their schools and teachers destroyed together, the people organized themselves into self-defense units. "Over a thousand groups of defenders of the revolution already exist in the capitals of provinces, districts, villages and sub-villages where tens of thousands of them defend the revolution with their arms." (Quoted by *Kabul New Times,* Jan. 24, 1983, from the Party paper, edited by Mahmood Baryalai, already interviewed by me, *Haqiqate Engqelabe Saur.)*

Counterrevolutionary terror was helping to unite the Afghan people more closely together and involve them directly in defending their revolutionary gains. This also included strenuous efforts to re-establish (and in some instances, to create) Afghanistan's cultural life. The National Museum of Afghanistan was repaired and re-opened in October, 1981. Workers had to rescue irreplaceable artifacts, surviving from ancient days, from where Amin had previously deposited them—outside in the open, lashed by snow and rain. A new national theater (the sixth) called *Meihan* (Motherland) opened in Kabul in February, 1981, where Afghan classical works as well as new works were staged. A first children's theater was due early in 1983. Art, music, dance, drama—all these children were being taught to appreciate as their illiterate (and superstition-ridden) parents had not been able, or free, to. Older artists were called on to work even more industriously to further Afghanistan's cultural productivity.

In October, 1980, the first, the "constituent congress", of the writers took place and out of it came the Writers' Union. Workers in art and other aspects of culture (architecture, music, cinema, theater, TV, and handicraft) also met and formed organizations to represent them. At each such conference, marked by revolutionary élan, all artists pledged their talents to the furtherance of the revolution.

Sport, too, was revived. Modern sports had not been well developed in Afghanistan. But by 1983, it could point to 17 national sportsmen's teams. Sportsmen, mainly wrestlers, had been sent to the Olympics in Moscow in 1980, though they won no prizes. But sports were already so popular in Afghanistan that when a team of soccer players that had visited the U.S.S.R. for friendly matches in April 1980 was ambushed on its return to Afghanistan and almost half of them slaughtered by the counterrevolutionary cutthroats, this crime, like the poisoning of the children's drinking water, aroused widespread anger among the people.

Thus, while counterrevolution worked to tear down, the revolution worked to create. In this contest, history has always chosen the side of the creators. While one side published books, the other side burned them—as they showed when they put the *Baihaqi* Bookstore in Kabul to the torch during the February counterrevolutionary *putsch,* feeding to the flames not only Marxist works but the holy Koran as well.

While one side blew up power lines bringing darkness literally to the people (as in December in Kabul in 1980), the other side labored to extend electricity to the remoter villagers and to bring it to work in factories and to ease the labor of the peasants on the farm.

WHO SUPPORTS THE REVOLUTION?

Now, when our house its mourning wears,
Do not thyself give way to tears:
Instruct your eldest son that I
Was ever anxious thus to die,
For when Death comes the brave are free—
So, in thy dreams, remember me.

Anonymous,
Pathan Warriors Lament

What of the Afghan army? In January, a few days after Amin had been toppled, Western newspapers would report that "...local Afghan troops ... are deserting their government's cause 'like so many disappearing soda bubbles,' diplomatic sources here said today." (IHT, Agency Dispatches, from Islamabad, Pakistan, Jan. 21, 1980.)

Further: "U.S. Intelligence sources in Washington estimated that Soviet dead, wounded, captured and missing in the war against anti-Communist rebels might now total 2,000." (*Ibid.*)

As late as January 1982 *The New York Times* would still report that: "Area experts [?] say that the Afghan Army has dwindled from 85,000 in 1978 to fewer than 25,000 men." (NYT, New Delhi, Jan. 19, 1982.) And again from New Delhi, Aug. 4, 1980:

> The Kabul-based diplomats, *who are themselves highly circumscribed in their access to first-hand information,* based their reports on several days of highly intensified air activity in the direction of Chazni coupled with "strong rumors" of a mutiny by at least a portion of the troops quartered in the town southwest of Kabul. (By Michael Kaufman. My italics.)

If this kind of "reporting" could be imagined to be a rope, and one's life depended on its holding firm, would one risk one's life climbing it? But, more or less typical, such stories would serve as the basis for the "rumor" that the Afghan army had completely dissolved. That the Afghan army had been subjected to all kinds of pressures nobody, least of all the Afghans themselves, denied. Charles Z. Wick, the chief grinder in Reagan's propaganda mills, the International Communications Agency, explains how to produce a veritable harvest out of such a grain of truth. "Propaganda usually means a cynical manipulation of a kernel of truth into some sort of conclusion that really doesn't square with reality." (NYT, Jan. 20, 1982.)*

The "kernel of truth" was, as Lt. Col. Rafi, then Minister of Defense, would himself put it: "Hafizullah Amin and other traitors did a lot of damage to the revolutionary Armed Forces. Yet that was cut short on Dec. 27, 1979. The fighting capacity of the people's Armed Forces has increased considerably during the intervening six months... Our Army, actively supported by the population, has inflicted heavy losses on these (counterrevolutionary) bands... We have done a good deal of work to create contingents of frontier-guards which are now holding key positions in borderline areas." (Press Conference, July 11, 1980.)

Lt. Col. Mohammad Rafi, like all the other leading Afghan personalities, has been variously reported as assassinated or killed in some shootout, and the fact that he would appear, after such reports, publicly in, for instance, Moscow (Nov. 10, 1981), as reported by *The New York Times,* never seemed to embarrass anybody nor modify their later stories with even a touch of caution, let alone humility. (After awhile one even detected a kind of impatience in the press as though, having prepared their funerals for them so hospitably, it was downright churlish of the corpses to fail to show up!)

Like many others in the Revolutionary Council, Rafi had been waiting in Pule-Charhi for the executioner's squad, brewing tea with a fellow prisoner (who later would be one of our interpreters). Only the uprising of December 27 saved him from the death already signed by Amin himself.

Quite young, this man in charge of the Afghan army is still learning his profession. The day we met with him in the Darulaman palace, where Amin had made his last stand, in July he was flanked by Gen. Abdul Kadir, who had also been in prison awaiting execution. Kadir had commanded the Air Force and Anti-Tank Forces which led the attack on Daoud on April 29, 1978. Now he was a member of the Revolutionary Council as well. He had been Minister of Defense in the Taraki government, and in 1982 would become "Acting National Defense Minister" in the present government, and soon after, Minister of National Defense.

Lt. Col. Rafi answered our questions this way: "Every day our army is scoring new successes. Our youth has taken an active part in the struggle against counterrevolution. Instead of being on the verge of collapse, our army is three times as strong today as it was in January. Soviet troops here

---

* In April 1984, Charles Z. Wick was exposed as having made (in some states) illegal recordings of private telephone calls to him—if you called him he would tape your confidential talk without telling you. He also was called to account for using government money for personal use, and was forced to pay it back.

hold back the invader by giving our soldiers backup support,* but it is our army which does the main fighting. The relationship between our soldiers and the Soviet soldiers is a friendly one. They are our brothers."

No doubt he would hardly have admitted that it was an unfriendly one. But independent evidence did back up his assertion that the Soviet troops did not play a leading role in repulsing the enemy, but for the most part supported the Afghan troops with helicopters and other technological assistance. The American military were trying out new and more sophisticated weaponry in Afghanistan, including plastic land mines which defied detection by the conventional mine detectors which reacted to metal. They also used gas, and Kabul would put on display captured gas and chemical weaponry at various times.

Meanwhile unexpected confirmation of the claim made by Rafi and the Soviets, that the role of the limited contingent of soldiers sent to Afghanistan in December was to support the Afghan troops, and not to replace them, came in an early dispatch by Richard Halloran from Washington, in January 1980, while the Karmal forces were still trying to sort out the situation, and agreement in Washington on what the American public should be told on such a key question had not yet calcified into dogma:

> Wash. Jan. 9 (NYT)—Taking issue with reports that Soviet troops had been battling Afghan insurgents, Defense Department analysts said yesterday that it was the depleted Afghan Army that was doing the fighting. They said that the Russians had limited themselves so far to a supportive position.

The real situation with the Afghan army was described by Karmal. Amin *had* purged the army ruthlessly, he *had* managed to demoralize it to a lesser or greater extent. But it was this same army which led the assault that overthrew Amin, and this same army which saw as its patriotic duty the defense of the revolution it had helped to bring into existence in April 1978, and then rescued it from betrayal in December 1979. At all times, however, the army was under the command of the civilian revolutionary leaders and responded to their authority. It was perhaps no small task to repair the damage to morale inflicted on the army by Amin. But the proof that it was nevertheless being accomplished came in the months that followed when fervent appeals from the counterrevolutionaries to desert, despite claims to the contrary, did not significantly succeed and did not "deplete" the Afghan army to the point of helplessness.

The crucial test of the army's reliability came when large assaults were launched on key cities by the counterrevolutionaries, at Herat and Kan-

---

* In an interview given to Sumit Chakravartly of the Indian daily *Patriot*, Karmal would still describe the Soviet army contingent as a "reserve force...guaranteeing the national sovereignty, independence and freedom of our country against...military aggression of the imperialist forces..." (*Kabul New Times*, April 27, 1983.)

dahar. They were repulsed by the Afghan army. Of course, the fact that there were elements of a civil war in the struggle—of Afghan against Afghan—complicated matters and strained loyalties. Of course, the ordinary Afghan soldier being no more than a peasant fresh out of the field only yesterday was susceptible to appeals to his superstitious and religious beliefs. After all, he too was either illiterate or barely literate—though he now, in revolutionary Afghanistan, attended classes to learn how to read and write. But he also knew that his family now had land, and that land would be his when he returned home. He had that to fight for, and it was no small thing. Besides, the monthly wages of a soldier were raised to 3,000 afghanis.

It was this army which carried on the grueling, merciless struggle on the "border" where the counterrevolutionaries lay in wait and set ambushes and traps for them at night. To dig them out they had to search through mountain passes, poke into secret caves and hidden pockets among the hills. But in fighting for the cause they came to believe in it even more. "You have set a heroic example in defending the gains of the Saur Revolution," Karmal told a group of young men who had just returned from the front, "especially in its new phase, safeguarding the national dignity and honor, the people's peace and freedom, the working-class ideology, the revolution, party and government... You are not alone. You constitute part of the tens of thousands of sacrificial party members and other patriots who have been engaged in fighting during the past two years." (*Kabul New Times,* July 12, 1980.)

But it is also true that in a country like Afghanistan, which cannot accurately, at least in the modern sense, be called a *country,* national patriotism was only in the making. For the country was divided into regions, into tribes and clans, into nomadic bands, each with its own traditions and even language. It was more natural for some Afghans to feel greater loyalty to their tribal chiefs than to a single president of a country that had not yet formed in their minds. The 3 million nomads did not, in fact, have a "country" in the precise sense of the term, passing as they did from "Afghanistan" to "Pakistan" with their sheep and cattle as the seasons changed, looking for pasture. The one thing that functioned as a unifying force was their religion, which in itself was divided into two unequal sects: the Sunnites (the majority religion) and the Shiites. Islam therefore was more their "country" than geographical Afghanistan.

In fighting against counterrevolution the Karmal forces were simultaneously fighting against feudalism itself—that is, they were carrying out a *democratic* revolution, though led by revolutionaries of the working class, or at least revolutionaries espousing working-class ideology. Because this revolution against feudalism and for democracy came so tardily on the historic calendar, it found among its enemies not only the native feudal lords but the "lords" of finance in the West, also "feudal" in their own way, who had long ago subverted with their hidden power the very institutions of democracy which originally had brought them into being. Now they stood opposed to their own past. Their own "past" was Afghanistan's present.

It was as though monopoly capital, once it had come into absolute power, had drawn a line across history and put it to the lagging colonial world: thus far and no further.

American reaction places a heavy bet on Islam, understanding its double character of a religion and a "national" unifying force in Afghan life. The counterrevolutionaries are called *Mujahiddin,* "holy warriors," not specifically patriots. They fight not primarily to regain a country but to clear their local areas of the infidel. But, of course, as history has clearly shown, no religious war is ever a war for religion alone. In calling on their serfs to die for Allah, the feudal landowners, the really rich ones now basking in the pleasures of Paris or Rome (as the last king of Afghanistan was doing when he was overthrown), expect to get back real material things: *land,* acres and acres of it (three percent had owned some 70 percent of the land before the revolution). For some strange reason, though God and Allah both live in heaven, it's necessary for Christian and Moslem alike to have a solid place on earth to worship them!

The PDPA therefore does not choose to confront Islam head-on. It has no quarrel with the *religious* aspect of Islamism, only its sectarian interpretation by reaction. The Afghan revolutionaries see no contradiction between a belief in Islam and a belief in socialism, and many of them are practicing Moslems. The fundamental charter of principles, outlined by the PDPA at the very beginning of the present struggle, declares the Islam religion to be *sacred*—the religion of Afghanistan. It is just as possible to believe in the revolutionary side of Islam as it is to believe in the revolutionary side of Christianity.*

---

* Interestingly enough, a similar problem had already arisen some 60 years before in Turkestan (in then Czarist Russia) when the Turkestan Communists refused to cooperate with the Young Bukhara Revolutionaries—made up of clergymen and bourgeois intellectuals—which declared its loyalty to Islam but championed in its program "the poorest masses" claiming that it "protects their interests against the role of the exploiters and world imperialism."

This "contradiction" between the religious and social aims of the Bukharan revolutionaries made the Turkestan Communists suspicious of their really revolutionary staying power. Their decision to sever connections with them for that reason was reversed by the Russian Council for International Propaganda, which found the action of the Turkestan Party too sectarian and argued that it is "illogical to destroy with your own hands an existing and functioning party...simply because after the revolution, in a new political and social situation part of it may end up in the ranks

109

So, by the end of 1981, the Afghan army had consolidated itself, was replenishing its forces with volunteers and by the draft. By 1983, the military situation was altogether different. Judging from Afghan reports, the intervening three years had not been wasted. If Karmal had inherited an army which had a morale problem in 1980, three years later much had changed:

> In the army, there are 600 chambers (clubs) of political enlightenment, 24 Afghan-Soviet Friendship chambers, and over 300 libraries with over 150,000 volumes of different books for the personnel.
>
> In order to promote literacy, over 2,100 literacy courses for a large number of soldiers are busy with their studies. The number of graduates from these courses, only in 1361 H. S. (1982/83) was over 40,000... Over 90 units of radio stations, over 119 film projectors, over 600 TV sets and a large number of radio and radio-cassettes are at the disposal of the army personnel...
>
> As a result of all this, in the trenches of armed defense of the gains of the revolution, a large number of officers and soldiers have joined the ranks of the PDPA (People's Democratic Party of Afghanistan) and the DYOA (Democratic Youth Organization of Afghanistan). The quantitative increases of the ranks of the PDPA in the first three-quarters of the current year (1982) is 45 percent, compared to the corresponding period of last year, and in the DYOA, it is 59 percent. (*Kabul New Times,* Feb. 14, 1983.)

Then at a press conference in Kabul in April, 1983, Maj. Gen. Mohammad Yaseen Sadeqi, Secretary of the Central Committee of the PDPA, and head of the Chief Political Department of the Afghan Army, would say: "Our National Army is growing in strength and numbers. It has trebled* in numbers in the past three years. The figure usually given in Western media reminds me of the story of the cow that dreamed of hay. Our enemies should not console themselves with illusions about the weakness and unreliability of our army. Besides, in nearly every village, the people, even women, have shouldered the arms given them by the state to defend themselves from the raids of the counterrevolutionary bands of cutthroats and maranders. The role of the limited Soviet military contingent invited by our government is confined mainly to safeguarding the security of Afghanistan from penetration by hostile forces from the territories of Pakistan and Iran." (Quoted in *New Times,* No. 19, 1983.)

---

of the counter-revolution." (*The Comintern and the East. The Struggle for the Leninist Strategy and Tactics in National Liberation Movements,* edited by R. A. Ulyanovsky, 1979.)

So precedent and experience on this delicate problem already existed in the revolutionary ranks.

* Depending on whose figures you use, that would put the army force at 60,000 or 190,000.

Not only that. As the war continued, more and more hostile groups gave up and came over to the government's side. If there had been desertions of government troops to the other side—and this had been enormously exaggerated—such desertions had occurred only in the early period (before 1979 and, sporadically, after). Now the tide had turned. Counterrevolutionary leaders, who had believed they were fighting Allah's sacred cause, had reached a dead-end. Burning down schools, killing teachers and students, destroying mosques, dynamiting irrigation systems, devastating crops —for what reason, for whom? If they were sincere patriots, such actions went more and more against the grain. And it seemed to reach no climax— next season the fields were resown, the schools rebuilt, the irrigation systems reconstituted. And what's more—this time such facilities had sprouted their own self-defense corps, which meant that not only were the peasants no longer afraid of them, but in choosing to defend their homes they had chosen the side of the revolution.

In March, "over 260 leaders of the armed groups from all the provinces of Afghanistan, who in the recent past were disillusioned and have joined the side of the revolutionary Government, attended a meeting at the headquarters of the National Fatherland Front (in Kabul)."

Why had they gone into opposition? "Ghulam Rasul, from the Herat province, who had with him over 1,000 armed men and who represented over 100,000 people of his tribe, said that it was the dark face of Amin and his tyranny that forced the people to fight for their lives even though they had hailed the Saur Revolution."

And, "other speakers, Mawlawi Azizullah from Helmand, Ishan Baba from Baghlan and Rajab Ali from Badakhshan, in their speeches, said that everyone now knows that the revolutionary party and the Government were working for the advance of Afghanistan and its people and for their prosperity, while the counterrevolutionaries were engaged in killing people and destroying public and state property." (*Kabul New Times,* March 10, 1983.)

At the end of their meeting the 260 one-time counterrevolutionary leaders adopted a resolution of support for the government and drafted a Call addressed to those who still remained in the ranks of the opposition to break with their past and come over to the side of the revolution.

Karmal congratulated them on their courage and welcomed them home. "We have struggled for truth and justice in our country and will do so until final victory," he told them. In April (1983) he announced that "tens of thousands of our deceived people, after realizing the humane, friendly and wise policy of our party and revolutionary state, gave up armed hostility against our party and state and surrendered themselves along with their arms to the state authorities." (KNT, Apr. 24, 1983.)

REVOLUTIONARY YOUTH REBORN

Rise and be born with me, brother,
Give me your hand from the deep region
of your far-flung sorrow,
You will not return from beneath the rocks.
You will not return from subterranean time.
Your stone-hardened voice will not come back.
Your chiselled eyes will not come back.
I come to speak through your dead mouth.

Pablo Neruda,
The Heights of Macchu Picchu

Was it true that the youth supported the revolution?

Though the bourgeois press would make a great to-do about demonstrations of students from Kabul University in May (1980), the truth was that not only was this the last arrow to be shot from the steadily depleted quiver of counterrevolution among the youth but it marked the end of *all* organized resistance in Kabul and, somewhat later, in other large cities as well.

In the beginning—in April 1978 and December 1979—Maoism and Trotskyism could appeal to some of the youth as genuine revolutionary expressions, since in their critical attitudes, and particularly in their rhetoric, these groups struck poses of super-militancy which to many youth is the beginning and end of revolutionary authenticity. They, too, claimed to oppose the counterrevolutionaries.

But as time went on their slogans and their anti-revolutionary actions coincided, first "independently" of the slogans and actions of the overt counterrevolutionaries, and then more or less in open tandem with them, as best proven in Herat in March 1979, when they inspired local riots with counterrevolutionary consequences.

Setting out to "purify" or "revolutionize" the revolution, they ended up in the ranks of those trying to burn it to the ground or destroy it by poisoning the drinking water of schoolchildren!

Finally, boxed off into a unit of their own, these Sholee Jawid and Sorha "revolutionaries," holed up on the Chinese side of the 74-kilometer (60-mile) border China shares with Afghanistan, make their raids into Afghanistan and harass the villagers in Badakhshan province precisely in the certified style of the cutthroat *Mujahiddin* who, in recognition for their efforts, refer to them as "third-rate Communists" and reserve for them no honorable place in their Islamic paradise of the future. Only the more tolerant CIA includes them—or reserves a corner for them—in the always elusive coalition it dreams of one day pulling out of the political hat. When we visited the headquarters of the Democratic Youth Organization one afternoon in July, we were stopped at the gate by about four or five teenaged "guards" carrying rifles almost as big as they were. One carried a submachine gun, however. When we came on them we had the feeling we'd interrupted some schoolboy game of theirs which they'd go back to the moment we left. They seemed to have mustered those solemn faces for us only with difficulty. Where did playing at soldier and being a soldier begin and end?

We met with Burhan Ghiasi, First Secretary of the Democratic Youth Organization, and with Sakhi Margan, Second Secretary, and Daoud Mazyar, also a secretary of the organization.

Their headquarters had once been a mansion belonging to a rich merchant, no longer at that address. In our discussion with these three and others, we had confirmed for us the fact that the university youth who had gone on "strike" in May had been trapped, polemically, into a political corner when they were asked to square their ideological opposition to the Karmal government with their *de facto* alliance with counterrevolution sent in from Pakistan. They couldn't. Some claimed that they had been pressured into joining with the others and had never really understood just what was going on, let alone who was behind what. Some said they had been terrorized by armed men who threatened to kill them if they didn't come out. At that stage of events it was no idle threat. All had been told that the Russians were taking over the country to make a vassal of it, and that Islam was being threatened by the atheist "green eyes" from the North.

Kabul University has long been a center of student youth political activity, and gave birth to the first Marxist study groups out of which Karmal himself emerged. In 1968—to take one year—Afghan students (from all schools) went on strike more than a dozen times, often in support of workers' strikes. Students date their revolutionary martyrdom on October 25, 1965, when a demonstration against the government of Dr. Mohammad Yusouf, appointed Prime Minister by King Zahir, was fired on by the Afghan troops, killing three and wounding many.

So there was a definite tradition of left activity among students, and the Youth League section of the PDPA (then about 2,000) had worked actively among the students during the period of agitation and "argued" with them, as Moneer, one of our student interpreters who was a Party leader of the student youth in Kabul as well, would describe to us with such authority.

He told us how, forewarned that counterrevolutionary attempts were being made to stir up the students, he had singled out the rebellious student leaders, whom he personally knew, and took them one by one into his office, where he sat them down and "argued" with them. This picture of two youths "arguing" in this context of an all-out war that in some of its features was so merciless struck us then as not so odd as it did later. There were many feckless aspects to events in Kabul then. While men were killing each other on the border, college boys were "arguing" in Kabul with one another about whether they should. There were, in and among the deadlier aspects of the struggle, such wayward pockets of amateurism, reflecting a kind of enduring naiveté among some sections of the people about what they were involved in and what they were really up against. It would cost them dearly, then and later. But for a long time there was a kind of amiable confusion between friend and foe, and the illusion that a logical argument would convince the other side to relent persisted.

When he got one of them into his room after all, someone he knew fairly well, Moneer told us that he then pulled up a chair and said: "All right. Let's argue. If you convince me I'll go with you. But if I convince you, you must go with me!"

So they "argued." They argued about whether Karmal represented a truly revolutionary force, what the intention of the Russians was, how dangerous, if at all, the Chinese were, and the role American imperialism played in their part of the world. Some he convinced—that a real revolution had occurred and had to be defended. Some he did not. None convinced him.

Later, those arrested were again "argued" with in prison, and the ones that sincerely recanted, or had their eyes opened by seeing where their abstract logic led them in real life, signed a statement to that effect and were released, and next day returned to their classes. (A bomb would be set off in Kabul University some weeks later, on May 9, and drew a huge protest meeting from university students.)

Some of the demonstrators were pre-teenaged boys who had been corralled into the demonstration with no real idea of what was happening or what they were doing. Their parents had been beside themselves with anxiety when these children failed to return home that night, as downtown Kabul seemed to be going up in flames, and gunfire could be heard.

Thus the youth were handled carefully—as a matter of policy. But not all the demonstrators had been youth. Some had been adults. Those who were caught were revealed to have been sent into Kabul from Pakistan—19 ringleaders were jailed—and some *were* Pakistanis who came equipped with submachine guns, with material printed in Pushtu and Dari, and with short-wave radio sets tuned to centers in Pakistan. These men were highly trained professionals. They had followed a carefully prepared plan and had a definite aim: insurrection. They knew how to manufacture Molotov cocktails to throw at buses. (This is an acquired skill. One is not born knowing how to do this.) They chalked slogans on walls: *"Allah-o-Akhbar!"* (Allah is great!") They taped the cry, "Allah-o-Akhbar!" and broadcast it over loudspeakers perched on dozens of roofs, giving the impression the whole city was crying "Allah!" They fired on firemen trying to put out the fires they had set. They settled scores with those merchants who had refused to cooperate. In short, they were trained counterrevolutionaries who, to a large extent, were dealing with amateurs, for those who opposed them in the streets were the youth from the Democratic Youth and volunteer groups formed almost on the spot. Self-protection corps from the factories resisted them most successfully.

Most of those university youth who joined in the demonstrations came from well-to-do families, they explained. Their fathers had been landlords or landowners, but this had not kept the children, on whom the sins of the fathers were not to be visited, out of the people's university. Nevertheless, when it came down to the crunch it was their class interests these young men instinctively rose to defend though, as is not unusual with well-to-do youth who become "revolutionary," they did so from the ultra-Left; in their case, from Maoist positions or from Trotskyite.

This February episode had taught them much, the leaders of the Democratic Youth told us, and they would make sure it could never be repeated.

The Democratic Youth were then growing by leaps and bounds. The July (1980) membership was around 20,000—2,000 more than the previous month, they told me proudly. By the end of 1982, the number had risen to 90,000—youth from all over the country.

Their influence was spreading among wider and wider sections of the youth, and not just among the university youth. During the February outbreak they had helped in putting down the counterrevolutionaries, but in an almost spontaneous, barely organized way. In October they sent their first battalion of voluteers to the Front, followed by still others.

They played an active role in the campaign to eliminate illiteracy, passing on their newly-won knowledge to their fathers and mothers. They joined in the mass movement to plant trees and other greenery in and around Kabul. Over 190,000 hectares of land had been set aside to establish a green belt around the city so that it could breathe more comfortably, helping to ameliorate the climate and hold moisture in the soil as well.

They replanted the denuded plains where trees had long ago been cut down and sold by mindless entrepreneurs for firewood, thus producing a desert, and wood had become almost as valuable as gold. Volunteer payless days, especially commemorating the anniversary of the Saur Revolution, when work was contributed to some worthy end, were enthusiastically backed by the youth, whom one would encounter with their picks and shovels all over Kabul.

And they, sons and daughters of peasants and workers, felt themselves literally reborn by the Revolution. They owed their very lives to the Revolution. From the children of peasants they were transformed into Prometheans—a new type of human beings—workers. As workers, their horizons expanded to embrace the whole future. For them, too, to become a worker was to become free.

THE END TO FACTIONS

The world has become peaceful
For both tiger and deer...

Daqiqi of Balkh

At a meeting with Kabul Party Committee members, among whom were Zohor Ramjo, secretary, Shahzar Livar, Karima Keshtmand (wife of Sultan Ali Keshtmand), Zahir Moafar, Azam Karigar, we would get a more focused picture of how the Party itself functioned in Kabul and what problems it faced.

First, the Party in Kabul (in July) had 9,000 members, including women, though these still represented a small portion of the membership. Compare this number to the number of merchants—30,000. The Party had taken on the responsibility of guaranteeing security, and with the regular militia helped patrol Kabul at night. Again, references were made to the events of February, which had become a kind of object lesson and living laboratory in the techniques of counterrevolution. They agreed, however, that this counterrevolutionary thrust ("foreseen" by Carter and Brzezinski) had been well contained by the police and the militia—the Afghan militia. (No Russians took part in putting the counterrevolutionaries down.) Groups of activists had gone out among the people with bullhorns calling on them not to join in with the counterrevolutionaries and explaining who they were. Others had pitched in with the militia to round up those they could catch.

February had taught them a great deal. I had been surprised at the ease with which counterrevolutionaries had been reported as boarding a bus, some on the Pakistan, some on the Afghan side of the border—at the Khyber Pass, for instance, from where Brzezinski could "see" straight down the valley to Kabul itself—and then had ridden on into Kabul where they registered at a hotel just like you and me! Once registered, and having washed up, they strolled out into the town and started burning down buses.

This was still part of the amateurism that was such a disconcerting feature of this revolution, and yet gave to its defenders—as unlikely as it might seem—a kind of charm. The Party people explained that the ease with which these deadly foes of theirs could come into town undetected and unchallenged, make their contacts, set up their apparatus, was due primarily to the problem of identification. Although Kabul residents did carry identification cards, it was useless to demand such cards from nomads and tribalists and even peasants, who were illiterate and, in fact, many of whom had no real addresses. Even in Kabul it was almost impossible for an outsider to locate where someone lived, since no reliable system of names and numbers of houses and streets existed. To find somebody you had to follow an elaborate set of directions. Nor could you be sure exactly who— or how many—lived in any particular home or hut.

Family ties are sacred blood ties. Every family owed hospitality to a blood relative, regardless of who he was and what his views were. Conceal-ment for criminals was therefore easy; the same for counterrevolutionaries. To ferret them out you had to depend on neighbors willing to help, even ready to break the "blood tie." In the beginning this was not to be depended on. Later it was. And if the population of Kabul was as hostile to the government as the Western press claims it is, then the uprising which was declared for the start of Ramadan, while we were there, could not have been nipped so neatly in the bud, as it was. This time the militia simply went out and rounded up the last of the conspirators where the people had pointed out they were hiding.

The efficiency with which the militia and Party workers had ferreted out the potential arsonists and water poisoners had won popular respect for them. Yes, some Party people had been assassinated since December. Yes, they all carried arms. Yes, they still had the problem of how to strain out the criminals from the stream of peasants coming into Kabul every day from the surrounding countryside. They learned their job, so to speak, on the job.

Nevertheless, what *about* the two factions, Khalq and Parcham, whose history did include bitter rivalries for more than a decade, and incessant back-and-forth polemical denunciations? Babrak Karmal would state at a press conference in Kabul (Jan. 24, 1980) that "an atmosphere of unity and cohesion now reigned in the ranks of the PDPA, the state apparatus and the army. Revolutionary order and legality were restored in the coun-try within less than a month."

Was that too optimistic? In any case, one fact was clear to all Afghan Party members, and that was that nothing could be more fatal to their country's hopes than factional divisiveness.

It was bitter factionalism that had paved the way for Amin's rise to such mordant power.

Though factionalism had been outlawed at the unity conference of 1977, there was more to it than just a decision to give up the old bad ways. The Party program, and the organization of the "party of the new type" in a truly Communist spirit in which the relationship between Party mem-bers and Party leaders was clearly defined, were objective standards based upon a scientific approach to politics by which any single person's—or group's—attitudes and actions could be precisely judged. Not his contribution to the success or defeat of rival factions and personalities, but how he carried out the Party program in defense of the country and in promotion of revolutionary ideals, was the measure by which any Party member was to be judged. The very names of Khalq and Parcham were dropped, and their designations as "leftist" and "revisionist" eliminated.

In April 1980, Nur Ahmad Nur, member of the Political Bureau of the PDPA, summing up the results of a plenary meeting of the Party some three and a half months after the December uprising, would say: "The period has been characterized by the stabilization of the situation in the country, restoration of revolutionary law and order, the creation of an atmosphere of trust and cooperation, the Party's persistent work to ensure the unity of its ranks, the further enhancement of the PDPA's role and prestige in society and the state, and the consolidation of the leading patriotic and progressive forces of Afghanistan... We are satisfied with the fact that we succeeded in *unanimously* adopting one of the basic documents of the Party—the Party Rules. The Rules determine the forms of the organizational setup of the Party, methods of its activities, and norms of Party life. Persistent work is now under way to further strengthen the political, ideological and organizational unity of its ranks and to rally it close around the Central Committee and the Political Bureau." (My italics.)

He reported that Party organizations had been set up in "provincial, urban and district" areas throughout the country. "On the committees are the most experienced and reliable activists of the Party. The Party bases its activities on the principles of scientific-revolutionary theory." (Apr. 20, 1980.)

The CIA would speculate on wished-for divisions within the Party and inspired stories would periodically surface in the press, claiming that the hostility between the factions, instead of dying down with Karmal's rise to power, in fact—and precisely at the Party conference in March 1982— had flared up with renewed virulence. "Afghan Party Supports Purge of Dissidents," the headline of a story characteristically reporting that conference in Kabul from New Delhi, would proclaim, "according to diplomats"—still there whacking away!—"and Afghan broadcasts and exiles". ... Planting stories like the one charging that the Khalqui actually had made "secret" contact (how "secret" is a newspaper account?) with the enemy was, of course, provocative, but in a diabolical way.

This is no more than a laboratory example of how the demonic art of sowing confusion and doubt is practiced by those who have studied the art. Sherman Kent, in his book, *Strategic Intelligence for American World Policy* (Princeton University Press, 1949) would write: "Black propaganda [there are 'white' and 'grey' as well] ... purports to come from dissident elements within the enemy's own population, but which is really carried on in great secrecy from the outside. Sometimes the black propaganda is done by radio, sometimes by leaflets, *by fake newspaper,* by forged letter, by any and all means occurring to a perverse ingenuity." (My italics). This reported "fact" that the Khalqui faction (though outlawed) of the PDPA made contact with the enemy was not a "fact" innocently plucked from the tree of life by a reporter the way you might pluck a cherry from a cherry tree.

Factionalism had indeed been a mortal enemy of the Afghan revolutionary party. In his Report to the 841 delegates to the National Conference in Kabul on March 14 (1982), Karmal would say:

> In the course of the discussion of candidates for nominations as delegates to higher Party conferences, above all, in the armed forces, the militia and some of the ministries, a resurgence of the malaise of the past, namely, factionalism was witnessed... It was clear that those people were echoing others, that they were serving our enemies who are anxious to split our Party and sow uncertainty, suspiciousness and enmity among its ranks.
>
> As you know, their plans were foiled... We are satisfied to note that the incorrect actions of certain persons were rejected by the absolute majority of Party organizations. With regard to these comrades I think that forbearance and care should be displayed. We should talk to them and explain the principles of revolutionary Parties to them and the importance of discipline and organization. If even this does not help them measures prescribed by Party Rules will have to be taken.

Here was no giddy dictator speaking, nor a man who has no confidence in his cause and in the membership of his Party. The delegates to the March conference were selected at nationwide Party conferences from a total membership (then) of 62,820. Some 58,000 members from all sections of the country participated in meetings, electing 16,000 delegates to further meetings and conferences at which 10,200 members spoke. Out of these grassroots meetings, the final 841 delegates were chosen to attend the Kabul Conference at which the Draft Program of Action of the PDPA and the Tasks in Consolidating the Party was to be adopted and (with some amendments suggested by the delegates) was in fact adopted, March 15.

Of the 841 delegates at the Conference, 106 were from the working class and working peasantry, representing 12.6 percent of the total number of delegates. Delegates came from the army, from the professions (teachers, students) and 56 women. This was a far cry from 1965 when, at the founding convention of the PDPA, there was only one woman!

By 1982, the revolutionary party of Afghanistan could point to the existence of 29 provincial Party organizations, two regional, 11 city Party organizations, 44 district Party organizations (in the cities), and 1,656 primary organizations.

By the time of the conference in March, 1982, it was clear that the Party, which had been torn apart by Amin, was fully restored, and despite lingering attempts to stir up the embers of an old factionalism, it was a united party—a party united on the basis of defeating factionalism, the position of factionalists—which had conducted a heated, open debate (in the midst of war) in which the overwhelming majority of the Party took part.

The main resolutions which came out of the Conference were adopted *unanimously*. These resolutions outlined the further strategy put forward by the Party for winning the war and for ensuring that the country, its factories and farms, also functioned. In time of war, the problems of peace were not neglected. Another great accomplishment of the Conference was to bring up-to-date the Party Rules.

WORKERS

> Labor is prior to, and independent of, capital. Capital is
> only the fruit of labor, and could never have existed if la-
> bor had not first existed. Labor is superior to capital, and
> deserves the higher consideration.
>
> Abraham Lincoln

The man we now met, Sattar Purdely, had been a member of the Parcham faction. He was now Chairman of the Central Committee of the Trade
Unions of Afghanistan, a very important position indeed, and an alternate
member* of the Central Committee of the PDPA.

He had been a revolutionary since he was 20. In fact, he was older than
unionism itself, which dated from 1968. Union organizers, who most likely
were PDPA members, were persecuted relentlessly, and attempts to form
unions were suppressed from their very beginning. After 1975, most trade
unions, which were underground, took the form of mutual assistance organizations which looked after the welfare of their members on an ostensibly
charitable basis. Only after the April (1978) Revolution were the conditions
for a mass trade union movement created.

By December 1980, unions had been set up in nine of the ten industrial
provinces of the country, and the tenth was in the making. Membership was
put by Purdely at 150,000,** which includes not only basic industrial workers
but office workers and "toilers." The basic working class—factory, mine and
mill, etc.—was put at about 60,000, though with construction and agricultural workers this number will increase several thousand. This was the
figure in July 1980. It has obviously increased since.

Sattar Purdely seemed to make a special point of stressing that the trade
union movement was solidly behind the Karmal government. He said: "The
trade union movement of Afghanistan needs to stand beside the new leadership of our country."

There were, he said, some 50 factories inside Kabul, and just five times
more outside it. Significantly, the counterrevolutionaries in February had not
tried, or not tried very hard, to attack those factories within Kabul itself, all of

---

* In 1983, he became a full member.
** Karmal would put the total at 160,000 in February, 1983.

122

which had their self-defense committees organized to defend themselves. Workers at the housing projects, incidentally, had worked on through all the commotion, refusing to allow the incendiaries to stop them. About 7,000 workers were in the private sector of Kabul's industries (much more were craftsmen, as we learned from Allam Namidi, director of handicraft production); about 9,000 (at that time) worked in the public sector. Kabul has a population estimated somewhere near a million, and thousands (30,000) of small merchants, outnumbering the workers, with an estimated million in the entire country.

The lowest monthly wage was 1,200 afghanis, and the highest, based on skill and performance, about 5,000. The average daily wage is a bit over 50 afghanis (then). A loaf of bread, its price fixed by the government, is 8.5 afghanis. Wages generally have risen from 40 to 50 percent for the lowest categories since January, 1982.

At the silo-bakery, which had been built with Soviet assistance long before the revolution (and once was attacked by an ultrareactionary mob), we found a tank guarding the entrance. We could see why Carter's "freedom fighters" would be discouraged from trying to enter here. But here is where we entered and met freely women workers without their veils.

It was of these women that Anahita Ratebzad was speaking when she said that the future full emancipation of women would start from working women. For women, more acutely even than for men, to be free meant to be a worker. What was true of the entire era—that the emancipation of mankind lay in its becoming the full expression of the working class— was to be seen here in microcosm but no less clearly. The contrast between the women they were, imprisoned behind their masks, and the women they now are—their faces as open as their minds—is dramatic. Only a workers' revolution freed them. Only a workers' society could guarantee that they would remain free.

These women earned an independent salary equal to the men's, had given up the *chadri*, and were, economically at least, independent of their husbands. Literacy among them was much higher than among women generally, certainly among country women. Political and social awareness was also correspondingly higher. They were, though perhaps still "backward" by absolute standards, infinitely more advanced than most women in the Orient, the Middle East, Africa, and certainly in other parts of Southern Asia, like their neighbors in Pakistan and Iran. The important thing was not where they happened to be at any moment one encountered them on the calendar, but that they were *in motion*. The working-class power which drove them forward was inexhaustible, since it was the motor that provided the energy on which history itself moved. For them, therefore, freedom had a very precise definition. It meant being a worker. *They* were the motor on which History moved!

All workers, through cooperatives, had access to cheaper goods, new housing, education, to health care and child care, to vacations, to cheap meals at their place of work; to a longer life, in short. Indeed, in a country still laboring under poverty and ignorance they were a kind of aristocracy—but an aristocracy whose aim was to raise everyone to their "privileged" position.

Needless to say, counterrevolutionary propaganda could make small headway with them. In fact, it was their example which counterrevolution held up to the women in the backwoods as the cautionary horror tale showing to what depths the godless revolution had already reduced the city women and would surely bring their own daughters and wives. When counterrevolution made its supreme bid in February, while downtown Kabul was smoking with burned buses and streetcars, peace reigned where they were. In the year that followed, 15,000 trade unionists took an active part in the defense and protection of the nation's industries. Soon, every factory had its defense corps.

"Believe me," commented Sattar Purdely, "now that they have political power in their hands (some of the women are on the City Council and others serve in other social capacities) and have a good leadership, they see a fine future for themselves. They're determined to push the bandits from the sacred soil of their motherland and continue the struggle until all the bandits are gone. About 700 of them were active in the factory's and city's resistance groups. . ."

At the time we interviewed Purdely there was still no central national trade union organization. The first Congress of trade unions took place on March 7, 1981. By that time they could count 400 primary workers' organizations and a total membership of 160,000 (including office workers, students and "toilers" not usually included among the "working class" in some countries). But this figure, too, would grow, and rather rapidly, in the months to come.

But though it was true that the first all-Afghan trade union would be established only that year, this is not to be read as meaning that worker militancy had not existed in Afghanistan in pre-revolutionary times, or that the factory working class (estimated at 60,000 then) had not already accumulated a history of struggle.

In one year—the key year of 1968—there would be a whole series of strikes and demonstrations by workers everywhere—in Jangalak, in the government printing press, bus and truck drivers in Kabul, at the Construction Company in Kabul, at textile and woolen mills in various other cities, in cement plants, oil fields, in the mines, by fruit workers, and others. The issues were wages, working conditions, vacations, and in this Islamic country a half-day off before the holy Friday, as well as many other demands varying from place to place.

But these demonstrations were often spontaneous, or directed by underground, illegal union leaders who had no central organizing working-class force behind them, except where the PDPA could provide it. Indeed, on a motion by Babrak Karmal, as far back as 1347-48 (H.S.) a decision to form trade unions had been taken by the Party, which raised funds and trained organizers to do so.

Now the workers were in *power*. But being in power and knowing how to exercize power are not one and the same thing. The shift of revolutionary gears from *against* to *with*—for now that workers were in power it was redundant to oppose themselves with strikes—took time and training. As an indication of how far Afghan workers had gone in the maturing process, one must note that thousands of them donated a free day of labor to the government on February 21, 1981, to welcome the First Congress of Trade Unions in March.

It is these truly liberated workers who are the most effective fighters against the counterrevolutionaries, and on their ears the cry of *Allah-o-Akhbar* is historically lost.

Organized, trade union centers became not merely the premises where strictly trade union matters (wages and working conditions) were considered. They also became schools where workers are taught not only to read and write but what to do with what they read and write.

By addressing themselves to social problems they learn that social problems can be solved and that, in fact, they are *social* problems. They are taught how to work and live cooperatively, beginning the dramatic, historic change in psychology which marks the transition from peasant to worker that has characterized our epoch in so remarkable a way.

Here, then, was how the working class is born. Out of the chrysalis of feudalism, from the peasant bound to the land emerged the man in overalls who attacked the mysteries of life with supreme confidence that he had found both the tools to change life, thus solving the "mysteries," and to change himself in the process. Taking hundreds of years to evolve in the West, this historic process had to be speeded up here in literally months. If a kind of half-peasant, half-worker, a centaur of our era resulted, this should not frighten mankind, though a pretense is made in the West that this pressure-cooker worker is a monster from the brain of a demonic communist Frankenstein.

He is not. He is merely developing quickly and carrying with him shreds and patches from his long, long past. Today the most advanced of them are taking the lead in organizing all the workers in Afghanistan, and in a single year unions for teachers, journalists, hospital workers, cultural workers (professions that had never been unionized before) would be formed. Organizations which brought tribal leaders, clergymen and others would also take shape, climaxed by the Fatherland Front.

Thus, the future (if the war could be ended) was bright. Every time a new factory is built new workers are born. For literally millions the road into the working class is the road to freedom. As Afghanistan industrializes itself it re-creates itself in the image of the working class which it simultaneously gives birth to.

PROBLEMS

> As I would not be a slave, so I would
> not be a master. This expresses my idea
> of democracy.
>
> Abraham Lincoln

Nizamuddin Tahzib is a member of the Central Committee of the Party and also Chief Justice of the Supreme Court. He, too, had been a marked target of Amin, and had seen the inside of a prison.

That being so, how was it possible for a member of the Central Committee of the Party to administer justice, particularly to those who had been unjust to him and his friends?

We asked him this pointed question, among others. He reminded us that in January (this was July), "after the second phase of the revolution we did not arrest anyone unless he had committed a real crime against the people.

"After Amin's overthrow, we had the problem of reassuring the people that his methods were buried with him—that the time of arbitrary arrests, torture, the disappearance of people forever with no word to their relatives about their fate was gone forever.

"We abolished the secret police force, Amin's KAM. We had to separate the judicial system from the government—to be independent of government, which does not mean that we are 'independent' of the revolution. Still, we had to take strong measures to regain the confidence of the people. I think we've succeeded.

"As for Amin's ministers, who have been arrested, they will be put on trial before the Revolutionary Court in due time."

Most of the present leadership had felt on their own bodies what Amin's "justice" was like and, though they were not overly sentimental toward real counterrevolutionaries, especially mercenaries, they did not seek for revenge even against Amin's henchmen, though Islamic law could be read as sanctioning "an eye for an eye."

On November 25 (1980), the PDPA Central Committee's Political Bureau and the Presidium of the DRA's Revolutionary Council, at a joint meeting adopted a resolution, "On Strengthening Revolutionary Legality."

The Resolution notes that "one important achievement of the new stage of the April Revolution was the adoption of the historic basic principles of the DRA, which guarantee broad democratic rights and freedoms to the people: immunity of the person and home, protection of life, secrecy of correspondence, etc."

And now: "To ensure revolutionary legality and to wage a successful struggle against any encroachments on the people's system and against other crimes violating the citizens' rights and legitimate interests, a new system of law-and-order agencies has been set up, consisting of a State Security Administration (HAD), special revolutionary and military tribunals, the Procurator's Office, and the people's militia. . ."

And it was resolved that "strict observance of revolutionary legality is a fundamental task of the new stage of the April Revolution . . . and the DRA government is to establish strict control over the fulfillment of the DRA's basic principles. . ."

From Mahmood Baryalai we would learn that it was no easy matter to expel American journalists, as they had to in January. "They came here not simply as journalists," he told me. "They also actively organized the rebels. They violated all the norms of journalistic behavior. Some came here with visas which they obtained by misrepresentation. They were not *bona fide* journalists: that was just their cover. They came to see what damage they could inflict on our country and our cause."

Mahmood Baryalai reminded us, when we referred to the Soviet army's presence in Afghanistan, "to keep Chile (1972) and Indonesia (1965) in mind! If the U.S.S.R. had not come in when it did, our country would have been a second Chile, a second Indonesia. We faced an enemy that is savage, that recognizes no human standards of behavior at all. Not only are they specifically enemies of communism—they are enemies of liberty everywhere, of culture, of science, all civilized values. They burned down schools and colleges and destroyed all they could lay hands on. They burned down our university at Jalalabad, killed hundreds of rural teachers, some after terrible torture, poisoned our children of six and seven years of age. They buried some of our people alive, flayed others until their flesh hung in ribbons from their backs. We faced that kind of savagery—backed by the U.S.A.—as inhuman here as in Vietnam.

"Our position is simple: we want to provide a poverty-stricken people with food, clothing and shelter. That's all."

The Social Science Institute, which opened its doors in October 1979—two months before the December events—stands on the outskirts of Kabul. Faroug Karmand, its president, explained that the purpose of the Institute is to train Party cadres, not only in Marxist-Leninist theory but in how to apply the Party program in practice.

Once its members had completed a six-month course—114 of them had just completed their course in January, and now in July 250 more soon would

—they would be sent to key areas of the country to put to work what they had learned in the lecture room.

The students, male and female, 750 of them, were all dedicated, devoted youth, familiar to us already from meetings of similar youth in many other socialist countries. The difference here was that they carried an historic burden on their shoulders, which it was both their luck to have been born to bear and their fate: some were killed.

Most, however, including the 180 young women, were welcomed by the peasants among whom they worked. It was also significant that most of the students came from the lower middle class, reflecting the fact that the working class, just lately awakened from its long sleep, was still relatively uneducated and could not yet provide the intellectual leadership which their revolution demanded.

Here we were witnessing, in Afghanistan, what was taking place in a number of other backward, newly liberated countries where survivals of feudal and even tribal relations existed, and where the working class is still in scarcely more than embryo form: members of the educated classes who, out of motives of deep patriotism, national pride, stung with anger and shame at the humiliation to which their country was subjected by colonialists, "stood in" for the working class until it could itself take over and produce its own educated cadres directly out of its ranks.

Minister of Commerce Mohammad Khan Jalalar certainly was unique among government ministers. He was one of three non-Party members of the government's top directing body (appointed in January). But this job of his was not new to him. He had held the same position in Daoud's bourgeois government, and was Deputy Finance Minister under the King! Now he was still at the same post, conducting the commercial trade relations under the Karmal government with apparently no major hitch in his passage from one government to another.

Trade was carried on with all countries, he said, except with Israel and South Africa. Surprisingly, he said that trade was carried on with Pakistan—one of the many paradoxes that one would run into here.

But the main trading partner was the U.S.S.R. Still, this was nothing new. Afghanistan's northern neighbor had been its main trading partner for a long time now, reaching far back even to Czarist times. Afghanistan's currency, the Minister said, was stable, and despite repeated stories in the Western press it would not be replaced by the Russian ruble. (As a matter of fact, the afghani in circulation at that time still had the face of Daoud on it.)

Export, he said, for the past year (1979) stood at 1.5 billion afghanis. Afghanistan exported natural gas, karakul wool, cotton, sesame oil, raisins, carpets, herbs, handicrafts. It imported petrol, fuel, tea, clothes and lemons, as well as machinery, transport equipment, tires, TVs, watches, etc. Carter's recent cancellation of the $ 15-million pending credit to Afghanistan had had little effect on the economy. Normal commercial relations with the U.S.A. continued.

Prices charged by the U.S.S.R. for Afghan oil were pegged at fixed world prices, based on 1967 but revised as world prices changed. Generally, all trade between Afghanistan and the U.S.S.R. was based on world prices, but specially favorable protocols did exist in some instances which benefited the Afghans. Total annual exports to the U.S.S.R. were put at 2.4 billion afghanis. Most of the foreign and domestic trade was in private hands. Private enterprise is encouraged to stimulate trade. Liberal credit from the U.S.S.R. at low interest rates helped to rebuild the country.

Piqued by the idea that he had been the Minister of Commerce through at least three different regimes, one of which was capitalist, one a royalist, King Zahir, when he was Minister of Finance, we asked him: "After 20 years, in which you served under three different regimes, which is best?" He laughed. "I'll give you my answer," he said, "when I retire." And left it up to us to puzzle that one out.

Afghanistan has something like 250,000 *mullahs* whose presence and influence saturate the social system.

But though they are servants of Islam, being close to the people they cannot entirely escape the problems of the people. Therefore, it is not surprising that the bitter struggle going on outside the ranks of the clergy should be reflected within their ranks in some form as well. Religion does not soar above classes, though it claims to. There are *mullahs* on both sides of the conflict, and each interprets Islamic teachings to suit—though they do not admit it—their class interests. It is as true of Afghanistan, Iran, Pakistan or anywhere in the East, where Islamic traditions are alive, that the class struggle in each country is fought out in religious form. That these "religious wars," coming as they do in a period of imperialism, of advanced technology and science, should seem anachronistic is due to the historic lag in social development in these areas, where feudalism has persisted into a world where capitalism itself is beginning the long decline into its last good-night.

That imperialism should try to adapt feudalism to its own ends under the guise of respect for religion is not surprising either. But there is no way of walling off whole countries in our day and age, when satellites can circle the globe in hardly more than an hour, as there is no way of bottling up modern social relations into forms that reflect a lower economic order.

American capitalism, in its moribund form of American imperialism, poses as great a threat to Iran (for instance) as it does to all Islamic countries anywhere in the world, and in reaction to this threat some of these countries (like Iran) have sought to strengthen their purely feudal traditions to protect themselves. But the threat is not to religion or tradition. The threat of American imperialism is to the material resources of these countries (oil, for one), and forcing women to go behind the veil again will not stop that threat.

As late as 1970 Afghan *mullahs* in Kabul had staged a month-long demonstration against girls wearing miniskirts, and some had even attacked them by throwing acid at their faces. Under King Mohammad Zahir Shah, women were required to wear the *chadri,* and few dared go out on the street without keeping their faces covered.

The *mullahs* (or, more accurately, the religious institutions which they served) had always stood athwart progress—or at least those did who most closely represented the interests of the landlords, which were often their own interests as well. But they had stood most immovably against progress for women. That any of the *mullahs* had found it possible to accept the new government despite the crudities of Amin, which had made life difficult for them, was in itself surprising. But what was extraordinary was that so many did. That very month (July) a conference of Ulemas, with 800 representatives, had taken place in Kabul.

We met four *mullahs* in their Maj Noonshah mosque in central Kabul. We took our shoes off and squatted in a circle around them. They were members of the Religious Scholars Association. Abdul Aziz Sadegh was their president and spokesman.

Our main question was why Moslems like themselves were supporting an "atheist" government, and whether they were persecuted by it or in any way discriminated against.

To this: "Are you persecuted?" Abdul Aziz Sadegh, a man in his late 50s, answered flatly: "Our only persecutors are the counterrevolutionaries."

It was they, not the PDPA members, who burned down the mosques and assassinated the *mullahs* who supported the government. He himself, as he would tell us later, was also on their hit list. Altogether, at that point, some 50 *mullahs* had been assassinated by the counterrevolutionary forces. (By 1983 this figure more than doubled.)

He insisted, however, that there was no contradiction between the goals of Islam and of socialism. Islam too wanted to put an end to poverty and oppression. Nor was the government anti-Islamic. The government not only did not interfere in the work of the *mullahs* but gave them funds with which to make repairs to their mosques and to rebuild those that were burned down. Declared Karmal in his Report to the Ninth Plenum on July 27, 1982: "The revolutionary state ... is paying great attention to the repair of mosques damaged by the counterrevolutionaries and the construction of new mosques. For this purpose Afs. 51 million were spent in

1360 H.S. (1980) and ... Afs. 53 million in the Budget for the year 1361 H.S."

"Before the revolution," Abdul Aziz Sadegh commented, "no *mullah* was ever consulted by the government on religious or social matters, nor sent abroad, as we have been to the Soviet Union to see with our own eyes how our brother Moslems live in that country."

What they had seen in the U.S.S.R. (in Uzbekistan, for instance, where the old mosques had been scrupulously restored in ancient cities like Samarkand) had impressed them. Alas for hair-raising anti-Soviet propaganda! One's own eyes are one's best guides to the truth.

At one point he said: "We belong to the country, not to the state." This seemed clear enough and explained to some degree how these religious men, who had seen many states come and go, could adjust to the new order.

As for the threats on his life, his answer was also simple: "I am not afraid of the enemy. I will follow God's will and He will not take me until He wants me. I shall be ready." (He would be reported assassinated later.)

He told us the government had helped about 8,000 pilgrims to go to Mecca, in Saudi Arabia, that year—6,000 by air and 2,000 by land. "A passport tax had been cut from 25,000 afghanis to 5,000." Later, Saudi Arabia would make such pilgrimages more difficult by cutting off diplomatic relations with Afghanistan.

Did he consider Carter, who just at that time (along with Brzezinski) had come out as a "defender of Islam," a true defender of Islam, using almost the same language as German agents did in World War I when they tried to convince the Afghans that the Kaiser was a friend of the Moslem peoples?

His eyes flashed. "No, for if he was, would he not have liberated Palestine and let the Arabs return to their country? He has done nothing to restore the holy place of Jerusalem to the Arabs."

One of the *mullahs* distributed pamphlets to us in Pushtu explaining the role that Moslems played in the new Afghanistan. There would be a conference of religious figures in Kabul before the end of the year and a *modus* for relations with the government further clarified. The organization that was formed at the conference also became part of the Fatherland Front.

Shah Mohammad Dost is Foreign Minister of Afghanistan. He is remarkable also as having served as a diplomat for previous governments. He made it clear to us that Afghanistan would accept no proposal for a settlement of the "Afghan problem" that violated Afghanistan's sovereign rights as an independent country. But everything else, he said, was negotiable, as the government's May 14, 1980 Statement (supplemented and added to by its Statement of August 24, 1981) had pointed out.

It is not to slight his meeting with us to say that what he told us we had already picked up from other ministers whom we interviewed before him. He repeated the government's position based on the May 14 proposition. He repeated the legal grounds on which the government stood in inviting the Soviets to come to their help. He repeated his government's willingness to reach a friendly agreement with Iran and Pakistan, much as it had reached an agreement with India. He was certain this would come about sooner or later. He explained that not all of the "refugees" reported in Pakistan were genuine refugees but, as we had already noted, thousands were in fact nomads stranded on the Pakistan side of the border, and thousands of others were villagers forcibly driven, lured or deceived into Pakistan, where they were kept against their wishes by terror and propaganda. There were people in Pakistan who had fled Amin. But, he added, Karmal's Declaration of General Amnesty had reached even into Pakistan and many, not without great difficulty and danger from the Pakistani border and camp police, had returned—200,000 so far that year (July 1980).

Thus, having met with dozens of administrators, high and low, Party officials as well as non-Party, being impressed by their youth (most of them in their 30s and early 40s, Karmal then having just turned 51 himself), having listened to their plans for the future as they outlined them in blueprints and figures, and seeing reconstruction going on everywhere, I found myself persuaded by all this and more that the government was in the hands of a very able, very dedicated and enthusiastic—perhaps naive, as yet—group of revolutionaries whose style and spirit breathed profound confidence in themselves and their mission.

So, with the government still in the early stages of formation, there was nothing sinister nor untoward in the fact that pesonnel was being shifted, replaced, promoted, demoted, acquired, retired. The new administration had to clean out not only offices but minds. Their aim was to forge an instrument out of the state, the government, which would actually serve as a tool for the people, and in serving the people serve the revolution: honestly, efficiently and self-sacrificingly.

Most of the 57 members of the Revolutionary Council, which was a kind of steering committee for the revolution, in July (1980) were veteran revolutionaries who had led the struggle for the liberation of Afghanistan for many years. Some had spent time in prison, others had been months in hiding, and still others had been in emigration. Some had been members of the Council under Amin but had responded to Karmal's call to overthrow Amin.

TRYING TO SNEAK
THE SUNRISE PAST THE ROOSTER

'Tis we, who lost in stormy visions, keep
With phantoms an unprofitable strife,
And in mad trance strike with our sprit's knife
Invulnerable nothings.

Percy Bysshe Shelley,
Adonis

In his book, *The Hidden History of the Korean War*, I. F. Stone made a number of startling discoveries about that war (which was not even a "war" but a "police action"). One of them was that there were "battles," luridly reported in the press as if by eyewitnesses in the most convincing detail. But the trouble was, *they never took place.* They were inventions by the supremely creative press corps attached to General MacArthur and under his command. These "battles" had been invented by MacArthur, as was later established, to prepare public opinion for the crossing of the Yalu and engaging China.

In the Afghan war, in which the U.S.A. does not officially play any role, battles also took place only in the imaginations of the newspaper correspondents, who also knew that they "were untrue." Untrue or not, they became "true" once they appeared in the press.

Though the intent was not, unlike MacArthur's, to prepare public opinion to enter the Afghan war directly, it did have an aim which, in the context of the times, contributed to "spreading the war" nevertheless. Though Afghanistan, like China, is not where the "real war" is to be fought, still it is one of the outposts of that war. It can be used to justify the termination of detente, for leaving SALT-2 on the "back burner,' and for a return to the Cold War in a new, more virulent edition than the old one.

In June, 1980, one of the most remarkable episodes in all of military history took place. Or rather, it did *not* take place, and that is what is remarkable about it. For at the very moment when it should have burst upon the world as a climax to the war, it disappeared utterly.

On June 9, AP was telling the world from New Delhi, under the banner headline that read: "Rebels Said to Approach Kabul; Soviet Troops Reported Ready":

> Moslem Resistance fighters have poured out of the countryside of Afghanistan to the outskirts of Kabul, and the Soviet military has moved to defend the capital, according to a foreign traveler with wide contacts in Kabul.

The account goes on—"sporadic artillery," "armed convoys," "fighter planes seen flying low over the city." "The traveler confirmed earlier reports of fighting in Paghman Mountain. . ."

On June 20 (1980), UPI was reporting (from Islamabad) that "Afghan insurgents have called for a general strike by storekeepers, students and other Kabul residents in a new protest of the Soviet presence in Afghanistan, rebel spokesmen in Pakistan said yesterday. . ."

But there's more. By June 10, the *Los Angeles Times* would report from New Delhi (now under the name of Tyler Marshall) that "Reports of heavy fighting between Afghan guerrillas and Soviet troops in the mountains around Kabul have signaled a new phase of the resistance to the Marxist regime of Pres. Bobrak (*sic*) Karmal and the Soviet military presence that keeps it in power. . ."

But uneasy lies the prose of a bourgeois correspondent, for Tyler admits in the same dispatch that the events in Kabul, gleaned from tales of "travelers" in New Delhi, might be a bit much, and suggests that the figure of 20,000 "insurgents around Kabul" is "discounted by political analysts as highly exaggerated."

Nevertheless, two days later, on June 12, also from New Delhi, also from the lips of "travelers," the *Herald Tribune,* whipping up various agency reports into a single souffle, came out with the new information that "martial law" had been declared in Herat and Kandahar, Afghanistan's two other major cities, and at the same time that "Soviet troops continued to station vehicles around Kabul because of a building of rebel forces."

This story went on to say: "A source [now, it is just a bleak 'source'] said that between 5,000 and 20,000 [a really big spread!] Moslem insurgents who gathered in the mountains outside of the city last week had progressed to the outskirts of Kabul. . ."

That's very close! Farther along in the same story there is an indirect confirmation of the fact that the Moslem insurgents had indeed successfully poisoned 488 of Kabul's schoolchidren, for it wrote: "Kabul radio claimed that 488 students in a number of schools in Kabul had been poisoned by 'anti-state elements and spies'. TASS said in a dispatch from Kabul that students and teachers were gassed."

No effort is made to deny the gassing and poisoning of those students. We shall deal in more detail with this later, but at the moment we pause merely to note that this fact is included in a context praising the resistance of the "rebels."

By mid-June, if the world (especially the American world) had believed these reports (and we see that highly sophisticated newspaper columnists did), so richly furnished with precise details, it could be forgiven if it also believed that Kabul was tottering on the edge of collapse, its Afghan puppet leaders cowering in panic (those not already assassinated), the two other major Afghan cities gripped in a general strike, also about to fall to the rebels, and that the end of the war had to be only a matter of days, perhaps even hours, away.

Why, then, would the Soviets, so beleaguered, so obviously at bay, choose precisely this moment—June 22—to announce that they were withdrawing "some military units" from Afghanistan because the situation there "has become more stable?" Were they mad, or so incompetent that they couldn't understand that Kabul was surrounded and about to fall any moment? Didn't they need every soldier they had to throw into the breach? In fact, as early as June 13, while the "collapse" of Kabul was still imminent in the press, TASS was apparently insanely reporting that:

> Kabul, June 14—Afghanistan's news agency, Bakhtar, has condemned statements by some U.S. high-ranking officials spreading tales about the situation in Afghanistan, including, among other, the report about an alleged "sharpening of tensions in Kabul."
>
> The news agency also stresses that a recent statement of the State Department spokesman, Hodding Carter, that a state of siege has been introduced in Herat and Kandahar has no grounds whatsoever. Such misinformation by Washington, aimed at misleading world public opinion, says the Bakhtar Agency's commentary, has become a daily practice and an organized part of the U.S. policy of subversion against the Democratic Republic of Afghanistan and its revolutionary government.
>
> "U.S. ruling circles," the Bakhtar News Agency continues, "do not wish to reconcile themselves to the fact that the Afghan people have assumed power and are building a new life independent of Western monopolies.
>
> "Imperialists and internal reactionary forces are doing everything to prevent the construction of a new society in Afghanistan, resorting, to achieve their ends, to barbarous means—from infiltration into Afghan territory of armed mercenairies who set fire to schools, hospitals and mosques, to abominable acts against schoolchildren, teachers and workers of state enterprises.
>
> "Why should, in this connection, the State Department spokesman abstain from commenting on a mass poisoning by terrorists of Kabul schoolchildren and workers?" asks the Bakhtar News Agency. "Hodding Carter had nothing to say about these abominable atrocities committed against the Afghan people, precisely because the United States and its allies are instiga-

tors of the use of chemical weapons, of gangs of mercenaries and terrorists to commit such atrocities.

"As regards the situation in Kabul," the Bakhtar News Agency points out, "it can be described in one word—normal. Counterrevolutionaries and mercenaries are sustaining and will continue to sustain one defeat after another until they lay down their arms. . ."

I left Kabul on July 16 unable to find a trace of the "rebel showdown" I had been promised by at least Ramadan. In fact, I had seen no evidence of anything more hostile than a monkey attacking a banana in the bazaar.

WAR BY RUMOR

"Is smartness American for forgery?" asked Martin. "Well," said the Colonel, "I expect it's American for a good many things that you call by other names."

Charles Dickens,
Martin Chuzzlewit

BBC had broadcast the night before (Jan. 14, 1980) that there had been a "civil disturbance" earlier that day in the middle of Kabul. Since I was in the middle of Kabul that night before, and had neither seen nor heard any "disturbance", civil or uncivil, I felt somewhat miffed. How could I claim to be a reporter when I missed gunfights right under my nose?

So I consulted with my student guide, who had been studying a textbook all morning, where a "civil disturbance" was most likely to occur. He couldn't tell me. So I decided to take a car and, with him as my interpreter, scour the city, stopping here and there to make inquiries. Which is what I did.

Nevertheless, the cab driver, the student and I saw nothing, and we heard no gory tales from those we interviewed, who were chosen at random as we went. People were not yet newspaper-men-shy, as later they would be when they learned how their words spoken in all simplicity and good-heartedness were actually reported. But nothing. It had snowed the night before and at one point I found myself watching children throwing snowballs at each other. Then I saw a man leading two camels by a string in their noses, and the sight of them plodding in the snow, when it had always seemed to me camels could not be imagined outside of desert sands in the hot Sahara day, struck me as something quite as weird, and somehow jimmied out of its natural context, as everything about the "war" now seemed.

Fareedah Hatif, a medical student home to Kandahar from New Delhi where she had been studying, told me when I confronted herewith a similar BBC and VOA report that there had been intense fighting in Kandahar just days before, that she had seen nothing, heard nothing. She had routinely taken the bus in Kandahar to Kabul and was now helping to interpret for foreign correspondents.

Later, when I asked her whether she had herself (obviously a liberated girl) ever worn the *chadri,* she said, "Yes. When I was 13." But, she added, only because her grandmother had insisted: her own parents had not. But by the time the revolution occurred she had taken it off. "How did it feel to wear it?" I asked. "Hot," is what she said. I asked her, too, whether Afghan men treated women fairly, and her answer was "No." "Progressive men?" "Better," she conceded, but only reluctantly.

Babrak Karmal, just days before on December 28, had issued a Declaration of Amnesty in which he declared: "I hereby declare a general amnesty for all political prisoners who have managed to survive the gallows of the evil Amin and in due course will take steps to abolish the death penalty."

Most prisoners had already been released, including one of our guides: also a medical student, whose name was Amad Shah. The final 2,073 were to be released that morning from Pule-Charhi, the main prison on the outskirts of Kabul, whose interior many of those now in power had known intimately. Some 500 Party members had been shot there, according to reports published in the press, and 2,000 others were scheduled to be.

This ride back to the prison was no routine excursion for Amad Shah Taghian. Hardly two weeks before he had been inside those grey walls himself, waiting for the midnight call that would have taken him from his comrades never to return.

No more than 27, he had been a PDPA member (from Parcham which was the wrong kind then) active among Kabul's students at Kabul University's Faculty of Medicine. Amin's men had had their eyes on him and caught up with him finally, as they did with 20 others of the 200 Party members in the University. They took him first to KAM special quarters where newly arrested political prisoners were taken for preliminary "interrogation." There his "interrogation" included bastinado beatings on the soles of his feet as a traditional preliminary, but he was also introduced to more modern means of torture, the contribution of the technological revolution —electrical wires were stuck into his ears, nostrils and testicles, and shocks were sent through them as a more direct means of persuasion. He was questioned about his Party affiliation, pressured to denounce Karmal, and when he resisted was sent to the prison to await execution. The arrival of soldiers on the evening of December 27, who shot open the prison gates, saved him. The so welcome voice of Karmal over the prison radio had let him know that Amin had been overthrown.

We were not destined to go inside the prison that day, as had been planned. For when we arrived at the high-walled prison we were to see a milling crowd gathered at the gate. On our way out of Kabul we had passed dozens of cars crowded with just-released prisoners whose families had been at the gate since early morning and were now all jubilantly going home to Kabul. But those people still here had not found their relatives. Although they had been told the prison was emptied of inmates they were clamoring to go into the prison and see for themselves. The prison officials had not had the heart to tell them that those missing were probably dead.

As we sat in our bus waiting for word we could move into the prison, suddenly we heard a shot, saw an armored car flash by and a rush of people follow. We were abruptly told to come back the next day, Saturday.

What had happened? We got only fragments of the facts then, but later we pieced the whole story together. It seems that the prison officials, seeing no other way of satisfying the upset relatives, had finally allowed them to go inside the prison to see for themselves. Illiterates live by rumor. Fear, panic and suspicion rule their minds. Convinced by centuries of deception to distrust authority, they search for truth in their own way, by sifting rumors and exchanging tales with their neighbors. Karmal's declaration of amnesty had been interpreted to mean freedom for *all* criminals. Real criminals were not freed. In addition, some new criminals—Amin's men—had been lately added to the prison rolls.

Nevertheless, no explanations would appease them. So the gates were opened to them and they surged in. They found the cells empty. Nobody was there—except in one section where not only 18 of Amin's ministers were now jailed but also 84 members of the Maiwandwal counterrevolutionaries, as well as members of the royal court and family, 16 Pakistani nationals—altogether about 150 to 200 prisoners.

When they came upon their tormentors, the ministers of Amin, aware by now that their sons and fathers had been executed, the crowd erupted into a mob ready to lynch these men. It was at this point that a guard fired a warning shot into the air that sent them (and those still waiting outside) running.

Next day—Saturday—we were back again. Amad Shah now led us through the prison complex with the assurance of an old tenant, which he had been a few weeks before. Moneer, who accompanied us, was also a Party member, but unlike Amad Shah had not been arrested. He had followed us mutely through the bleak yards. I said to him at one point, as we passed under the grey *pisé* walls: "Here is where Amin's men would have put you if they had caught you in time. How do you feel now?"

He gave me a swift, hot glance, his amber cat-like eyes flaring. "Free!" he burst out, as though the word had been shot out of him.

The guards were still at their posts—guarding an empty prison! We passed through the long, desolate, whitewashed corridors between empty cells, and they saluted us, their faces impassive, these young men who had come to the city from the country and had become tormentors of the very people dedicated to freeing them! For they had been in prison, too—locked in a policy that had been perverted by unseen hands. They thought they were doing their revolutionary duty as it had been explained to them by Amin's men. Now the prisoners they had guarded were free, and the question in their eyes was: would we be in those cells tomorrow?

Amad Shah led us to his cell, which had been crammed with three times as many prisoners as it was built to hold, and showed us a slogan he had written with a felt-tipped pen that had been smuggled in to him: "Long Live Menkind!" Moved, I could only say: "You misspelled mankind." He explained that he had written it in English because "it is a universal language."

He pointed out other slogans written by other prisoners: "I've fallen in love with you, Freedom!" "Damn those who have arrested and executed innocent people!" "Humankind is born free."

Then he pointed to another one ironically and said: "This Amin's people put up." It was a card neatly printed in red. It said: "Today everything is for the benefit of the people." He looked at me to see if I had registered the irony.

Suddenly he threw his arms around one of the guards we came upon and then introduced him to us, explaining that he had been the friendly guard who had helped him in prison, and it had been he who had smuggled in the felt-tipped pen. When we questioned the guard, Habib, he told us that he had been repelled by how the other guards treated the prisoners and he himself had been put into a punishment cell for refusing to cooperate in torture after his first experience of it in which he had been forced to hold down a prisoner while another guard beat him. At the moment however he was more worried that his sister was alone at home in the village.

This, then, was the whole thing. In Moscow I would read in my *Herald Tribune* the following story headlined: "Two Killed by Guards, Afghans Storm Prison in Kabul."

> Kabul, Afghanistan, Jan. 11—Hundreds of Afghans stormed Kabul's main prison today after the government failed to release all the prisoners that it had promised to free. Guards opened fire, killing at least two persons.
> About 1,000 family members and friends then rushed the prison guards, who opened fire. Diplomats (!) said that only a small percentage of the 12,000 to 15,000 political prisoners reported detained throughout the country had been freed despite the pledge of Mr. Karmal that all prisoners would be released except supporters of the regime of Hafizullah Amin...
> "No more than 2,000 have been released," an analyst (!) said. "Most of them have been Parchamists. The prison remains very full..."

Amazing story! I was there. On the spot. I heard the shot (one!). Nobody was reported killed—then or later. That was Friday. Next day, without benefit of diplomats or nameless analysts, I had visited the prison itself, walked through acres of empty corridors and looked into dozens of empty cells, and saw that the whole section which had held more than 2,000 prisoners (Thursday) was now empty (Saturday).

Our guide was a real-life Afghan, himself a recent prisoner, who had a name, an age (27), a profession. His was no disembodied "voice," no anonymous "observer" or fleshless "analyst." He had lived, felt, agonized, triumphed.

That was January. I came again in July and spoke with other inmates. Their stories checked with those I heard in January. They would confirm the fact that Babrak Karmal's announcement of a general amnesty on January 19 had indeed been carried out and that all political prisoners, with the exceptions noted, had indeed been freed.

COUNTERATTACK IN FEBRUARY

These are the wounds whose open mouths cry out
The midnight hours when ghosts and diplomats
Walk on the scars of graves and all await
The terrible surgeon: either ours or theirs.

Thomas McGrath,
Wounds in the Rain

Early in February (Feb. 3, 1980) Zbigniew Brzezinski unexpectedly showed up at the Khyber Pass on the Afghan-Pakistani border. The Khyber Pass had been the scene of many a movie and novel (one by Kipling: *Kim*) and in real life had been the gateway south for traders and north for invaders, who were always the British.

With TV cameras watching, Brzezinski threw open his U.S. army jacket to show a dagger stuck in his belt which the Pakistani officers had given to him as a present. What did that gesture mean? In any case, he now asked one of the border guards to hand him his submachine gun and, with the TV cameras clicking away, aimed the weapon at Afghanistan! The pose, that could have been cast in bronze as it stood, was so classically melodramatic that they egged him on to carry it through to its logical end— to really shoot. But presumably sensing that drama had indeed passed into melodrama—in any case, the point had been made—he turned the gun back to the Pakistani border guard and asked him to shoot instead. And the guard, after jamming first, finally managed to get out a burst. The gun bore Chinese markings.

Standing there with a garland of flowers draped around his neck like a racing horse in the winner's compound, on the "free soil" of Pakistan, Brzezinski predicted confidently that the Afghan counterrevolutionaries would be in Kabul "soon."* Carter had been more specific. It was at the end of January that he had "proposed that the world's athletes boycott the Moscow Summer Olympics or that the event be moved to another country unless the Soviet troops are withdrawn from Afghanistan *within one month.*" *(Herald Tribune,* Wash., Jan. 30, 1980. My italics.)

---

* In June, 1983, Zbigniew Brzezinski announced the appearance of "Americares" with plans to send $2 to $4 million worth of "medical supplies" (poisons for drinking water?) to "refugees" in Pakistan. "It is not a political effort, it is not designed to advance any foreign policy objective," announced this modern Pinocchio whose nose has grown terribly long since he came to and left Washington.

This adamant, "unreasonable" insistence on the precise date on which the ultimatum would expire, at the time went by almost unnoticed. But it became enormously significant after February 22. For on the 22nd the counterrevolution made its supreme bid for power and for two days spread arson and sabotage in an organized and concerted manner, in an insurrection that failed.

But it had been well organized up to and including the very moment when it struck—February 22. Both Carters (President, and State Department's Hodding Carter), and Brzezinski of course, knew precisely what they had in mind when they made such a punctilious, even niggling, issue of the date. Hodding Carter, 3d (speaking for the State Department), had been almost Prussian about it. For February 20 was to mark not merely the beginning of the Olympics boycott but the beginning of the counterrevolution. The date had been set, everything was in place, and the conspirators couldn't afford to temper with what were already the concerted plans.

As events proved, no better moment could have been chosen than those last weeks in February. The Karmal regime was still struggling to consolidate itself. A certain amount of confusion still reigned, even in Party and government ranks. Kabul was virtually an open city into which counterrevolutionaries could move in and out with remarkable ease. The Pakistani border was but a few hours away. Streams of peasants and merchants moved into the city in the morning and out in the evening. The Kabul merchants had been terrorized on previous visits by sinister strangers who had threatened them with death if they didn't close up their doors on February 22. (And proved it by setting fire to the shops of those who showed reluctance.) The Kabul militia was still disorganized, or at least considered to be. And as for the Afghan army, reassuring reports had reached Washington by boomerang (for it was out of Washington that the first report originated) that it had "disintegrated as a fighting force" and would constitute no serious obstacle. (NYT, Feb. 22, 1980.) As for the Karmal government, it was isolated and could "command no significant followers." (*Ibid.*)

As for the Soviet forces, which kept their distance, whatever they did would be wrong. If they didn't intervene they would be faced in the morning by a Kabul in rebel hands. If they did intervene they would pay a high political price for that, too.

For months a team of CIA "experts," working out of Peshawar, headed by John Reagan but operating under the direct orders of Robert Lessard (the team also included David Turman and Richard Jackson), had been busy on a master plan for the uprising, coordinating inside (the American embassy in Kabul) and outside forces that would strike at the same moment. (Robert Lessard, a one-time staff member of the U.S. Embassy, had been expelled from Kabul in 1974 for precisely this kind of conspiratorial work.)*

On paper it looked foolproof. In fact, Washington was convinced that chaos ruled in Kabul and, as a reporter in the city would put it, "Bobrak's Soviet-backed government ... (had) ... virtually broken down." So that all that was needed to make it tumble was one good push.

So they pushed.

Here is how this particular episode was treated in the press. First, from the IHT, which, in a roundup of its news services (AP, UPI, Agence France-Presse, Reuters, etc.), wrote:

> New Delhi, Feb. 22—The Soviet-supported regime in Afghanistan today declared martial law in Kabul after gunfire and mass demonstrations erupted during a dramatic national general strike, reports reaching here from the Afghan capital said. Soviet forces were reported called in to Kabul to prop the weakening authority of the regime of Bobrak Karmal...

From a certain Michael Goldsmith, actually in Kabul:

> Kabul, Afghanistan, Feb. 28 (AP)—Soviet and Afghan troops and bands of heavily armed civilians patrolled the Afghan capital today, but President Bobrak Karmal's Soviet-backed government appeared to have virtually broken down...

All references to the actions of the storekeepers** closing their doors were referred to as "strikes." Here is how this "strike," which is usually not a hearthside word in *The New York Times* offices, was hailed there (Feb. 25):

> By slamming the gates and shutters of their shops, the merchants of Kabul gave voice last week to the anger of the occupied peoples of Afghanistan. That simple but heroic civil disobedience cried defiance against Soviet tanks and troops. It is also a cry of anguish that pierces the indifference of other cultures which had been debating every interest in this crisis except that of

---

* Every tumultuous event throws up its jetsam and flotsam. During the February events a certain American, Robert E. Lee by name, was reported as having been captured and having confessed that he was a CIA agent and now wanted to go over to the Afghan side as he denounced the CIA. The Left papers had featured this episode—as naturally they would—but after a while references to Robert Lee disappeared from the press with no explanations given.

Now it turned out that Bashir, representing the Bakhtar News Agency, had actually questioned Lee—knowing American English as he did. He told me that the CIA agent turned out to be a nut. Lee had asked the Afghan authorities to accept him as a defector, that he wanted to join the revolution, and that he didn't have the money to pay his hotel bill. The authorities were bemused by him—didn't know what to do with him. They finally had him deported. So ended this episode, too neatly cut to fit the anti-CIA pattern to have been accepted on face, but the temptation to do just that is, of course, overwhelming. Such a propaganda plum falling into one's lap can only be seized, not examined! Alas for the too-pat and the too-true!

** An estimated 30,000 in Kabul alone. An estimated million in the entire country.

the people most directly concerned. It was indeed, as one shopkeeper put, 'a great victory.'
The silent strike of businessmen...
For all we know, the mountain guerrillas and village youth who are ambushing Soviet armor, sawing down telegraph poles and sabotaging electrical lines...

One expected the editorial to go on: "and poisoning the drinking water of pre-teen-aged schoolchildren and setting off gas bombs in the schools..." but at that point the typewriter keys had gotten stuck.

But in actual fact, the storekeepers, on the whole, to whom a "strike" is a novel, in reality an altogether alien, idea, closed their shops because they had been threatened by counterrevolutionaries who had appeared the day before all over the city and had *ordered* them to close down their shops or have them burned down. At this point—two months after Karmal had come to power—these shopkeepers, who were hurting from the early end of the tourist trade, had no way of knowing which of the contending forces was going to come out on top. The new government had not yet shown that it could control the situation.

I have already reported on how the Kabul leadership had handled the situation. Now I want to go to a first-hand report from one of the university students who had serviced us in January. This was Bashir, brother of Moneer, who had learned his English at the American Center.

We sat together before a TV set because an Afghan documentary was on and he had promised to interpret and explain things to me.

As it happened, the documentary dealt with the events of February 21-22. He started out by saying that he had taken part in putting down the insurgency. We looked at him with disbelief. *Our* Bashir shoot a *gun*? (He was already "our Bashir.") He nodded—well, he hadn't actually shot one because he had driven an armored vehicle, but he did carry one that day. (Moneer, also busy among the students, had no gun—and regretted it, saying that if he had had one he would certainly have used it against the vandals breaking windows of the university. But they had been strictly forbidden to use weapons, though the other side did not hesitate to use theirs.)

The counterrevolutionaries had organized a march on the Party headquarters of the university, and Bashir had been assigned to protect it. The university has an enrollment of about 12,000 students and this "march" consisted of hardly 500, but not all were legitimate students. Some, it later transpired, were in fact outsiders who had come in to organize the demonstration, and others were pre-teen-age children. In fact, the organizers of the march had stationed the children in front of the march to serve as a shield, aware that the Communists would not fire on children. And they were right. What they did instead, Bashir told us, was to call on the children through a bullhorn to disperse at a given signal, and when they did the university defense corps closed in behind them and, after a tussle in which some of Bashir's friends were wounded, subdued the leaders.

The camera was meanwhile showing us children who had been swept up in the excitement the day before and "arrested." This was now the morning after and their parents, half mad with anxiety, were there at the prison gates reclaiming their children with tears and cries as they emerged, themselves crying, from the jail. They were bundled home quickly—and to the paddle which cured most of them of their love of adventure.

The TV showed interviews with some of the children (no more than 10 or 12 years old) who had been used by the counterrevolutionaries and had no idea what they were getting themselves into. The TV also showed an interview with a shopkeeper who told the camera how he had been visited by a mysterious stranger the day before, a man pretending to be a customer but who, at one point, suddenly opened up his coat and showed him a big revolver stuck in his belt, warning him to close down his shop or else. The camera moved in on shops that *had* been burnt to the ground and the woeful merchants picking among the ashes for what bits and pieces they could salvage.

The TV showed us a segment of new recruits to the army, and Bashir told me that he knew most of them—they were Party members, ex-students or now still students, workers and so on, all of whom had answered the call of the government to join the army. He translated for me when I asked him one of the slogans that the counterrevolutionaries had written on the wall. "God is great."

The considered approach to erring students and other weekend counterrevolutionaries who were judged to be confused and misinformed reported by Bashir and others was actually Party policy as confirmed by Sultan Ali Keshtmand, later:

> Even in the most tense situation, where counterrevolutionaries provoked riots in Kabul and elsewhere, the Party leadership and the government did everything to protect innocent people who had been deceived by the reactionaries. They allowed these people to go home after brief questioning. The only ones jailed were counterrevolutionary ringleaders, foreign agents. (WMR, Sept. 1980.)

Western reports would outdo each other in a kind of macabre dance around casualty figures for those two days. The estimates (never verified) would go from 300 to 600 in the same dispatch, and one of them charged that 1,500, another that 1,000 (a nice round number) had been executed, and 2,000 jailed. For confirmation of these "estimates" they cited each other. But all of them could have cited, if they had been more precise, the godhead of information from which they all fed: the mysterious "diplomat" who commuted so often between Kabul and New Delhi, whose clairvoyance was matched only by his remarkable diffidence in admitting to a name.

Later it would be revealed that those "patriots" who had climbed to the roofs of houses and shouted "Allah-o-Akhbar!" had not thought the idea up themselves. They were asked to do it—for 50 afghanis apiece (a day's wages). Those storekeepers who had hesitated about closing their shops had them burned down. *U.S. News & World Report* (Mar. 10, 1980) would comment disingenuously that the "seemingly spontaneous anti-Soviet demonstration" was just as "seemingly" the act of "unarmed men, women and children" who just happened to find Molotov cocktails all prepared and handy to throw at streetcars and buses. Somehow, they also "happened" to have leaflets, printed in Dari and Pushtu, which they circulated calling on the people to revolt.

Among the "unarmed men, women and children" later captured were 19 Pakistanis, who only a day before had been living in Peshawar. Two Afghan counterrevolutionaries—Mohammad Kasin, a former landlord, and Abdul Khakin—were also captured. Mohammad Kasin's home disgorged 400 grenades, automatic rifles and guns; and in Abdul Khakin's house were found foreign currency and anti-government propaganda literature. The Pakistanis had grenades, walkie-talkie and other paraphernalia which, the odds are, do not come easily to hand in a "spontaneous" situation. Of course they talked, and made it quite clear that they had not come to Kabul out of a sudden impulse to visit relatives or to take in a show.

So the February *putsch* had failed. It was not true that the government had no support. The intention, it was clear, had been to show that it did not. But the result had shown the opposite.

For, though the merchants and some students responded, as much out of fear and misplaced militancy as anything else, the workers did not. Nor was the militia as disorganized as expected. Self-defense groups had been set up in the bakery and at the big auto repair works of Jangalak as well as among the construction workers. Here the counterrevolutionaries were rebuffed. The militia had been supplemented with volunteers from the Democratic Youth and effectively contained the havoc.

But for all that they were amateurs against professional, CIA-trained saboteurs and arsonists. They worked under difficult conditions. Firemen trying to put out the deliberately set fires were shot at. Boys working with the militia had never handled a gun before. As we would learn firsthand from one of our January student guides, it took skill and courage for the young defenders of the revolution to suppress the uprising with a minimum of damage and injury. They, too, were amateurs.

The experience had taught the Party forces that security measures had been too lax. In January, when I had noted the ease with which travelers (and quasi-newspapermen) had been able to leave Pakistan and ride into Kabul with nobody checking their identity at any point along the way, I was told that because there were so many illiterates a man's signature—an X—could not identify him. Also, physically there was little to distinguish an Afghan from a Pakistani, so what could they do? And if they were nomads, they had only the changing seasons for an address.

By December of the following year it was clear that they had solved the problem, and *The New York Times* would now be reporting from Kabul:

> Unconcealed weapons are visible on every street as grayuniformed Afghan soldiers patrol, often picking out passers-by at random to demand identity cards. In an attempt to curb the movement of guerrillas from the countryside, the Government of President Bobrak Karmal has issued residents with *pink cards that contain their photographs,* names and occupations. Inspection of these cards, while frequent, are brief and cursory. (NYT, Dec. 29, 1981, by Sanjoy Hazrika. My italics.)

But this by no means is the end of the story. Newspaper accounts of the February events, magnified with repetition, took as their theme the notion that the people of Kabul, inspired by a profound hatred of the oppressive Russians and by their love of Allah, had risen in one convulsive mass in an heroic effort to overthrow the foreign tyranny and liberate their country.

Most of the stories that came bounding out of Afghanistan were based on sources that were themselves based on even more spectral sources: "Western diplomats," "travelers," "area specialists," etc. Such reportage violated, at least before Afghanistan, all the hitherto known canons of journalism but were published with the air of a bully's indolent insolence: "So what are you going to do about it?"

Bad as all that presumably was, even worse were the "ripple" effects. In due course the swamp of misinformation generated in the press swept over its fragile dikes into the presumably more conscientiously defended realms of Academia.

Before the year was over, books began to appear, authored now by professors and others who had spent usually some prior time in Afghanistan (under dubious auspices in most cases). Now, in a poker-faced "All-I-Know-Is-What-I-Read-In-the-Papers" prose, they reproduced in ostensibly more measured terms, but now as historical fact, the same harrowing newspaper tales that we had laughed over with our morning's coffee.

No one illustrates how this process works better than Nancy Peabody Newell and Richard S. Newell, both of whom had spent time in Afghanistan and are billed, one as "independent researcher on societies of Afghanistan and South Asia," and the other as "a specialist on Afghanistan" who is "currently Professor of History at the University of Northern Iowa."

They describe Kabul in February (1980) in their co-authored book, *The*

Struggle for Afghanistan, as boiling with (counterrevolutionary) rage against the Russians, as "Resistance groups worked together to stage a crippling strike," as *"shabnamas* (night letters) calling on demonstrations against the government were distributed," and as "mobs" poured into the streets and quickly "overran police and militia strong points, raided police arsenals and marched on local Afghan army posts, calling on the soldiers to come and join them. Some from the Kargha Afghan army barracks did. Parchamists [our Bashir and Moneer?] were hunted down. [But not Khalqui, presumably.] In the early stages of the street fighting the police and some military units became demoralized by the fury of the demonstrators. Men are reported to have walked up to Afghan soldiers, one after the other, asking to be shot. After shooting several, the soldiers ran away unnerved."

At this point the reader could be forgiven if he now had the definite impression that counterrevolution had triumphed. "Government control over most of the city was quickly lost. . ." and "thousands of citizens" climbed on the roof tops of the buildings and all cried, "Allah-o-Akhbar!" and this "powerful sound ringing through the silent city" was, it seemed, "spine-tingling."

The city was gripped in a strike, the police and militia "strong points" had been overrun, "thousands" of people were up on the roofs yelling, the Afghan army, or what was left of it, was surrendering to the demonstrators, some of whom had come up to the soldiers and apparently begged them to shoot them (and apparently some did), the buses and streetcars and buildings were in flame, Karmal and the puppet government were cowering in terror in the Soviet Embassy, the stupid Russians, in an Abbott and Costello comedy, were running into each other in their confusion and cordoning off areas of Kabul where nobody lived, and so on—surely a picture of the absolute collapse of the Karmal regime and the triumphant return to power of the people! The situation was exactly as the schemers in Peshawar (out of Washington) had planned it: insurrection had overthrown the puppet government. Word could now be confidently sent to Brzezinski, still waiting garlanded at the Khyber Pass with his Chinese submachine gun, to let Zia Nassery, relieved of his CIA 9-to-5 informer's job, come home at last and take democratic control!

As the account of the February events stumbles from the ludicrous to the grotesque to the finally imbecilic, scholarship stumbles faithfully after it, the willing participant in a farce in which it plays a demeaning role, its cap firmly on its head, its bells tinkling merrily.

But pity the poor undergraduate (not only in Iowa) who goes trustingly to his college's library card catalog and conscientiously notes down the titles of books in which he is sure he will find the unflawed pearl of truth about Afghanistan! Never has trust been placed in less trustworthy hands! The myth, whose origins are forgery and class hatred, takes on an independent life and emerges on the academic scene as hallowed fact, predictably reincarnated in dozens of college term papers, all decorated with approving A's, and finally finding its resting place in the encyclopedias of the land.

Confronted by such weighty tomes in which audacious fiction is enshrined as granite fact, never to be questioned this side of TV, how was a mere undergraduate (not even a PhD.) to know that those "night letters"—thought-up, written and duplicated on this year's model Xerox machines by Afghan "patriots" fired up with such hatred of the Russians that they forthwith invented them—were actually thought up, written and duplicated on Xerox machines already invented by men in the American embassy whose literary talents had been shaped in that amazing school in Langley, U.S.A., where "patriots" of every stripe and calibre are turned out as the occasion demands them?

And how are they to know that those "thousands of patriots" who had climbed up on the roofs of the buildings all over Kabul and had all begun crying "Allah-o-Akhbar!" were not only paid (50 afghanis) to do so, but that their voices had been taped in advance and were now monstrously magnified by loudspeakers which they had brought up on the roofs with them?

TODAY I WILL TELL YOU A TALE

> Be a craftsman in speech that thou mayest
> be strong, for the strength of one is the
> tongue, and speech is mightier than all
> fighting.
>
> *Maxims of Ptahhotep*

Hardly three weeks after all of this I was in Kabul again (it was now July 9, on the eve of Ramadan). And the war for a showdown that was imminent just days before was nowhere to be seen. The ring of steel around Kabul had evaporated. The 40,000 troops inside the city had dwindled down to one (Afghan) traffic cop on our corner. The tanks at strategic cross-points still were less visible than the one tank perched on its granite base in Revolutionary Square. No merchants were on strike, no students were demonstrating. If travelers were still slipping in and out of Kabul, it was not in the dead of night but by bus in open daylight (or by plane).

In fact, the whole dire situation had vanished—miraculously. And as for the press, out of print, out of mind. [But not for long!] Hardly had we registered the fact, once we looked into it, that the masses of rebels surrounding Kabul had disappeared like ghosts into the typewriters of their creators, than the BBC gave us a fresh theme to muse upon. It now told us that there would be a new uprising within Kabul on the eve of Ramadan, just a couple of days away!

While waiting for the start of Ramadan, however, we took a trip to Pargham, the city so often mentioned in the dispatches of the bourgeois journalists as being under "insurgent" control, and there saw a pleasant town where we met with the local Party officials in the yard of their head-quarters and asked them questions which had become much-chewed in our mouths by now. We looked for evidence of "fierce battles," and thought we'd found at least one such bit of evidence—even with a sense of relief! —when we saw a Party activist come into the yard wearing a bandaged head. Surely here he was, the first rebel victim we'd encountered, in the damaged flesh! But when we asked him what had happened, he smiled sheepishly and refused to explain. It was one of his friends who explained. "He drank too much last night and fell in a ditch." At least this much could be claimed by the "insurgents"—the night was dark and lights were not lit too often because of them, with ensuing casualties.

That was July 1980. One year later, on November 3, 1981, I would read in *The New York Times* a story authored by Michael T. Kaufman that an "Afghan source was quoted as having painted (!) a similar picture of how Soviet-supported Afghan units were able to gain a foothold recently (!) in Pargham, a resort west of Kabul that had been controlled by the rebels since spring.

"Although the guerrillas were said to have suffered only light casualties, most of them withdrew and, as a result, Government forces were able to enter and establish at least the appearance of civilian administration in the town."

I wonder if that fellow who fell into the ditch and wounded himself when we were there "painted" that story!

One more. This goes back to January. On my way out of Kabul, on the 17th, I spent an hour in the airport waiting for my plane, which was late. and as I waited I kept eating peanuts. The takeoff, once the plane arrived. was normal, my flight back to Moscow routine, my peanuts undigested and complaining.

What was my surprise when I landed in Moscow to learn, as I checked on my Telex, that I had been in the middle of a raging battle at the very airport, at the very time I was there, and I had missed it all!

Planes spitting bullets had zoomed over me and I had not seen them! Artillery had been firing somewhere nearby and I had not heard. Armies had clashed by day but where my senses were, it was night! All I heard in the midst of this military pandemonium was a bird singing!

I knew that the story of a battle at the airport was true—had to be true—because *The Washington Post* had headlined it, and if *The Washington Post* of Watergate fame headlines a story, it's *got* to be true! In addition, the State Department, through the lips of Hodding Carter 3d, would "confirm" it.

Which left me in a somewhat difficult position!

That was July 17. On August 24—just in time to restore my faith in my five senses—came this story by Stuart Auerbach, who had fathered the earlier story which the *Post* had headlined:

> Even the best of sources produce errors. In the Pakistan capital of Islamabad in January, a reliable (!) Western European diplomat told an inquiring reporter that his country's embassy in Kabul was reporting heavy fighting around the airport, with Soviet Mig fighters seen striking around the city. In an interview later that day, President Mohammad Zia ul-Haq confirmed (!) and elaborated (!) on that report on the basis of information he said he received.
>
> *The Washington Post,* acting on two different sources, including the one who allowed his name to be attached (!) to the report, carried a frontpage story of the fighting. The only problem is that it never took place.

Yes, that certainly is a problem! And yet, this was by no means a single case, but only one in which the reporter was caught *in flagrante delicto*. Auerbach could have flipped back to many other of his past stories and beat a hole through his chest with his *mea culpas!* But to go on:

> The recently arrived traveler settled himself against a cushion and began: "Today I will tell a tale."
>
> Indeed he did, spinning during the next hour what appeared to be a highly fanciful account of his journey by road through the rebel-held area of Afghanistan. He was not deliberately trying to mislead but rather was following a great Afghan tradition of story telling...
>
> Thus, reporting the *major East-West confrontation* under way, in the world today, has become a second- or third-hand affair—a combination of seeking out diplomatic sources with information from Kabul, gleaning tidbits from Radio Afghanistan and trying to separate fact from exaggeration in travelers' reports...
>
> According to correspondents who were in Kabul, in January (1980), soon after the Soviet intervention began, some of the *most hysterical and unreliable* reports on activities within Afghanistan came from daily briefings given by U.S. diplomats... (My italics.)

"Hysterical and unreliable!"—and these from U.S. diplomats! Surely this was biting the hand that fed it. Not that the derisive adjectives weren't deserved.

Ben Bradlee in the *Boston Globe* (January 1980) would note that many Western embassies got their best information from their servants, whom they sent into Kabul's bazaars every morning where, along with the fresh vegetables, they picked up the freshest of gossip. He then listed the following *caveats* for his readers: "If a report comes from a 'guerrilla' source in Peshawar, it should be ignored altogether. If there's a reference to 'diplomatic sources,' the item as likely as not is based on information obtained at the embassy of the correspondent's own country. If a report cites a 'reliable Afghan source,' the information most likely originated with a taxi driver." (*New Times,* March 1980, quoted.)

These "reports," acquired by such labor and research, are then broadcast by BBC, VOA and other unimpeachable sources of world news back to Afghanistan, where it is not unlikely that the originator of the first report will hear his own report returned to him second-hand but now immensely magnified.

Now, contrast the way in which the airport story was handled by the *Post* and by *Pravda*—that is, by the "free" as against the "unfree" press.

Pravda's correspondent in Kabul, after reading that a furious battle had taken place in and around Kabul airport on January 17, asked Mohammad Rafi, Minister of National Defense of Afghanistan, just what had really happened. Was the report in the bourgeois press true? Here is Mohammad Rafi's response:

What nonsense! There was no such clash, just as there was no mutinous regiment. The imperialists are conducting a propaganda war against us because we are one of the contingents of progressive forces. They dislike the changes in Afghanistan and our friendship with the Soviet Union. But we are glad that the Soviet Union is on our side at this critical moment. Afghan officers and soldiers treat their Soviet comrades as brothers. *(Pravda, Jan. 28, 1980.)*

Meanwhile, some two years later I would finally find out (more or less) what really happened in June when Kabul had found itself surrounded by rebel forces and hung there, overripe for plucking, except that when it actually came to claiming the fruits of their victories the rebels unaccountably vanished into thin air again, leaving Kabul as they found it. Again I would discover that the historians and scholars—the Newells—were helpful here. We would read now (in their book published in 1981): "The reportedly large massing of mujahaddin around Kabul in early June 1980 appears to have been intended more as a show of strength, and perhaps as a device (!) to infiltrate the capital, than a prelude to an attack...."*

They were saying *boo*, that is.

Both Anthony Lewis and the Newells would have profited if they had read an earlier dispatch in the London *Daily Telegraph* (Jan. 22, 1980):

> The departure (from Afghanistan) of American journalists has been accompanied by a sharp drop in the stories of armed clashes and murderous incidents usually attributed to "diplomatic sources."
>
> I could find no one who has actually witnessed a military engagement, seen a body or a helicopter gunship in action. The shops are open, people queue at the cinema and, apart from the 11 p.m. curfew—which was in force before the Russians arrived—life in Kabul seems normal... The American Embassy in Kabul has been consistently putting out exaggerated reports of rebel victories which other diplomats consider reflect badly on United States credibility and provide an over-optimistic impression of insurgent capability.

---

* *The Struggle for Afghanistan,* by Nancy Peabody Newell and Richard S. Newell.

THE STRANGE CASE OF THE AFGHAN REFUGEES: NOW YOU SEE THEM, NOW YOU DON'T

Heaven stops the nose at it...

William Shakespeare,
Othello

Deputy Secretary of State Walter J. Stoessel, Jr, would explain: "About three million Afghan refugees have fled their homeland seeking freedom, principally in neighboring Pakistan. Almost one-fifth of the pre-invasion population of Afghanistan—the largest group of refugees in the world—has so voted with its feet." (NYT, Mar. 8, 1982.)

But whatever the figures, nobody denied that "refugees" existed. Amin's actions had indeed sent many Afghans running to Pakistan because they believed, and with some justice, that they might be imprisoned by the regime. Some who fled *knew* they would be. They had been money-lenders who, at last count, held 11 *million* peasants in a debt that under no circumstances they could ever hope to repay. Others were bride-buyers who, for prices ranging from $1,400 to $4,500 would buy as many girls (at any age) as the buyer had money for. This slaver naturally ran to Pakistan and became a holy warrior on the spot. Landowners, 3 percent—40,000 of them —who owned 70 percent of the land, also fled: they, too, became not "rebels" but "freedom fighters." Others were *mullahs* (almost half a million of them who lived off the peasants and themselves owned land or served landowners).

There were other "refugees" who are unwilling refugees because "they hold the sons of tribal sheikhs and chiefs, and relatives of the leaders of large family clans as hostages," to prevent them from returning to Afghanistan. (Faiz Mohammad, Minister of Border Affairs of Afghanistan, quoted in *International Affairs,* 1980.)

Amin's undifferentiated policy of lumping all landlords into the same invidious category—middle with rich and poor with middle—succeeded in alienating sections of the landowning class that were not exploitative and posed no threat to the revolution. These too had "fled."

Sections—not all—of the omnipresent clergy, the Moslem *mullahs,* saw in the attacks on feudalism, the foundation on which they stood, unproductive members of society that they were, being undermined. Some were landowners themselves. Some just "belonged" to landowners. In both cases they identified their interests with the interests of the feudal landlords. It's not overly difficult for people to persuade themselves that their private interests are identical with God's! Their influence over the illiterate peasant was absolute, or so it seemed. They were able to persuade many villagers to flee from the infidel, refusing to accept free land since Allah forbade taking the landlord's property, condemning it as "stealing."

But there were refugees who were not refugees in any sense at all. These were the 3 million nomads whose seasonal trekking from Afghanistan to Pakistan and back, in search of pasture, took no account of borders, or indeed of nations or states. They belonged to tribes and followed tribal customs and tribal leaders. Not only was religious influence heavy on them, blood ties weighed just as heavily. They were forced to stay in Pakistan by one means or another, including, as we have just noted, the taking of hostages to keep them there.

Nevertheless, they were not refugees in any reasonable—and certainly not in the Stoessel—meaning of the word. And when news reached them that the Karmal government bore no ill will toward them, at first cautiously and then in a gathering flood they returned home, usually illegally, and there pledged their allegiance to the Karmal government when they reached their home villages.

Returning home was no easy matter. Not only did they have to overcome physical barriers, which included Pakistani and rebel guardsmen and police. They also had to overcome the massive and unrelenting propaganda brought to bear on them from every source that a return to their homeland meant their death. However skeptical you might feel about what you hear on the radio, a certain quotient of doubt does enter your mind if you hear it repeated often enough.

At a press conference I attended on February 20, 1981, in Moscow during the 26th Congress of the Soviet Communist Party, Babrak Karmal, who was there as a foreign guest, told a CBS-TV reporter that:

> Of the Afghans now living in Pakistan some are ready to come back home right now. We keep our arms open to those who want to return. On the other hand, there are camps in the territory of Pakistan where the mercenaries, smuggled into our country, are trained and equipped. Pakistan does not have as many refugees as it claims to have. They are mostly nomads who move between two countries and the government of Pakistan is now preventing them by force from moving into Afghanistan. For centuries such nomads have gone to Pakistan in winter and returned later. So one may say that for one or two million nomads both countries are their native land.

Newsweek had already reported early in 1979 that a meeting on what the Administration's attitude should be toward newly-revolutionary Afghanistan had been held in Washington, presided over, at least ideologically, by then National Security Adviser Zbigniew Brzezinski but joined in by the

CIA—if that's not a tautology. "Refugees" had by then become a political issue. Twelve camps (later, more than 100) were already established on the Pakistan side of the Afghan border, and some 5,000 counterrevolutionaries, the first of thousands, had been given the peculiar training for "refugees" found necessary at that time—how to burn down schools, blow up bridges and poison drinking water.

From the very beginning, therefore, the word "refugee" was to carry a decidedly ambiguous meaning. By whatever route they got there, and whatever reasons they originally had to go there, once they were inside the camps in Pakistan they were turned into something else than what they started out to be. The camps, it soon became clear, were not havens where refugees could passively wait until their homeland was "liberated" by others. They were expected to take direct part in its "liberation."

It is "interesting" that so many of the "refugees" were single men. These left their families behind in Afghanistan. In camp they drew a monthly pay of $5 per person, with $50 as a maximum payment for an entire family, if indeed they had brought their families along. Pakistan paid those families whose breadwinners were killed in counterrevolutionary activity 500 Pakistani rupees* in compensation. To judge the value of these payments one must remember that, according to U.N. statistics, the average Afghan earned less than $200 a year.

But wherever money is doled out, especially for mixed reasons, it arouses an appetite in that part of the *Mujahiddin* which merges its patriotism with its greed for gold. By 1981, the number of "refugees" was put at 2.1 million, and a year later the irrepressible Deputy Secretary of State was putting it at "almost three million" without taking the trouble to cite where he got that figure.

But a close counting of the real refugees tended to diminish these figures and to unfix the image of an entire nation fleeing for its life before the savage brutality of the Russians. Jere Van Dyke, who had spent time with the "refugees," would note in his *New York Times* report (Dec. 24, 1981): "Officially, Pakistan and the United Nations High Commissioner for Refugees put the number of those who have sought sanctuary at close to 2.5 million, but some of the aid officials privately doubt this number. Some of these people say that many of the refugees register more members of their family than have actually come to Pakistan, and draw benefits fraudulently...

"Some people are said to collect this amount while actually spending most of their time in Afghanistan working their farms and coming across regularly to collect the benefits"—a double-dipping arrangement not unknown in the States.

---

* A Pakistani rupee is worth $ .10 to $ .12.

158

Strange refugees, but nevertheless "counted!" And what really motivates them? "If," the same writer continues, "patriotic passions motivate men to fight, so, too, does a monetary gain." Black market dealings among each other, as well as with the "enemy," were also rife: "Many guerrillas talked openly of their bizarre black market collusion with the Soviet* and Afghan troops who are their battlefield adversaries... Certainly for most of the hardy and poor people of Afghanistan the war has meant a steady diet of bread and tea, often without sugar. For some, willing and eager to run the risks of conflict, the war has brought relative riches, mostly from an active trade in guns and hashish." (*Ibid.*)

The Afghan Minister for the Tribes and Nationalities, Suleiman Laiyek, a renowned poet and author of Afghanistan's national anthem, would have something to say about "refugees" as well: "Imperialist propaganda is inflating the refugee figures to discredit democratic Afghanistan. In addition, the Pakistani government has a special reason for doing so. In this fraudulent manner it seeks to trade more financial aid from China, and the U.S. and other Western states. The counterrevolutionaries too deliberately exaggerate the figures." (quoted in *New Times,* No. 33, 1981.)

American affluence is the petard by which the genuineness of political claims is hoisted. Just as the American GI after World War II could be followed through Western Germany, France and Italy by the trail of Mickey Mouse watches and Hershey chocolate bar wrappers he left behind, so, too, the typical consumer items of the West could be found everywhere in Pakistan, reducing fierce *Mujahiddin* into Black Market hustlers practically on contact, and turning the "holy war" on certain days into something that looked more like a bargain basement rush at Macy's in New York City. Holy warrior fought holy warrior for stereos and digital wrist-watches and tape recorders. The same writer, already quoted, found such exotic items even in the remotest mountain village bazaars, frequented by the "rebels" ... "drinking glasses from France, ballpoint pens, Russian cigarettes, rubber slippers, and razor blades." (*Ibid.*)

Philip Jacobson wrote in the London *Times* (Jan. 20, 1980), after visiting a number of "refugee" camps in Pakistan and after examining a number of reports and graphs, that "it [a report on refugees] makes clear at a glance that the vast majority of the 300,000 people registered with the refugee authorities arrived weeks before the Soviet invasion of Afghanistan and that the flow since then has slowed significantly. This is an awkward discovery, because virtually every foreign journalist—including myself— had unquestionably accepted..." the figures of "refugees" that had been handed to them by the camp authorities, including the figure of 60,000 Path-

---

* There is no independent confirmation of dealings with *Soviet* troops.

an nomadic tribesmen who were in Pakistan only because it was now winter and they had come for pasture.

Confirmation of the ambiguous nature of Afghan "refugees" would arrive discreetly sandwiched between paragraphs in the same dispatches that charged the opposite, as in one by William Stevens from Islamabad, Pakistan, much later (1982): "It is widely but quietly recognized that the Pathan tribesmen *who account for most of the refugees* do not consider themselves foreigners in Pakistan. 'For them, this has always been their homeland,' one Western diplomat said. 'They don't recognize the border.' " (NYT, Sept. 21, 1982. My italics.)

In the same story a hint as to the kind of problem Pakistan had taken to itself with these Afghan "warriors" was also dropped: "For the first time, the diplomats say, some Pakistanis are privately expressing concern that the Afghan refugee population will become a permanent fixture in their country. That would be no small matter, according to these Pakistanis, because the Afghans are warlike, highly skilled in martial pursuits, heavily armed, independent-minded, impossible to dislodge except at high cost, and an international force to be reckoned with." (*Ibid.*)

Minister of Foreign Affairs Mohammad Dost had told us in July 1980, some 200,000 Afghan "refugees" had come back home already, braving all obstacles, and more were arriving every day. We, too, could see them drive into Kabul in their colorful traveling vans decorated in bright colors and covered with intricate designs—into which whole Afridi families had piled, and eluding the guards at the phantom border, threaded their way back through the innumerable passageways by which they had made their way to Pakistan months before.

In January 1981, the Afghan government issued a new statement of policy on refugees in which it declared that all "refugees" who, "influenced by the false propaganda of the enemies of the Afghan revolution" had left their homes earlier because of "the atmosphere of violence and fear brought about by the Amin government," were welcomed home. "All those who have left Afghanistan under the influence of the lies and threats of the enemies of the motherland and the revolution, and whose hands are not stained with blood," were urged to return, taking advantage of the amnesty declaration "steadily put to life" and assuring them that "the necessary conditions for life, fruitful work and social activity... will be created for those who return."

The Statement went on to ask "the neighboring countries to stop anti-Afghan activities and stop placing obstacles to the seasonal migration of nomads and to the return of Afghans to their homes..."

Did any refugees respond? Granted it wasn't easy, even if one chose to return, even if one's doubts and fears were overcome—who came back?

Here is a sampling of reports from the Bakhtar News Agency of such returns as they appeared in the press (1908): Dec. 11: "...838 people and 85 families returned home via Islam Kala border ... who had left their homeland due to the tyranny and dictatorship of the blood-thirsty Hafizullah Amin and his terrorist bands..." Dec. 12: "The number of Afghan citizens returning home is increasing with each day... Bakhtar Agency reports that more than 800 people returned last week to Herat province..." Dec. 15: "Sultan Shah, Abdul Rashid and Abdul Hadi, inhabitants of Malil village, Mooristan Moloswell, Lagman province, who had been deceived by counterrevolutionary elements ... surrendered themselves to Noristan High Commissioner, laid down their arms and expressed penitence for their past actions..." (1981) Feb. 16: "...in recent days more than 300 people returned to Afghanistan through the Islam Kala border post..." Feb. 24: "...another 200 persons have returned home in recent days..." Feb. 26: "...more than 100 families returned ... a total of more than 10,000 families returned to the country in the past year..." Mar. 6: "...more than 100 people ... have laid down arms and surrendered to the organs of power in the Afghan province of Herat..."

And so on, in what seems like an endless stream.* The returnees included active rebels as well as nomads and landless peasants who, for one reason or another, had found themselves on the Pakistani side of the border when hostilities broke out in April 1978, or escalated after December 27, 1979. (The 1893 Durand Line often cut Pushtun villages in half—one half on the Afghan side and the other half on the Pakistani side.)

The fact that argued for the return of the refugees was the simple one that it was in their best interests to do so. Land awaited the ordinary peasant. To the small merchant or property owner, or even middle peasant who was not an exploiter, what had been theirs before Amin had taken it away was now to be returned, and what couldn't be returned or replaced would be compensated for. *Mullahs* could resume their religious life and nomads could lead their flocks to pasture.

Against this the leaders of the various "rebel" groups could put up nothing more compelling than the fear they had implanted in everyone under their direct influence that if they returned to their homes the "Russians" would kill them. Now obviously the "Russians" had no reason to "kill" anyone who returned to Afghanistan from Pakistan, for in returning these "refugees" were weakening the feudal landlord resistance to the Karmal government. Of course, the more who returned and were not killed, the easier for those still in the camps to make the same move. By the end of

---

* A reading of *Kabul New Times* in 1982 and 1983 reveals the same phenomenon continuing.

1980, force was needed to held refugees in the camps where they no longer wanted to be.

Meanwhile, when the first Spring came in 1980 and the nomads from Paktia, Paktika and Nangarhar now stranded in Pakistan tried to return to their traditional grazing grounds in Afghanistan, they met concerted resistance. Some were arrested for "cattle stealing" (taking their cattle back over the border); others for "smuggling goods" (their household effects); or simply illegally crossing the frontier. Hostages were taken—wives and children were held by the authorities to guarantee the return of fathers. Tribesmen were harried in a dozen other ways, ending up as demoralized members of camps from which they could "escape" only if they agreed to enlist as mercenaries.

Here are some pictures of life in the camps. The first is from *Pravda* (Sept. 4, 1980), written by its correspondent in Pakistan, V. Baikov:

> A gloomy tale of physical and emotional suffering experienced over the last few months was told to us by Ismail Ali, Niyas Khan and other people from the village of Khel in the Afghan province of Nuristan.
>
> Late last year (1979), the village rich man Rakhim Khan loaded his possessions on camels and fled abroad. By promises and threats he made nearly half of the villagers leave their homes, too. At the moment Rakhim Khan is well off, living in Peshawar, where he has bought himself a house. Meanwhile, the peasants that had gone with him have found themselves in dire circumstances. They are not given good pasturage, the cattle have grown thin and their reserves of food have dwindled to almost nothing. The money allowance of about two rupees per man per day is so miserable that nothing can be bought for it except tasteless flat cakes. The worse the situation grows, the more often they are visited by mercenary recruiters who offer them money for fighting against their countrymen.

In October 1980, U.N. representatives who had come to inspect the camps in Pakistan would be quoted by the correspondent for the London *Guardian* as being appalled at how much "aid" had disappeared into the corrupt hands of the Pakistani and Afghan go-betweens. Often, aid channeled through the "camp commander" system ended up on the Black Market, enriching the local chieftains and warlords. The same "system," incidentally, had proved equally profitable in Thailand to the same type of "camp commander," a Pol Pot man, who managed to line his pockets from "aid" intended for women and children, genuine "refugees," but from Pol Pot gangs that had lured or driven them from their homes in Kampuchea.

It was to the interest of such "commanders" to inflate the number of "refugees" under their control, for the size of the "aid" that came to them —and therefore their "cut"—was determined by the number of "refugees" they could produce on their books.

The "refugee" in the camp is completely at the mercy of such "commanders." In Thailand, revolts among the Kampuchean refugees against this system broke out in 1980-81 inside the camps, until finally the U.N. had to stop channeling aid through the hands of such bandit types. It was arranged to get the aid directly to the women, who then would make certain their children at least were fed.

But if these sources from *Pravda* and Bakhtar News Agency cited here are considered biased against the counterrevolutionaries, here is another source, thoroughly biased indeed, but *for* the counterrevolutionaries. His name of course is Stuart Auerbach, and the newspaper is the much-abused *Washington Post*; the camps are at Aza Khei, Pakistan. We shall nevertheless scrutinize his story with "rabbinical care:"

> The Afghan refugees are settling in. A miniature city of mud huts, the usual housing in Afghanistan, has sprung up here to replace what a few months ago was a rat-tailed collection of tents pitched in privately owned fields.
>
> Now this highly visible refugee settlement has taken on a sense of permanence. It has become a visible symbol to residents of the northwest frontier province, who are becoming increasingly upset with the influx of Afghans, that the refugees appear here to stay.
>
> "The people of the frontier have been very tolerant, but our sympathies are wearing out," said one Peshawar resident who poured out a litany of complaints against the Afghans. His view was echoed by a dozen residents interviewed in Peshawar.
>
> He said that the anti-refugee feelings have intensified during the summer and added that he feared open clashes could break out between the residents here and the Afghans who flooded over the border since a pro-Marxist regime seized power in a bloody coup in April, 1978...
>
> The two million head of stock—mostly sheep—had what the United Nations High Commissioner for Refugees termed "a miracle" lambing season this spring. But the great increase in the number of sheep, he said, "is most likely to cause severe problems" of overgrazing during the coming winter months...
>
> Moreover, the rapid arrival of camels as pack animals is expected to aggravate the grazing problems. Since there is little publicly owned land in the frontier country, the arrival of refugees is impinging on private property and long established grazing rights. (Sept. 1, 1980, WP.)

So the problem of "private property" raises its sinister head! To this, the Karmal government would respond (Jan. 17, 1981) that all those refugees who returned home, if they *could* return home, were guaranteed not only "the free use of pasturage on a just basis but also their right of free movement around the country's territory"—a far different perspective from what they were presented in Pakistan where they lived on sufferance, the prey to bandits, disease and homesickness.

Dissention and friction rose in the camps, not only because the rights of private property were being violated but the U.N. Commissioner (as quoted by the London *Guardian*) would also note that "Generally people are upset because the refugees are sitting around doing nothing and are being paid as much as people who are working. We found families from Quetta (the Baluchi capital) who went to live in refugee camps as they could get money, food and clothing."

TASS, from India, reported that "There is growing discontent in Pakistan over the presence of Afghan mercenaries in the country," quoting the newspaper *Indian Express*. "Many of them are engaged in contraband trade, usury, brigandage and murder. The people of Pakistan want these unwelcome 'guests' to be expelled from their country. As is known, the *Indian Express* goes on, 'the center of the Afghan counterrevolution is in the Pakistani city of Peshawar where the headquarters of six Afghan counterrevolutionary organizations are located. These gangs are abundantly supplied with arms by the United States, China and a number of West European countries and Egypt.' " (TASS, Oct. 13, 1981.)

William Branigan, after a visit to Matasangar Camp in Pakistan in January 1980, would note that "Conditions here are among the most miserable of the Afghan refugee camps... Another reason for concern is a growing resentment among Pakistani Shiite Moslems against Afghan refugees, who are almost entirely Moslems of the Sunni sect. 'The Shiites are not happy with the influx of Afghan refugees in this area,' said Taj Mohammad Khan, the federal administrator of the Kurran Agency or district in Parachinar." (*The Washington Post,* Jan. 30, 1980.)

Discontent, mutual bickering and even gun battles—why doesn't Pakistan's government which runs the camps do something about creating order and discipline in them? Here we get a glimpse of the wheels within wheels that sometimes make the picture we are trying to focus on nothing but a blur. The camps are the source for counterrevolutionary forces, and there are six major rebel organizations vying for power among them. Zia likes it that way. In fact, "a diplomat," quoted by Michael Kaufman in an interview, would say "that having rising and falling coalitions [among the counterrevolutionary groups] seemed to be in Pakistan's interest."

Disunity, battles among each other, one holy warrior tearing the other holy warrior apart? How could that be good? Confided the diplomat, who for once can be taken as an authority: "Having a disunited group of organizations connected to nearly two million refugees is much better for Pakistan than having a united leadership that might some day raise the issue of a homeland for all Pushtu-speaking peoples on both sides of the border." (NYT, Aug. 31, 1981.)

Zia had not forgotten the revolt of the Baluchistani in 1972-77, which had taken Pakistan's entire army (with help from the Shah of Iran) to subdue. There were even more Pushtuns divided between Afghanistan and Pakistan than there were Baluchis, and voices raised in demands for national autonomy had never been silenced.

Finally: "Karen Bagger, the aide, who is based in Islamabad, says the organization (Office of the United Nations High Commissioner for Refugees) is worried about a possible outbreak of communicable diseases in the camps. Immunization is alien to the refugees, and unsanitary conditions, lack of safe water, and crowded conditions continue to pose health hazard. The men and boys have some access to health facilities but most women would rather die than let themselves be examined by a male doctor.

"An effort is being made to arrange some schooling for the boys, but mothers will not allow daughters to learn and many cite education as one of the 'terrible' things the new Afghan regime tried to foist on them." (NYT, July 4, 1980, by Mehr Kamal.)

In Kabul, meanwhile, the new (then) Minister of Education was telling a journalist:

> A few months ago, a group of tribal men came to me, asking what we wanted to make out of their girls, opening literacy courses for them or sending them to school. I said, "Well, it's not required; it's voluntary. If you want, we will open them. I know your traditions, and when your women are sick, even unto death, you won't let them be seen by male doctors, even though these men are Moslems. So I wanted you to have your own woman doctors, nurses and midwives, and then you won't have to let your women die in front of you and leave your children motherless." (*New World Review*, July-August, 1981, by Marilyn Bechtel.)

In a radio speech marking the eve of Eid-ul-Fitr (Feast of Martyrs), Karmal could say:

> Lately, thousands* of our compatriots, who had left the country under the effect of hostile propaganda, have returned to their country, to their homes and have resumed their peaceful and honest work in the interest of the country and the revolution.
>
> Likewise, hundreds of armed individuals, who were deceived by the enemies of the revolution, have laid down their arms, joined the ranks of the defenders of the revolution and announced their desire to cooperate with the revolutionary government.
>
> This state of affairs reflects the fact that our countrymen increasingly realize the falseness of the poisonous propaganda of the counterrevolution and every day greater numbers of the deceived persons become aware of the futility and harmfulness of cooperating with the counterrevolution. (*Foreign Affairs Bulletin*, July 31, 1982.)

---

* 21,000 reported in February, 1983.

MORE SANCHO PANZA THAN DON QUIXOTE

> Where there's no more bread, boon companions
> melt away.
>
> Miguel Cervantes,
> *Don Quixote*

A more hapless pretender to the vacated throne of Afghanistan can hardly be imagined than the one whose star glimmered so brightly in the weeks after December 27 (1979), and whose fortunes the State Department labored, though with diminishing enthusiasm, to promote: Zia Khan Nassery.

From the pomp and circumstance of red-carpet receptions by top officials in the State Department, where millions of dollars were casually tossed into the conversational air between them, to his political demise in the prison of Khomenei, where appeals to Allah and to Washington were (for a time) equally futile, Zia Khan Nassery can be said to have led a chequered career. Nor is it only a bad pun to say that many "cheques" played an important role in that career. For if ever there was a monster created by the CIA—though one which Frankenstein would have disdained as a scientific miscarriage—it was Nassery. Born in Afghanistan, and a loyal subject of the King, whose father, Nasrulla Khan, had been chief of intelligence for King Zahir, and in whose service, while he was still King, Nassery himself is said to have played some part, he became an American citizen (1977) almost at the same instant that he became a ward of the CIA. The Asia Foundation, an out-and-out CIA creature, would become his banker and godfather.

Nassery had been a school exchange student who arrived in the U.S.A. in 1963, still in his teens. Without too much ado about it, he found himself working soon after for (at first) the FBI and reporting industriously on the activities and private opinions of his fellow Afghan students, thus fleshing out his student's stipend. Hafizullah Amin was already in the States, and what their relationship to each other was is still to be revealed: for Amin was the head of the Afghan Students Association, funded by the CIA, and Nassery was a student working for the FBI in the immigration service.

For an Afghan to be an American citizen should have been formidable obstacle to any hopes of playing a leading role in the country he had given up. But it shows how empty the barrel was then and how hard they had to scrape the bottom of it if the U.S. government could only come up, in

166

the first weeks after Amin had been toppled, with this ex-Afghan but hard-at-work spy!

Before one had located Afghanistan firmly on the map, as Art Buchwald complained, in those hectic December (1979) days one would be assured by the American press that a replacement for Karmal, who had barely reappeared on the scene in Afghanistan, had already appeared in the U.S.A.! And a genuine Afghan at that!

That Nassery was taken seriously—at least at first—was shown by the fact that he was received by various presidential advisers to the White House and the State Department, particularly in February 1980, some weeks before the February "revolt" in Kabul.

At a press conference he gave to newsmen after one of these meetings at the White House, he made certain admissions whose indiscreet nature aroused some doubts in that quarter, not so much about his reliability as a certified anti-communist but about his political judgment.

The problem of supplying Nassery with money (to buy guns) presented some sticky legal problems to those masterminding his ambitious schemes. But only momentarily. The Afghan Relief Committee was promptly invented for him, headed by Theodore Eliot, another ex-ambassador to Afghanistan (who had been in Kabul when Taraki came to power and "recognized" the new government), and through its generous and humanitarian offices Nassery received almost immediately a donation of $19,500,000 authorized by Carter himself, as "food aid"—an extraordinary compliment to Nassery's appetite. But this was still only a piddling amount: Nassery and his friends had tossed figures like $20 and $40 million between them as no more than appetizers.

Nassery was a Don Quixote and his own Sancho Panza at the same time. Schooled for great drama, he was prone to Keystone Cops pratfalls. No sooner was he clothed in the distinction of a White House audience than he tripped and almost fell on his face when the press discovered that this Islamic leader of the Afghan masses was actually an American citizen. How much this revelation embarrassed his backers—whose stoicism in the face of even greater embarrassments was nothing short of Spartan—is not known.

Nassery had claimed to be the representative of Sayid Ahmad Gailani, head of the United Islamic Revolutionary Council, but in January (1980) he would turn up in Peshawar, where he proclaimed "a free Islamic Republic in four provinces of Afghanistan today and appealed for foreign military help." (IHT, Jan. 25, 1980.)

By then, Nassery had been promoted, in some mysterious way, to the "chairman of an Afghan Islamic and Nationalistic Revolutionary Council," and told reporters that "his forces are in control of the four provinces except for a handful of cities occupied by Soviet troops." *(Ibid.)* To *The New York Times* he had already confided that he had "150,000 fighting men in Afghanistan." (NYT, Apr. 16, 1979)—incidentally, well before the Soviet troops' entry into that country.

It had taken this spy for the U.S. Immigration Service hardly four weeks to rise from informer on Afghan students to where he could now confidently call for "foreign military aid!" He took pains to make it clear that "This is not a government-in-exile. This is a government of liberated Afghanistan!" (IHT, Jan. 25, 1980.)

He had dined on strong meat indeed—far from the days when, as head of a group called NASR, he had bombed Soviet property in Paris and Brussels!

Shortly after he had proclaimed his "government," he was boasting to Germany's *Der Spiegel* that he had met with Anwar Sadat and Menachim Begin at Aswan and there Sadat had fallen in with his scheme of supplying training and arms to Afghan counterrevolutionaries (which he immediately did), as Begin nodded his approval and promised similar future help. Of course Nassery could not have hoped to reach such eminent ears if his introductory letter hadn't borne prestigious Washingtonian signatures!

That his intention was to knock together a mercenary army was no secret once he blurted it out to *Soldier of Fortune* in April 1980, to which he also confided some of his problems persuading the *Mujahiddin* to cooperate with him: "On one occasion tribesmen captured a number of (light tanks), drove them home and refused to give them to us. . . I had to get the religious leaders to talk to the tribesmen and tell them it was their religious responsibility to give us the tanks to fight a holy war."

But this would be the least of his troubles. For in Pakistan, where he had made his grandiloquent statement that he had "liberated" practically all of Afghanistan but a few cities, he would run afoul of Zia ul-Haq who, being one, knew one, and find himself ordered out of the country "within 24 hours!" To this hard-to-misunderstand piece of information Nassery replied with hurt dignity that he would "appeal"—a proposal in Zia's Pakistan that had little room for traveling.

So Nassery, an instant "freedom fighter" and "liberator" of most of Afghanistan, whose bags had hardly been unpacked in the Khyber Hotel in Peshawar, had to repack them forthwith and return to Washington for further advice and consultations.

There, he was received with due respect by R. Maddock who, perhaps by this time, had smelled a loser, though he was still willing to talk. Now plans for February 22 were cooking up a tempting-smelling aroma. Nassery saw his future role rekindled in these plans. He had a rendezvous with history—he would be in Kabul by the end of February, his path paved for him by a strike of storekeepers who, on his arrival, would greet him: "Your maximum!"

His "maximum" was the whole country, with that little 12-year-old merchant thrown in, and at that time it really did seem, in some crazy way, quite possible. A power that could make and unmake rulers by a waft of a CIA wand—a Shah for a Mossadeq in Iran, a Pinochet for an Allende in Chile—could also replace a Karmal with a Nassery if a Nassery was there in the right place at the right time with the right backing. Why not? Who had a better claim to this country than the scion of a once-rich Afghan family?

He had gone to Teheran to drum up support for his own activities, and perhaps for more than that. With Sadegh Ghotebzadeh, later (Sept. 15, 1982) to be executed for conspiring to assassinate Khomenei, as Foreign Minister, and with Abolhassan Bani-Sadr, later to head the Iranian counter-revolution from Paris, as President, Nassery had every reason to believe that the ears he spoke into would be receptive to his message.

Already some 14 training centers for Afghan counterrevolutionaries existed in Iran, which was openly hostile to the new Afghan government. Though Karmal had immediately corrected Amin's superleftist hostility to Khome-nei's power and pledged cooperation and friendship early in January, there was no perceptible lessening of hostility from Teheran when Nassery got there in March. At the Islamic Foreign Ministers Conference in May 1980, at which the Afghan issue was to be discussed, Ghotebzadeh would bring with him a group of "anti-Soviet guerrilla leaders" (NYT, May 20, 1980) and insisted that they be heard. His ready denunciations of Karmal and the U.S.S.R. obviously warmed the cockles of the hearts of those monitoring the Iranian situation from Washington.

And yet, April, a cruel month for Carter, would come and go, and take with it Carter's hopes not only of a return to the White House trailing clouds of Hollywood glory but also the collapsed master plan that Brzezinski had concocted for retaking Iran in a rush of helicopters. Liberating the imprisoned embassy personnel was only a minor part of it. There was an "arc" that needed mending and the cornerstone of it was Iran. Between Iran and Pakistan little Afghanistan could be squeezed into pulp. But Nassery, a cork tossed on these troubled waters, wound up in Evin prison in Teheran, arrested as a CIA spy!

The New York Times would note somewhat dolefully that "One of the three Americans held by Iran after the 52 were allowed to leave is still said to be in a Teheran jail. He is Zia Khan Nassery, a naturalized American born in Afghanistan, who was arrested at a Teheran hotel in March 1980 on suspicion of being a spy. Mrs. Nassery, who lives in New York, said her husband was a travel agent who was arrested while trying to help Afghan refugees." (NYT, Jan. 21, 1982.)

From head of a "revolutionary" army which had freed four whole provinces in war-torn Afghanistan, from the exalted eminence of "His Excellency" who had been greeted like future royalty at the White House and State Department, from the heady heights of a man who had presided over a "government of liberated Afghanistan" just a few months before, the descent to the modest status of "travel agent" as attested to by his New York wife, was as swift as it was anti-climatic.

Nassery had timed his visit badly. He was caught in his hotel room with $25,000 on him—quite a sum for a "travel agent" (as his wife characterized him) in cash! He claimed he wanted to use the money to set up clinics for the Afghan counterrevolutionaries. Somehow, his story didn't quite wash, and he was led away to prison, where he was slated to be shot. Fortunately, as an American citizen, his plight commended itself to the State Department in Washington which "sweated" to get him out. How they managed it remains unknown, though obviously the inducement to stay those itchy hands of the executioners must have been very impressive. "Immense efforts" (NYT, Jan. 17, 1983) finally paid off. To have let their "travel agent" perish would have struck a blow at the tourist trade.

This is the saga of one man. But there are others whose personalities and doings deserve more closely looking into. And we shall proceed to do so, mindful of the fact that while they might enter the mysterious Hall of Mirrors of our jarred times with one image, they might quite possibly emerge from it with quite another.

KINGS, DUKES AND LOW-DOWN HUMBUGS

> It didn't take me a long time to make up my
> mind that these liars warn't no kings nor dukes
> at all, but just low-down humbugs and frauds.
>
> Mark Twain, *The Adventures of Huckleberry Finn*

But exactly who are the counterrevolutionaries? In fact, is it correct to use the term at all?

Nothing about the war for the counterrevolutionaries was simple to define, including what to call themselves. It was clear that the war itself was defining them. But meanwhile, the question remained: who were these men coming out of Pakistan in the dark of night to fall on a peaceful Afghan village which they then put to the torch and killed (after torture) those villagers who resisted?

Chided image-conscious President Reagan, addressing some newsmen: "You've used the term 'Afghan rebels' and sometimes I think the Soviet Union has been successful in their propaganda* with getting us to use terms that essentially are incorrect." Having gotten the attention of the newsmen by this not so subtle hint that they had been duped by "Soviet propaganda," Reagan went on to elucidate: "Those are freedom fighters. Those are people fighting for their own country and not wanting to become a satellite state of the Soviet Union, which came in and established a government of its choosing there, without regard to the feelings of the Afghans." (NYT, Mar. 11, 1981).

J. Edgar Hoover had called his Communist villains "semantic saboteurs."

Somewhat semantically jumbled as it came to those Soviet-duped reporters from *The New York Times* and *The Washington Post,* et al., still the idea was clear: Mr. Reagan, a champion of "packaging" the truth (as he would later make equally clear) is also a purist in political "semantics." Freedom-fighters—*not* rebels, and certainly not counterrevolutionaries. Not even "guerrillas." And "bandits!" (basmachi).

The term the counterrevolutionaries gave themselves might have somewhat discomfited President Reagan also—"holy warriors," *Mujahiddin.* After all, in neighboring Iran the holiest warrior of them all, Ayatollah

---

* The same thesis hammered in *The Spike* by Robert Moss and Armande Borchgrave.

Khomenei, in his war against the American infidel had caused America a great deal of grief.

Nevertheless, " 'This is a Jihad, a holy war,' the commander of the camp [in 'rebel-held Afghanistan'], a *mullah*, or Moslem priest from the area said. 'For all Islamic countries fighting Communism it is a holy war.' " (John Kinfer, NYT, Jan. 9, 1980.)

"They wanted to send everybody to their classes, even the old men and women with 10 children, so we killed the teacher, who was a Communist, and fled,' a guerrilla said, explaining what happened in his village." *(Ibid.)*

Exactly how to characterize these and other combatants puzzled correspondents like Tyler Marshall of the *Los Angeles Times*, who had been looking into the various counterrevolutionary groupings that came into existence like summer midges, particularly after the December 1979 events (though some had already been functioning even before April 1978). Peshawar, in Pakistan, meeting at the Kazafi hotel, would be the center of counterrevolutionary politics: all the groups had their headquarters or representatives there. In fact, what happened in Peshawar was to prove more important to their futures than what happened in the mountain valleys of Afghanistan. Born in fierce inter-group rivalry, their mutual hostility reached its peak soon after December 1979, and the attempts to weld together (begun in January 1979) the disparate elements of the counterrevolutionary "Committee of Struggle" into one effective political and military force then and afterwards inevitably foundered on the rock of personal ambition, tribal rivalry and naked lust for power. Though the generally agreed upon goal was to establish an Islamic republic in Afghanistan, the means to achieve it proved to be extremely brittle.

Looking closely at these various groupings, Marshall would find himself at odds with his typewriter. Though his ideological "sympathies" pointed west, his facts went east. "How much of the success against government forces is the result of banditry is impossible to determine. Guerrilla groups often form brief ad hoc alliances with local tribesmen to attack an army installation or road traffic in return for a share of the goods." (Loot?) (LAT, Jan. 2, 1980.)

TASS quoting France-Presse would report (June 15, 1981) that a scandal had broken out within the Islamic Revolutionary Movement where its leader, Maulavi Nabi Mohammadi, had been accused by Nasrullah Mansoor, at a press conference, of having stolen $300,000 from the "sacred war fund." Maulavi Nabi Mohammadi managed however to retain his post, boasting of a following of some 25,000 though the figure, possibly inflated to bolster his claims for money and arms, has to be taken cautiously. Very reactionary in his political orientation, he claims the support of "ulemas, tribal chiefs, landlords, pirs and sufis." (*Arabia*, April 1982.)

Bandits? It seemed to fit some of them at least. Barbarians? One can imagine the teacher "who was a Communist" might have thought so as he watched strips of skin flayed off his back, before the final blackout.

But the problem of just what to call whom was solved, according to Sayid Ahmad Gailani, the leader of the National Front of Islamic Revolution, the day the Soviet troops entered Afghanistan. That event instantly transformed "bandits" into "holy warriors," and in Washington to "freedom fighters." "Formerly," according to the same Sayid Ahmad Gailani, "those we were fighting were Moslems and Afghans. Now we know who we are killing, and we will do it to our heart's content." (*Ibid.*)

At least three of the most active counterrevolutionary leaders—Burhanuddin Rabani, Gulbuddin Hekmatyar and Sebgatullah—had begun their careers as counterrevolutionaries much earlier—earlier even than Taraki's coming to power in April 1978.

Some of them had gone into opposition when Daoud overthrew King Mohammad Zahir Shah in 1973, for they had been Royalists. Daoud had declared Afghanistan to be a republic, and had proposed a number of social reforms, and this was enough to send these worthies into a bloody rage.

But even they had enemies. For there were fundamentalists—the Moslem Brothers—among the counterrevolutionaries so extreme that they considered even the King to have betrayed Islamic principles, and their aim was to create an "Islamic state" governed by the clergy. This "state" would be such a throwback to the past that Europe's Dark Ages would seem like the Age of Enlightenment by contrast.

So who they were and what they were remained a problem. Their motives were different, and often opposed to each other's, and their aims were different. But the entry of the Soviets into Afghanistan did confront the disparate "holy warriors" with not only a military problem but a political one.

They would be fighting now not just "Afghans and Moslems," who were actually illiterate peasants armed by the government to protect their lands. Some of these they managed to terrorize and confuse. But they would now face an organized body of soldiers, and though the Soviets would serve mainly as a back-up to the reorganized Afghan troops, a "reserve", as Karmal characterized them, still their presence was a solid fact that had to be taken into serious consideration.

Secondary matters of tribal loyalty, regional attachments and inter-group rivalry and jealousy now hampered matters more than ever. Over and over the various leaders of the armed groups were urged by their Washington advisers to set all differences aside and unite into one disciplined army. But how were these groups of "warriors," suspicious of one another, milling around Peshawar, attacking each other not only with words but on more and more occasions with guns—how were they going to unite? They were all pulling in different directions. Each wanted to go its own way—one to a restoration of the King, another to setting up an Islamic republic, a third to restoring another Daoud to power.

Still they tried: "Afghan rebel leaders have held private meetings here this week (May 30, 1980) with much talk about unity, but the goal of a common political and military front for the rebels appears as elusive as ever." (Marvin Howe, NYT, May 30, 1980, from Peshawar).

It would seem that with the "enemy" invading the country it should not have been difficult to convince like-minded patriots to set aside their differences and rise as one man to throw back the oppressor. But it became increasingly clear, as time wore on, that the various groups could not agree on who would get how much of the spoils after victory. It is interesting to note that it was of the defense of Islam against the infidel that they most often spoke, and not of the defense of the country. For it was the *devil* they were fighting, and as is often the case when one is fighting the invisible devil, one tends to find him everywhere, even among one's own friends and allies, even in one's self.

As for the country, they saw it not as their Homeland but only as the intangible framework within which their great estates had once existed and had been expropriated by the devil. They wanted a social system reclaimed, not a country. "Country" as a modern concept did not exist for them. "Country" meant surrendering their personal power and privileges to strangers—to a state—to their enemies. They were feudal lords and their social boundaries were reflected by the boundaries in their minds.

This much, however, they grasped. With the Soviets now in the country they could no longer depend on slipping into hamlets asleep at night and slicing the throats of the peasants' leaders who had helped distribute the land to other peasants—and then out again into the hills while the dead buried their dead. Terror was not enough.

So, from holy warriors they transformed themselves, for the time being—after January 1980—into holy salesmen, and began to visit friendly capitals of the world where they presented themselves as being able to sell a better war than their competitors.

This same Sayid Ahmad Gailani would hotfoot it to Riyadh (Saudi Arabia) early in January with that aim very much in view. "We hope the Moslem world as well as the Free World [he didn't explain the difference] will realize we are fighting a just cause. Many nations have condemned the Russian aggression, but I hope they are convinced they should now support us *materially* too." (*Ibid.* My italics.)

A year later, in February (1981), this same Sayid Ahmad Gailani would

174

turn up with a companion Moarubi in Washington where he had come to discuss getting arms—specifically, ground-to-air missiles—for his Islamic Revolutionary Front warriors, and though the White House issued no statements commemorating the visit, Gailani himself had no qualms about telling the press that he had had a "very useful exchange of views on all aspects of the Afghan situation" with "high-ranking State Department officials."

Soviet sources would reveal that another leader of the counterrevolutionary grouping, Professor Burhanuddin Rabani, head of the Jamiat-e-Islami Party, had been "linked with the special services of Pakistan and the American CIA since 1973" [when the King was ousted]. TASS revealed that Rabani was getting money from the United States and Saudi Arabia "through Oman, where an account has been opened in an Omani bank in the name of Tufail Mohammed, a close associate of Rabani." (TASS, Apr. 23, 1981.)

The Jamaat-i-Islami Party was very active in Kashmir, too, where it claimed to have more than 30,000 members and apparently limitless funds. It conducted schools free of charge—apparently from the 8.5 million rupees it received as a "donation" to its cause from Saudi Arabia and the U.S.A. In Kashmir, which is part of India, it is behind the religious battles that are chronic in that stretch of land so close to China, as well as the inspirers of demands for "autonomy" from India. Arson, assassinations, riots—the Party is expert in creating chaos where an uncertain peace had reigned before. In any case, it was an open tool of Zia* both in Kashmir and in Afghanistan, and it was no organization an honest fighter for Islam would want to become part of, as the following story bears out.

In August 1980 (soon after I left Kabul), the Afghan Foreign Ministry called a press conference (as it does from time to time) to introduce to the press its latest counterrevolutionary prisoner Moshen Rezai by name, who had seen the error of his ways and was ready to tell the journalists about it.

"Under the influence of the Islamic revolution in Iran [Moshen Rezai is an Iranian citizen], I wished to take part in the struggle against American imperialism and Israeli Zionism"—motives which still activate even those counterrevolutionaries who find themselves in camps being instructed by Zionist teachers!— "...and so I asked Bahbani [whom he had contacted] to assist me in going to Palestine to help the Palestinian people. Instead, he introduced me to an Afghan, Husseini. They both started telling me that in Afghanistan, just as in Palestine, the struggle for Islam is going on, as they said, against Communist unbelievers.

"Husseini brought me to the city of Meshed where he introduced me to one of the leaders of Jamiat-e-Islami, a certain Deldtu. Thus, I became

---

* On March 25, 1981 he "outlaws all political parties except the neo-totalitarian Jamaat-i-Islami..." Eqbal Ahmad, Prof. of Political Science, Dec. 6, 1982 (NYT).

involved through deception in the struggle against the Afghan people, siding in fact with American imperialism...

"Carrying Deldtu's letter of recommendation I left together with other Afghans, members of Jamiat-e-Islami, for Quetta in Pakistan, and then for Peshawar, where I was introduced to the head of the organization, Burhanuddin Rabani...

"Rabani advanced the task of stepping up subversive activities by the Kabul group of Jamiat-e-Islami... We were to set up a military committee for carrying out acts of subversion and terror in the city, organizing strikes and mass unrest, forcing people under the threat of death to miss work and students to stay out of classes and close the *dukans* (small shops), setting off explosions in buses and schools, printing and spreading antigovernment leaflets.

"On being smuggled into Afghanistan we delivered to Kabul, for the future military committee, submachine guns and pistols, anti-tank grenades and mines, hand grenades, explosives and detonators, delayed-action fuses and Bickford fuses, as well as ammunition and strong poisons. The bulk of these weapons were delivered by us from Surhab ... the boxes containing submachine guns and ammunition were labeled 'Made in Egypt'. The head of the military committee of Jamiat-e-Islami in Peshawar, Major Ayub Khan, told me to burn those boxes in case of danger to prevent them falling into the hands of the DRA [Democratic Republic of Afghanistan] authorities. At the military committee at Peshawar I saw weapons of American, British and Pakistani makes, as well as submachine guns manufactured in China."

He had set out to fight the Zionists in Palestine and had wound up fighting the Afghans in Afghanistan. "It became clear to me," he said, "that the struggle inside Afghanistan which was imposed by the imperialists is directed at restoring the old order in the country. The heads of the antigovernment groupings are planning to return to rich people everything the people's power had taken away from them..." *(Pravda)*

It is not unusual for an ordinary Islamic citizen to speak familiarly of "imperialism," nor does he need to attend advanced classes in Marxism to acquire that language. To most of the world "imperialism" is a living reality, and in ex-colonial countries the distinction between the rich and poor is sharply drawn, and what may appear like "propaganda" to an American ear lulled by talk of American philanthropists abroad is breakfast language to an aware peasant whose heritage is the bitter one of poverty and suffering.

Meanwhile, Tyler Marshall of the *Los Angeles Times,* who had looked into the various groupings, came away with a number of conclusions: "While rebel leaders are reluctant to discuss the results of the renewed plea for help, there are indications that at least in certain Moslem countries the idea of aiding the rebels materially is being discussed more seriously than at any time in the past." (LAT, Jan. 2, 1980.)

But there was always that one major obstacle—the different organizations could not get together. "The divisions appear to be mainly personality clashes couched in vague ideological terms. Sometimes poor relations between groups are described simply as a difference in tactics. 'The leader of every rebel group wants to be king of Afghanistan,' said Aziz Ulfat, the cultural committee chief of a breakaway faction of the Peshawar-based Hezbe-Islamic Afghanistan...

"In the field this lack of cooperation often has been disastrous. There are numerous accounts of rebels from one organization standing by rather than aiding guerrillas from another group under attack." (*Ibid.*)

James P. Sterba, who had looked the "rebels" over closely, would come up with some unorthodox reactions: "The best-known and most discredited (!) of the insurgent groups are those with rear bases in Peshawar. Theirs has been a game of king on the mountain that diplomats expect will break into internecine warfare if and when Soviet troops pull out of their homeland..." (NYT, Mar. 3, 1980.)

If one reads this correctly, one can reasonably deduce from it that Soviet troops should make a point of staying in Afghanistan if for no other reason than to keep the various "rebel" groups from each other's throats!

But to go on: "Most of the groups want to turn Afghanistan into an orthodox Islamic state. The largest and most fundamentalist of them is Hezbe-i-Islam, the Islamic Party of Afghanistan. It is headed by a former engineering student at Kabul University named Gulbuddin Hekmatyar, whose piety is manifested in a facial expression that foreigners have never seen creased in a smile."

It should be noted that Gulbuddin Hekmatyar at least had further recommendations, which he expressed in other, perhaps more smiling, ways. Openly identified as an agent of Pakistan's secret service, he considered his own grouping Hezbe-Islami to be a part of the Jamiat-e-Islami (Islamic Society) on which General Zia ul-Haq leans so heavily for support. Hekmatyar has the further distinction of having spent two years (1970-72) in prison for the assassination of a fellow student. His chief source of funds is to be found in Saudi Arabia. His outstretched hand will not be unknown in Washington either.

Connected with the notorious Moslem Brothers gangs, Hekmatyar had not sprung, like some of the others, fully grown from the head of the CIA in April 1979. Expelled from military school for homosexuality, he had long been involved in subversion, including against President Daoud in 1975 because he considered Daoud (as did the Shah of Iran and the American "experts" there) as "dangerously leftist," according to Selig Harrison (NYT, Jan. 13, 1980).

According to Fred Halliday (NYT, May 18, 1979), Hekmatyar's party makes no bones about the fact that it "calls in its program for the reinforcement of purdah restrictions," which would mean that the thousands of women who had cast off their veils would have to put them on again and return to their ghettoes.

Not incidentally, it was the Hezbe-Islami that passed out photos to newsmen showing the *Mujahiddin* shooting "Communist high school teachers" near Farah in southern Afghanistan (NYT, Jan. 11, 1980). Other photos showing "Communist high school teachers" with their feet tied to the bumpers of trucks being dragged to their deaths were not published in the West, in order to spare the squeamish stomachs of their readers.

One of the rare instances on record of what the counterrevolution will do if it regains power over the country was reported by UPI (Feb. 14, 1980). A spokesman for Hekmatyar's Hezbe-Islami claimed that it had retaken the town of Share Jadid in Baghian province, and says UPI: "The spokesman said the new government was returning the land nationalized in land reform campaigns... The rebels seized the cotton-processing Springer Company and 'put to fire' all 'Communist' workers and officers. The workers and officers" whose 'Communism' was presumably easily readable in their faces, were burned together with the plant.

It is also to Hekmatyar that we owe precise information on the dollar value placed on lives of peasants who opposed him. By 1983, his money problems solved by the generosity of Saudi Arabia and his American friends, he would publish—or make known—what the going rate for murder and assassination in that part of the world was—and, by local standards, they were munificent indeed.

According to two of Hekmatyar's former supporters—Abdul Gaffar and Nasrullah—Hekmatyar was ready to pay any "holy warrior" who could prove his claims, the following:

For every Afghan army soldier killed—5,000 to 7,000 afghanis. (How did one prove he had killed a soldier? He brought in an ear—anybody's ear—man, woman or child—as they had done in Vietnam to prove a "Cong" had been killed.)

For every Party activist (a more important bag): 10,000 to 15,000 afghanis.

For every Army officer (still more important): 30,000 afghanis.

For every destroyed tank—100,000 afghanis. (*New Times*, No. 13, 1983.)

In 1980, 43-47 afghanis were worth one American dollar, officially. The average annual income of an Afghan peasant was hardly more than 8,600 afghanis. You could get a year or more pay in one afternoon!

The paymaster for these "ears" was, among others, the Afghan Relief Committee, with its bank (American Express Bank) in Basle, Switzerland, where $150,000 of a donation of $300,000 were deposited to Hekmatyar's personal account. Hekmatyar's financial problems were understandably minimal. Even Toyota relieved him of the worry of getting a new car—the company donated him one, seeing in this holy warrior an even holier automobile salesman one day, assuming he could return to Kabul.

This much can be said for the Hezbe-Islami Party. It has made its principles quite clear. "Afghanistan is an exclusively Islamic state where all non-Islamic ideas or practices are forbidden," Hekmatyar has been quoted. In power, it would return all confiscated lands back to their original landowners and presumably condemn those peasants caught working the land to death. Women would again be forced back behind their veils and into their previous state of servility and ignorance. Military education on a "holy war" basis would be universally enforced. One language would be declared compulsory, with Arabic as a second language.

As for Gailani, Selig Harrison, in the January 13 (1980) issue of *The New York Times*, would call him "more of a businessman than a practicing saint," the source of whose counterrevolutionary passion could be located in the fact that the revolution had "dispossessed him of his lands and properties." A man like that, who is also head of the Quadiriya sect of Islam, shunned by the Sunni and Shiite Moslems as heretical, who had been a one-time Peugeot car dealer in Kabul, finds it difficult to convince Moslems of his other-worldliness, especially with "his two glamorous, jet-setting daughters." More than that, his ancestry was not Afghan but Arabian.

A monarchist, he himself points to the fact that his father was hanged for resisting Afghan independence in 1919. This has not prevented him from becoming enormously wealthy as a landowner and businessman in independent Afghanistan. But he kept his options open with Allah as well, for he posed as a religious man, a "Pir," dubbed so by the British who originally smuggled his family into Afghanistan to overthrow the king, who had struck out for independence against Britain.

Gailani was no stranger in Riyadh (Saudi Arabia), London or Washington. He had entry to sheikhs, kings, members of Parliament and senators. But whatever he had to offer, the fact was clear that nowhere was he chosen as the main pillar on which to erect the "West's" counterrevolutionary hopes, and to gain a confidence in those quarters that mattered, so he fought, not so much the "enemy" in the hills of Afghanistan as his own "friends" in Pakistan.

In fact, so notorious was the inter-group fighting (in which Hekmatyar's forces played a leading part) that it wasn't long before the real reason for it was discovered: the hand of Moscow. In September, Michael T. Kaufman would report from New Delhi that "Amid widespread reports that the Soviet-backed Afghan government is exploiting old tribal vendettas to divide the Islamic rebels, one insurgent leader [Mohammad Amin Wakman] today in New Delhi told of violent fighting between his men and other Islamic guerrillas." (NYT, Sept. 2, 1980.)

Why should they fight each other? The answer was forthcoming. Quoting an "Afghan exile"—a most remarkable "exile" indeed, with "access to both rebels and (Afghan) government officials"—this "insurgent leader" would report that his informant had told him that the Soviets had worked out a plan to infiltrate the rebel groups with "people between 14 and 22" who "are being paid $162 a month—more than deputy ministers were paid before the Soviet intervention" (and more than most Afghans made in a year) to pit one group of rebels against the other.

And indeed, it seems that one of those rebel groups which had been so successfully infiltrated—whether by the 14-year-olds or the 22-year-olds or a combination of both isn't specified—was none other than the most fundamentalist, most militant and unyielding of all the "rebel" groups, Hekmatyar's own Hezbe-Islami group!

One night, presumably on Moscow's orders, his men fell on Wakman's group and the ensuing battle raged all night. At dawn, 13 of Wakman's rebels lay dead and 32 of Hekmatyar's. And what reason had Hekmatyar given for attacking this group, which was also pledged to the same goal of liberating Afghanistan from Soviet occupation? "They call us third-class Communists," said Wakman unhappily.

Mohammad Amin Wakman, it seems, heads a group which is called the Afghan Social Democratic Party. Wakman protested: "We are all good Moslems and we also are fighting against the Russians." *(Ibid.)*

But there was no room in the holy war for a united front with the Social Democratic Party! To fundamentalists who dreamed of driving women back into their pre-revolutionary subservience, a Wakman who believed in the education of women was no better—perhaps worse—than the Communists themselves!

From not too far a distance it looked more like gang warfare in Peshawar than a war of liberation in Afghanistan.

As late as May, 1983, *The New York Times* military analyst, Drew Middleton, whose pipelines to the military top brass and the CIA are generally unclogged, in an article conceding that "experts in (the) West appear to favor the Soviet Union" as winning the war, put forth their reasons for this judgment. The main one for their successes was still that the counter-revolutionaries "lack unity of command and training. Generations of tribal and personal enmities remain strong. After one recent operation in which two insurgent groups combined, the Afghan guerrillas fired on each other as freely as on the Russians, according to Western sources." (NYT, May 1, 1983.) It was obviously more dangerous for some rebels to meet other fellow-rebels there on the street in Peshawar than it was to meet Afghan Army forces in the mountains, who at least did not kill you if you surrendered, and even if you didn't, it was possible to do some bartering with—you could perhaps sell your K-47—Soviet Kalashnikov automatic rifle (sent in from their surplus by Egypt) for a consideration. (Fred Halliday, *The Nation*, Jan. 26, 1980.)

So much for cooperation in a holy cause.

Other of the six groups of counterrevolutionaries with bases in Pakistan, officially "recognized" by Zia ul-Haq, are National Liberation Front of Afghanistan, headed by Hazrat Sebgatullah Modgaddadi; Islamic Revolutionary Movement of Afghanistan, headed by Maulavi Nabi Mohammadi; and another group which had split off from them. Ideologically they followed the lead of the Moslem Brothers, whose Islamic fundamentalism is so extreme that it has been a political liability for the Americans to identify openly with them, especially since as terrorists, their brothers-in-spirit, they have no hesitation about assassinating the "wrong" people, like Anwar Sadat.

Such leaders, incidentally, were not poor *mullahs* who owned nothing but their sandals. They were sharp businessmen and landowners whose financial exploits efficiently dovetailed with their religious devotions. For them, reading their bankbooks took equal importance with reading the Koran, if not more.

In Iran, counterrevolutionary bases had also been organized after April 1978. Soon some 14 major ones had been set up where 1,200 men could be trained at any one period. The Iranian newspaper, *Islamic Republic,* a supporter of Khomenei, would reveal (June 30, 1980) that "these U.S.-backed counterrevolutionary groups comprise the Islamic Party of Afghanistan headed by Yunus Khalis, the National Liberation Front, Jamiat-e-Islami, the Islamic Revolutionary Movement, National Unity and Islamic Revolution of Afghanistan, which have been to Egypt... All these groups are treacherous and mercenary ... serving the U.S." (Quoted by KAR, *International,* No. 6, Oct. 1981.)

But these "holy warriors" also dealt in drugs and in the arms traffic, and sometimes ended up in prison or even at the wrong end of a firing squad, as would be reported in November 1981, by the Iranian newspaper *Meshed,* announcing the arrest and death sentences of nine persons, including two Afghans, for drug trafficking. But found on their persons were cards identifying them as Islamic fighters against the Russian "invaders". Such reports of opium smuggling by such "revolutionaries" were a daily occurrence in Iran, but such allies in no way embarrassed the Americans.

In addition to these counterrevolutionary groups, whose militancy against the enemy as "holy warriors" shaded imperceptibly into their hunger for dollars as drug peddlers, there were some smaller, Mao-oriented groups that operated out of China on the Afghan border: the Sholee Jawid and Sorha, which were reputed to have been behind the riots in Herat in March 1979.

Ever since the various groups, with their anarchic, wild and disordered leadership and irregular, not to say eccentric, forms of organization and leadership had made their appearance on the scene, it had been the main assignment of Robert Lessard, America's CIA man in Southern Asia, to knock them together into some kind of united, organized front that would come to heel when they heard him whistle. But it was like caging the wind. He always failed.

This has been troublesome in the extreme to the Afghan desk in the State Department. Its recipe: "To succeed, these efforts at coordination will require setting aside deep divisions between fundamentalists and moderates, traditionalists and leftists, tribal chieftains and mullahs, Pushtu and minority ethnic groups, and among numerous rival tribes." (NYT, Aug. 31, 1981.)

A tall order! If the "leftist" Social Democratic Party continued to object to Gulbuddin Hekmatyar's warriors tying high school teachers to trucks and dragging them to death, it could never hope to find a common ground with them and would have no option itself but to sleep with one eye open at night, always with guns in easy reach!

UNCLOAKED, UNDAGGERED

O ye, who lead,
Take heed!
Blindness we may forgive,
but baseness we will smite.

William Vaughn Moody,
An Ode in Time of Hesitation

The charge that the CIA was extremely active in Afghanistan before, during and after the revolution in 1978 has relentlessly pursued American policy there.

Some pinpoint the beginning of its stepped-up activity in that part of the world to a meeting of top American officials held in Annapolis in June 1978 as part of a NATO command symposium. The main topic before the assembled generals, admirals, foreign diplomats and others was how to respond to the April 1978 Revolution in Afghanistan.

By the beginning of the "second phase" of the revolution, in December 1979, counterrevolutionary organizations were already operating in 18 of the country's 26 provinces. These were not spontaneous flare-ups of hard-pressed peasants responding to unendurable oppression, but clearly organized groupings, armed and financed from sources outside of the country and already finding in Pakistan a haven for their activities. By November 1979, some 30 bases and 50 centers for training (15,000 by then) rebels had been set up.

The outlines of a counterrevolutionary policy were already quite visible by the beginning of July 1979, so that *Le Figaro* (Paris) could write: "The United States wants to use the developments in Afghanistan as a lever for making the countries and parties deeply committeed to the Moslem political concept join the camp hostile to the Soviet Union." (July 3, 1979.) And the same paper would declare that the U.S. had chosen Pakistan to be the base from which hostilities would be launched against Afghanistan, a charge also made by Pakistan's *Millat* in July, 1979. In any case, the CIA moved its headquarters from Teheran to Peshawar directly after the Shah's downfall, which had had such traumatic repercussions in Washington.

Robert Lessard was the CIA's man in charge of anti-Afghan activities from the American embassy in Pakistan. He had trained the Shah's secret police in the techniques of subversion and torture, after the CIA's overthrow of Mossadeq in 1953, which the CIA, after a certain point, made no attempt to deny. Kermit Roosevelt, who had been in political charge of the overthrow, openly admitted it in his later book, *Countercoup: The Struggle for the Control of Iran.*

It is interesting to note that one of the cover organizations used by the CIA to conduct its activities was the Narcotics Control Authority, centered in Lahore, whose announced objective was to "control" the narcotics traffic between Afghanistan, Iran and Pakistan, as the "golden crescent" now rivalling the golden triangle, but whose "control" had nothing to do with eliminating this profitable and deadly business, but to exploit it.

In November, 1982, Attorney General William French Smith toured Afghan "refugee" camps, reportedly to discuss means of curbing the drug trade, while offering inmates "firm support in these difficult times." He had wanted to visit areas where the drug situation was most flagrant but his Pakistani guide, Lt. Gen. Fazie Haq, refused to guarantee his personal safety if he let it be publicly known that he was investigating the drug trade— so Mr. Smith beat a hasty retreat and left the area as quickly as decency and armored vehicles would allow.

After April 1978, Pakistan teemed with CIA men. Publications like *Counterspy* have enumerated and named some. But they constantly change. Among the early ones, in addition to Lessard, was Louis Dupree, the CIA man in Kabul, whose activities there among the counterrevolutionaries made him *persona non grata* to the Afghan government, and he was forced to leave in 1978, but only as far as Peshawar where he resumed his work directing counterrevolutionary forces in an attempt to bring a happy ending to his book, *Afghanistan,* otherwise so woefully unended.

All this, however, is cited only as background the better to focus the center piece of this chapter. For we are at last ready to take off one of the cloaks and examine one of the daggers. If at times it seemed that the CIA might in fact manage to rule the world—as harrowing a science-fiction nightmare as the nightmare vision of ants overwhelming us with their sudden multiplication of forces—the history of George B. Griffin is at once a reassuring episode in the story of human resilience and a cautionary tale of some practical use.

Griffin came to dramatic notice in October 1981, when India stirred up a considerable tempest by refusing to accept him as "political counselor, the third-ranking post in the United States embassy". As the newspaper report put it: "It is unusual for a government to block a foreign diplomat from taking up an assignment. Ambassadors are subject to scrutiny, but lower-ranking diplomats generally take up their posts without prior agreement. As a result, the Indians' refusal to accept Mr. Griffin is being described by State Department officials as 'unprecedented'." (NYT, Sept. 1, 1981.)

Unprecedented! If such a step was so unusual, what motivated India in taking it, risking the inevitable retaliation, which duly came? Relations between India and the U.S.A. had indeed been strained for some time, and Reagan's appearance on the scene, with Secretary of State Haig ordering the world to come immediately to America's heel, had not improved matters. In the several wars which Pakistan had waged with India, American power had always backed the Pakistans, with whom America had a military pact since the 50s, and Reagan's recently stepped-up massive military aid to Zia (and China), including his barely tacit agreement to look the other way as Zia created an atomic arsenal, did not sit well with Indira Ghandi, nor indeed with any Indian, high or low.

Indira's statement soon after the Soviet entry into Afghanistan that she "understood" why the Soviets had to go into the country, implying that it was as much to counter American power intrusion in that area as it was to rescue the Afghan revolution, did not help matters either. This statement from a leading member of the non-aligned movement helped bend the non-aligned ranks which had shown some anti-Soviet animus in the U.N. vote on Afghanistan in January. India's further decision to recognize Kampuchea had also been unwelcome in Washington. Attempts to convince the Indians that America's massive fleet in the Persian Gulf, its massive military build-up in the island of Diego Garcia in the Indian Ocean, commanding entire Southeast Asia from there, were all to protect India from the Northern Bear did not persuade that country at all. India had watched for years as China, which it charged, had seized 36,000 square kilometers of Indian territory by arms in the 60s, kept on building its massive Karokorum military road to Pakistan, over which arms for that country endlessly flowed. Arms for Pakistan had always meant that war with India was not far off.

But how did all this affect George B. Griffin? How did it affect Afghanistan? We had asked the question: who was the "hysterical and unreliable" anonymous "diplomat" so often quoted by bourgeois correspondents from Kabul, but always without identification? Some of his "information" had been hairy indeed!

Now we can bring him out from under his cloak. His name is George B. the same Griffin, "political counselor" and CIA man extraordinary whom India had refused to accept. Griffin had been listed as a second-ranking officer in the embassy in Kabul, though he was also simultaneously included on the embassy personnel list in Islamabad as well. One of the oddities of his behavior was that he was a regular commuter between Kabul and New Delhi where, for some unexplained reason, he had parked his wife. Nevertheless, as a good husband it was his duty to visit her from time to time. His passing from Kabul to New Delhi so easily and so often, and apparently through raging battles and "bands of steel," is explained by the fact that he had diplomatic immunity. All he had to do was board a plane in Kabul airport (about a ten-minute drive from the embassy) and, passing through customs unhindered, fly to New Delhi in less than two hours, there to meet with eager correspondents anxious to receive information hot off the griddle, along with the marvelous injunction that they were free to send on any tale to their home papers, no matter now wild, as long as they didn't precisely name the source, referred to austerely only as "a diplomat." This arrangement had the further extraordinary advantage of making journalists sound as if they had entry into private and privileged sources—and therefore were on the *inside* of events—without being burdened with any responsibility for the truth or accuracy of the cited facts. Their stories often made the world's headlines, like the charge in January 1980, that the "Soviets had massed 10,000 troops on the Iranian border within striking distance of Iran's oil fields." But it was impossible to verify their truth independently of the mysterious "diplomatic" source, and he refused to be identified, much less questioned.

That Griffin was the "diplomat" so often cited as the source of many of the most harrowing tales about Soviet atrocities and even nightly executions was all but admitted by the *Times* itself. For while in New Delhi, it wrote: "he (Griffin) occasionally briefed reporters on the situation in Afghanistan". But he also "briefed reporters" in Kabul as well (as a captured Afghan spy would confess), although after January 1980, when most of the Western reporters had been booted out, his journalistic audience tended to shrink there. But his stories, and the stories of his colleagues, grew so increasingly wild that they provoked the London *Observer* (not bound by any old-school-tie loyalties) to say tartly: "The American embassy here (in Kabul) has been feeding wildly inaccurate information to American journalists, exaggerating the number of Russian troops in the country, the number of Russians killed, and the extent of the engagements."(Ian Mather, *Observer*, Jan. 20, 1980.)

The Indian weekly, *Blitz*, ran stories that charged Griffin with being the moving force behind all intelligence activity in Afghanistan working out of Pakistan. TASS added that Griffin was "a major specialist of the CIA who, from Pakistan territory, guided secret operations of the American spy department against Afghanistan..." And: "Griffin's duties, which were concealed under the roof of the United States Embassy in Islamabad, included the supply of weapons to the hands of the Afghan mercenaries who had found refuge in Pakistan."

Finally, when Washington sent Griffin to India as a "political counselor" in the American embassy, a member of India's parliament, Bhupesh Gupta, demanded that Griffin should be asked to leave the country as *persona non grata*, which is precisely what he was asked to do.

The Indian government denied—and "resented"—the published charges that its rejection of Griffin was due solely to left-wing pressure. The decision was made "after a careful evaluation of his activities during his various postings in India and the subcontinent."

Griffin had served in Calcutta in 1971 as war with Pakistan loomed over Bangladesh (East Pakistan), with the U.S. supporting Pakistan while India, backed by the U.S.S.R., supported Bangladesh. "Pro-Soviet newspapers," noted the *Times* (Sept. 3, 1981), "in India have frequently used his (Griffin's) name in connection with activities attributed to the Central Intelligence Agency."

But naming Griffin as a CIA man was really no great triumph of investigative journalism. Anybody who saw or heard him perform in Kabul could hardly misunderstand his antecedents. Other CIA operatives would also be as easily identified, like the already-mentioned Robert Lessard, who was in charge of the feckless task of uniting two of the main counterrevolutionary organizations, headed by Burhanuddin Rabani and Maulavi Muhammad Nabi Mohammadi.

Inside Afghanistan before 1979, the CIA functioned in various ways and under various covers. One of its conduits was Asia Foundation, whose activities turned out to be more malign than benign. According to Joel W. Scarborough, Asia Foundation's representative in Afghanistan for some time, the Foundation "has closely collaborated with other American governmental agencies in Afghanistan, especially ICA [International Communications Agency, which runs the Voice of America and other government propaganda organs, as a CIA collaborator]..." (Quoted by *Counterspy*, Vol. 4, No. 1, 1980.)

"Humanitarian" organizations of one sort or another in Asia were almost all of them CIA conduits, or in some degree CIA collaborators and, after the April 1978 Afghan Revolution, sprang up like mushrooms after rain.

These included the International Rescue Committee and CARE, already in existence, as well as a newly-minted organization, the Afghan Relief Committee, set up by Robert Neumann, one-time U.S. ambassador to Afghanistan, along with the widow of Adolph Dubs, Mary Ann Dubs. Another humanitarian organization that became busier than ever with the onset of the Afghan events was Catholic Relief Service, which, under Cardinal Spellman's control, had funnelled moneys to support Ngo Dinh Diem* in Saigon during the 50s. All of them (and others) in some degree served not only

---

* Ngo Dinh Diem had been groomed to take over leadership in South Vietnam by the Maryknoll Fathers while he lived in New York State. Eventually, he was assassinated on America's orders when he proved to be an obstacle to Pres. Kennedy's plans there.

the needs of the refugees in Pakistan but the political ends of the faction which ran the American government at the time. That food had become a political weapon (if nothing else) by now had become a commonplace in international politics, and few humanitarians were so humanitarian as to shrink from using it toward that end. As William McCullough, Washington representative of the Afghan Relief Committee and one-time economic adviser to King Zahir, would put it when asked if the "aid" of his committee might end up in the hands of the rebels, "I certainly hope so." (*Counterspy*, Spring 1980.)

Rebel leaders ferried back and forth between Pakistan and Washington and found many doors otherwise impenetrable to ordinary Americans flung wide open for them. Both the then Senators Frank Church and Jacob Javits (whose wife was a paid agent for the Iranian Shah) maintained cordial contacts with organizations whose aims were more than dubious and with personalities whose antecedents were no more honorable.

As time went on, and it became even more clear that the U.S.A. was the main force behind the counterrevolution, visitors to Kabul wondered out loud what role the U.S. embassy now played. True, since the death of Dubs no full ambassador had been named to replace him. In any case, there was little legitimate business to be done with the Karmal government. Nevertheless, the embassy was choked with people in all stages of activity. What in the world were they so busy about?

Part of the answer came very early. When Amnesty International representatives showed up in Kabul early in 1980, on the prowl for "prisoners of conscience," they showed extraordinary indifference to the accomplishments of the regime and enormous interest in who the new regime was putting behind bars.

To find out, they went to—the American embassy. And whom did they meet there who turned out to be a partial keeper of the world's conscience? None other but our "hysterical" friend, George B. Griffin, who promptly gave them a long list of the new "prisoners of conscience" he felt ought forthwith to be freed if Karmal wanted to be included in the good graces of Amnesty.

Lo and behold, when the Karmal people looked at the list, they found it to be a very complete list indeed. It included all the so far arrested counterrevolutionaries, Amin's bully-boys, and CIA misadventurers! All "prisoners of conscience"!

A further idea of what the Americans were up to in Afghanistan came in May, 1983, when Afghanistan kicked out Peter Graham (to be followed by others later). Graham was the U.S. "second secretary" whom the Afghans accused of selling pornography, a term which probably was applied in a very broad sense. At the same time, "most of the white-collar Afghan employees at the embassy" were arrested. (NYT, May 8, 1973.) And thereby hangs a tale.

Earlier, in December, the *Kabul New Times* published the confession of a spy, Mohammad Daud, "son of Ghulam Mohammad, a resident of Ghasni province", who revealed that he had worked for the American embassy under George Griffin.

Griffin had maintained close contacts with Gulbuddin Hekmatyar's counterrevolutionary gangs when he was in Kabul. Louis Dupree, the peculiar historian, was named by others as coordinating the counterrevolutionary bands working out of Peshawar.

The arrest of Ralph Pindar-Wilson, "a British archeologist", in Kabul early in March, 1982, revealed further details about anti-revolutionary activities. According to the *Kabul New Times,* Pindar-Wilson, who had remained in Afghanistan after December, 1979, had been charged not only with trying to smuggle out antique coins, but spies and counterrevolutionaries as well.

But the most detailed description of counterrevolutionary activity centered in the American embassy in Kabul came from Mohammad Esa.

Mohammad Esa had been put in touch with the American embassy official, James Mitchell Crowe, in 1981, through an Afghan national, Ahmadzai, and it was through him later still that he received money and orders from the embassy:

> Usually, these orders concerned collection of military intelligence, information about the subversion carried out by counter-revolutionary bands in various parts of Afghanistan, organizing explosions and sabotage. These orders were sent through me to the members of the Jamiat-e-Islami, who were outside the embassy.
>
> I gathered intelligence through my contacts among whom Mohammad Akbar was responsible for gathering intelligence in the Miaden and Wardak regions, Sayed Baquer for the Logar region and Lal Jan, known as Mashal, for the Kota Sangi and Paghman areas.
>
> I passed on the information thus gathered to Ahmadzai. He would translate and type it in English in the premises of the U.S. embassy and handed these reports over to Crowe.
>
> From what Ahmadzai said, it appeared that these reports were sent through diplomatic mailbag by embassy staff to the U.S.A. and Pakistan.
>
> Crowe and [CIA man] Morris paid me and other members of Jamiat lots of money for carrying out intelligence assignments... Thus in the year 1360 HS (begun March, 1981) they paid a sum of AFs 200,000 to the Jamiat-e-Islami group inside the embassy. Usually, the money was distributed through Ahmadzai among the group leaders, and these group leaders, in turn, would hand it over to their contacts. Part of this money was used to recruit new agents.
>
> The diplomatic staff of the embassy had placed three taxicabs at our disposal for gathering intelligence. Moreover, a number of false passports, pre-

pared by the U.S. embassy, were also made available to us. Through these passports we sent a number of our contacts to the United States for learning intelligence work. . .

Once every fortnight the staff members of the U.S. embassy went to Pakistan and brought from there revolvers, hand grenades, and powerful explosive mines. These weapons were distributed through Ahmadzai among the members of the Jamiat-e-Islami outside the embassy. Once I was also given four powerful explosive mines so that, through my contacts, I could get them planted and exploded in places which were determined in advance by Crowe. Those were residential buildings and shops located in the densely-populated city streets. . . .

The U.S. officials in Pakistan have close and friendly relations with the leaders of the Jamiat-e-Islami and give more attention to Jamiat-e-Islami than to other counterrevolutionary bands in the context of providing aid. . .

He (Morris) gave me the assignment of delivering the propaganda and organizational printed matter which was in the possession of the U.S. embassy staff to members of Jamiat-Islami outside the U.S. embassy. This printed matter included anti-state night letters, posters and photographs of the chief of Jamiat-e-Islami. . .

So when the American journalists filed obediently into the embassy in Kabul and made a little respectful circle around the "unnamed spokesman", the "Western diplomat", they were told tales of how the valiant rebel "underground" had bombed a restaurant in Kabul, and yes, there had been "many casualties"; or had sabotaged the power system, and how the people of Kabul had found "night letters" under their doors in the morning denouncing the "Karmal puppet regime", and how—as cherry to the cake—"internal resistance to the Moscow-installed regime" was increasing as proven by these remarkably spontaneous outbursts of indignation. . .

PAKISTAN'S CANDLE

> ...a little candle burning in the free world.
>
> Zia ul-Haq

On July 5, 1977, the Pakistan government headed by Prime Minister Zulfakar Ali Bhutto was overthrown by a four-man military junta in a coup led by General Mohammad Zia ul-Haq—a man so trusted by Bhutto that he had promoted him to be chief of staff of the Pakistani army. There is no gratitude in politics. In return, though many leaders of the world pleaded with him to spare Bhutto's life, Zia had his chief hanged in April 1979.

Thus, on a note of treachery Mohammad Zia ul-Haq made his entry on the modern scene, uniquely equipped to attract the attention, and even affection (as we shall see) of Washington.

After chafing for a few months as one-fourth of a military junta, Zia ul-Haq, in September 1978, impatiently threw off whatever Constitutional restraints were still hampering him in July 1977 and assumed full dictatorial power as "president." He promised "free elections," however, in 90 days, and when the first 90 days were up he promised to have them somewhat later, but most certainly on his dictator's word they would be held—until finally, in 1982, he let it be known that Pakistan could not expect so exotic a luxury as "free elections" in *any* foreseeable future.

For those Pakistanis who didn't take to this way of doing things, Zia had a cure: prison. By the end of 1981, 3,500 such dissenters were officially admitted to exist, but non-government sources put the figure closer to 10,000 and, in 1982, to 15,000. (*World Marxist Review,* Jan. 1982.)

Exact figures about such sensitive matters are notoriously hard to come by since those to be counted remain invisible to the would-be counters. But quite visible to all with eyes—visible because they, too, became *invisible*—were the disappearance of opposition newspapers and opposition parties. To compensate for that was the heightened visibility of the military.

Visible, too, were beggars (400,000 of them), the rise in the numbers of the lame, halt and blind. Visible were the soaring prices and the despair of the people. Always visible was the general himself.

Zia had early developed the qualities which American power would find so irresistible. But his charm reached its zenith only after Afghanistan. When

191

it first became apparent that Zia was busy gathering material to construct an atomic plant that could manufacture atomic bombs, the Senate recoiled and, in moral indignation assembled, passed a resolution which forbade the sale of arms to Pakistan until Pakistan promised that it would cease and desist. But then, having marched up the hill in 1979 (before Afghanistan), it just as smartly marched down again (after Afghanistan) in 1981.

"Afghanistan" was the ostensible reason. "Afghanistan" had magical powers. It had become the philosopher's stone which turned all political dross to political gold. Situated "strategically" between Afghanistan and the U.S.S.R. to the northwest, with a border on China, with India to the southeast and touching Iran with its boot, today's Pakistan has inherited all the problems which its geographical position seemed to make inevitable, but apparently no solutions to any of those problems. "Afghanistan" seemed to offer at least the hope of a key to an exit from its historical dilemmas.

Pakistan had gained its independence from Great Britain in 1947. Almost from the very moment of its "independence," and possibly as a "reward" for it, it managed to pick a quarrel with India. Between that time and the present it succeeded in fighting three wars with India and remains at daggers drawn with that country to this day.

In 1971, it "lost" East Pakistan, which became Bangladesh, a loss to which it could not reconcile itself (at least its ruling clique could not), and for which it blamed both India and the U.S.S.R. The U.S.A. had supported its efforts to keep East Pakistan tied to it, as did China. Its parliamentary system, originally modeled on the British but denatured by colonial accommodation, inaugurated in 1956, flickered feebly, giving way to military coups one after the other, with Zia ul-Haq leading the most recent.

Its chronic problems, which never seemed to advance or recede, throb around a number of organic wounds, like the drive of the Baluchis for autonomy, the Pushtuns as well, and the endless deadly enmity between the Moslems and the Hindus, which has resulted in several ghastly massacres. *Cui bono?* There is also the constant problem of the Kashmirs, claimed as her own by India, a tempting plum for Pakistan and/or China.

Religious wars have cursed the country. But, as even the greenest of tyros now know, religious wars—grotesquely anachronistic though they are—are still wars not over whom or what people shall worship which god in which heaven, but who or what people shall rule on this earth—how they shall live in what kind of social system. And this problem remains unsolved in Pakistan, as it does in its neighbor, Iran.

In its foreign relations, practically prescribed for it by John Foster Dulles in the 50s, no matter which cabal ruled in Pakistan it always seemed to have the same cards to deal, and it always dealt them in the same way. There was always the same combination of the U.S.A., China, the U.S.S.R. and

India: all of them forces to contend with. Early on, the ruling forces in Pakistan "tilted" toward the U.S.A., signing a defense treaty with it in 1959. Cooperating minutely with Dulles, who was one of the pioneers in arc-mending, Pakistan rushed to "found" SEATO and CENTO, both organizations intended to firm up the "arc" of Southeast Asia, both threatening to collapse almost immediately they were formed, and finally doing exactly that.

Relations with Afghanistan, its permanent northern neighbor, were strained no matter who ruled in Islamabad. At one time, in 1961, Pakistan had actually broken off diplomatic relations with Afghanistan over the Pushtun issue, a never-to-be resolved problem, an eternal threat.

There is a constant pulse of anxiety in the ruling circles of Pakistan that the 5 million Baluchis will one day manage to separate themselves into a nation of their own, with borders that would include part of Iran as well. There are in addition 14 million Pushtuns and they, too, feel oppressed by the majority Punjabis, who represent 58 percent of the population—the ruling percent.

The attitude of the Pakistani ruling clique (landlords and feudal lords, the military, etc., the almost mirror image of the original Afghan ruling clique) toward its minorities mimicked the attitude of the British ruling clique toward themselves before independence—though even then they were given *compradore* status. While oppressed themselves (at least to some extent) they dreamed of freedom to oppress others. The real exit from this moral and political dilemma they always shunned, and so, instead of solutions to their inherited problems, they simply piled up more problems.

In fact, Pakistan seems to have nothing *but* problems. Endemic poverty, which was Great Britain's imperial gift to the colonial world—a poverty on which the sun never sets—has driven hundreds of thousands of skilled and semi-skilled workers (badly needed in Pakistan itself) abroad in search for jobs. Hardly any country has suffered more from the "brain drain" than has Pakistan. Nearly 3,000 (annually) graduates of Pakistan's medical colleges are jobless; most go abroad, according to *Muslim* (Apr. 19, 1981). The educated see their future not in their home country but in any country but their own. And yet, workers who had gone abroad sent home (in 1979) $1.7 billion in wages—while all of Pakistan's exports brought in only $2.2 billion!

Pakistan's foreign debt (in 1980) had reached a staggering $8 billion, which comes to 41 percent of its gross national product. Military costs have zoomed, especially since the declared Afghan "crisis."

After his move in September 1978, as we have already noted, in which he emerged as sole dictator, though still "president," General Zia assured the world that he would soon hold "free and fair elections".

But he put Pakistan under martial law* and in quick order disbanded all opposition parties, arrested their leaders, placed newspapers under his censorship (those still operating), and, in short, became the very model of a contemporary police state with Dark Ages trimmings. "Consumption of alcohol has been banned. Drinking is punished by flogging.** Other Koranic punishments such as cutting off of hands for robbery have also been adopted but have yet to be carried out... Furthermore, an Islamic Ideology Council, appointed by the government, is reviewing almost all the laws of the country to determine whether they are 'repugnant to the spirit of Islam.' Family law, elections and business dealings are all being reviewed in this light. In some respects the puritan movement goes beyond the practices of Saudi Arabia or Iran." Still, none of this ran contrary to Zia's notion of democracy. " 'What we would like is democracy as close to Islam as possible,' he said." (Michael T. Kaufman, NYT, Oct. 21, 1981.)

Resistance to martial law was widespread and reports of new arrests began to surface increasingly in the world press. In February 1981, over 2,000 students would be reported boycotting classes in Peshawar, even exchanging gunfire with the police. That same month the Union of Cooperatives, with a membership of more than 4 million, protested against the government's attempt to turn these voluntary organizations into government tools.

Marches of students occurred in Multan, Lahore and Rawelpinda protesting martial law. Bhutto's daughter, Beanazier Bhutto, was placed under house arrest after a Pakistani airliner was hijacked by some members of her father's outlawed Pakistan party, People's Party, and flown to Kabul and then Damascus in March 1981. Protest meetings of journalists denounced

---

* "On Sept. 27 (1978), General Zia decreed, by Martial Law Regulation 53, the death sentence for 'any offense liable to cause insecurity, fear, or despondency amongst the public.' Crimes punishable under this measure, which superseded civil law, include the following: 'Any act with intent to impair the efficiency or impede the working, or cause damage' to public property or the smooth functioning of government; abetting 'in any manner whatsoever... the commission of such an offense'; and failure to inform the police or the army of the 'whereabouts or any such information about such a person.'...

"Martial Law 53 reverses the fundamental principle of justice: in Pakistan, you are guilty until proved innocent. The law provides that 'a military court on the basis of police or any other investigation alone may, unless the contrary is proved, presume that this accused has committed the offense charged with'...

"Significantly, this assault began in earnest in early 1981, after Reagan Administration had offered him a five-year, multi-billion dollar armaments package." (Eqbal Ahmad, "a Pakistani, is a visiting professor of political science at the University College of Rutgers University." NYT, Dec. 6, 1982.)

** "We have floggings, but there is a style of flogging." (Zia ul-Haq, NYT, Dec. 9, 1982.)

the censorship of the press but got nowhere. A demonstration of 25,000 teachers in March 1982 was broken up by the police with tear gas and riot sticks, with 100 arrested and at least 15 wounded. The same number of teachers had demonstrated in Lahore earlier and a demonstration of 15,000 teachers in Islamabad was stopped by the police. It is noteworthy that the Pakistan National Federation of Trade Unions, with 200,000 members, sent a message in March 1980 of solidarity to the Afghan workers opposing the use of Pakistan as a staging ground for counterrevolutionary activities.

In January 1982, "the authorities have arrested about 450 suspected members of an organization that wants to overthrow the military Government of President Mohammad Zia ul-Haq..." (Reuters, Jan. 14, 1982.) From New Delhi the Central News Service (India) would charge that thousands of opponents of the military regime had been thrown into jail, quoting the Pakistan newspaper, *Imrose*, as admitting that in Punjab province alone there were more than 5,000 prisoners.

With all this—and much more—the General could nevertheless assert that Pakistan was "a little candle burning in the free world."

Nor did there seem to be any voice raised in the U.S.A. to dispute him— or more, to denounce his regime. *Realpolitik* now reigned supreme in the newspaper editorials, as witnesses *The Washington Post*:

> One answer to these dilemmas is to allow the pluses and minuses to cancel each other out and, with a certain cold-bloodedness, to do essentially nothing. That is the wrong answer. The right answer is to accept Gen. Mohammad Zia ul-Haq for what he is—the man running Pakistan now; to give his regime the kind and amount of help that will make plain that the United States understands the larger stake in the security of Pakistan, and then— eyes open—to try to limit the collateral risks. That the choices are painful does not mean they can be avoided. (Jan. 11, 1980.)

The New York Times, though opting for the same eyes-open realism, did strike a note, sounding querulous in this context, that nevertheless expressed a certain uneasiness: "As Iran attests, selling costly hardware to a country cannot of itself assure the stability of a vulnerable regime. Pakistan's Gen. Zia is so unsure of his hold that he has postponed elections four times. He has been unable to quell Baluchi and Pathan insurgents, and has filled prisons with dissidents." (Jan. 9, 1980.)

Filled prisons with dissidents! Wasn't an excoriation of precisely this kind of thing the heart of American "human rights" policy—to refuse any kind of political or military aid to a country which jails dissidents? Wasn't its entire anti-socialist policy based precisely on that allegation? Nevertheless: "Carter may sensibly conclude that the circumstances nonetheless justify immediate military help to Pakistan.... The test for U.S. aid ought to be whether it meets specific, practical requirements that justify bending (!) present restrictions." (NYT, editorial, Jan. 7, 1980.) Military aid to Pakistan meant military aid—"bending"—into the Afghan counterrevolutionaries, not to speak of escalating India's fears.

Not to be outdone, James Reston, head of the Washington Bureau of the *Times,* would come up with this equally hard-as-nails advice: "The president's decision to lift the embargo on arms for Pakistan and his express determination to defend vital U.S. interests in the oil-rich Middle East may have some practical value both in Afghanistan and Iran." (Jan. 7, 1980.)

With a "sagging economy, an inflation rate that would hit 15 percent this year" (*U.S. News & World Report,* Feb. 1, 1980), the General had seen in the Afghan crisis which he had had a large part in bringing about a golden opportunity to recoup his position and improve it even more. America had poured money into Pakistan before 1980—about $5.6 billion in all. Air bases had been created for American military in the 1960s. In fact, it was from one of these—Badaber air base near Peshawar—that Gary Powers had launched his ill-fated U-2 spy flight in 1960 over Soviet territory as a provocation that resulted in torpedoing the Summit Conference between Khrushchev and Eisenhower scheduled to be held in Paris that summer.

Hand-in-glove with the American military, immediately after the overthrow of Prince Daoud in Afghanistan in 1978, Pakistan had taken a hard line against the revolution headed by Taraki, and had immediately extended a haven for the ousted feudal lords and medieval landowners.

By December 1979, there were at least 30 fully-equipped military camps— still pretending to be no more than "refugee" camps, though for some reason overwhelmingly peopled by young men—in Pakistan and some 50 additional strong points serving the counterrevolutionaries. Between June and November 1979, it was estimated that 30,000 counterrevolutionaries had received training there. By 1982, over 100 camps, most training counterrevolutionaries, were in existence mainly in Pakistan. A year later (May 1, 1983) Drew Middleton, *Times* military correspondent, would declare that "200,000 Afghan rebels are under arms."

An army trained by the Chinese, Americans, Egyptians and others was already in the field even before Karmal came to power.

Of course, after the overthrow of Prince Daoud those in Pakistan did not fail to put two and two together. Over 80 percent of the cultivatable land in Pakistan is owned by a fraction of the large landowners, just as was the case in Afghanistan before the revolution. Poverty and backwardness are no less widespread in Pakistan than they were in Afghanistan, according to U.N. statistics, listing Pakistan as among the 32 poorest in the world, and the opposition revolutionary parties were raising the same demands as the PDPA had raised so successfully in Afghanistan. The tears, therefore, of brother Afghan landlord burned like acid on their Pakistani shoulders. "Behold thy fate in me! Tomorrow thou wilt be as I am now, shorn of wealth and lands, unless thou immediately launch *jihad* (holy war) against the infidels from the North, who have stolen the wits of our pious peasants who now impiously long for our lands. *Allah-o-Akhbar!*"

Allah is great, but he doesn't have much money. A power equal to Allah exists across the water in that born-again Baptist (a pork-eater!) who can send thunderbolts against the enemy, as well as cash, in his determination to defend Islam.

Unfortunately, the Baptist's offer of cash to Zia ul-Haq in December 1979, of $400 million so offended that General that he denounced it as "peanuts"—a new measure of value, learned from the peanut farmer Carter, by which kings and countries, freedom and enslavement could now be precisely determined.

Anyhow, as a Pakistan journalist would confide to *The Washington Post:* " 'You need us more than we need you. . .' A government official put it less bluntly when he said, 'If we go, the entire Mideast goes for you.' " (Jan. 13, 1980.)

Zia wanted to be paid as a man worthy of his hire, and not in peanuts. And then, once Carter was given his walking papers as a result of "free elections"—an outcome whose import was not lost on Zia himself—he found that he could deal better with Carter's successor and a man after his own heart: the ex-actor Ronald Reagan, who dealt now not in peanuts but in jelly beans laced with napalm.

In an interview which Mohammad Zia ul-Haq had with Arnaud de Borchgrave, then *Newsweek's* "senior editor" working out of Paris, Zia sounded the alarm and laid the issue face up on the table: "We need a major qualitative improvement in our defensive capability . . . (and) would like to see the United States assist, as China had done, in improving [Pakistan's] economic stability. . ." He asked rhetorically: "Is the nuclear issue now out of the way? What is to happen to the Symington amendment? Will it be rescinded by congressional act or suspended by executive order? Is America going to restore its credibility through words or with practical steps?"

These questions were quite pointed, for in Zia's eyes they represented the message he was now signaling to the U.S.A.—"You need us more than we need you"—signals which, as we would see, were picked up by Washingtonian ears and hearkened to.

The ever-resilient Congress, which had passed a law in April 1979—actually an amendment to the Foreign Assistance Act, called the Symington amendment, which "forbade" "aid" to countries suspected of building nuclear plants—neatly reversed itself in 1981. The moral obstacles that had seemed so impenetrable in April had become remarkably porous by December, as Zia developed more and more of those charms which are so irresistible to the White House and to Congress. The adjectives attached to his name in *The New York Times* changed from "bloody tyrant" to "strong-willed" defender of the faith. When Zia dismissed the pleas of many of the world's leaders, including the Pope and Brezhnev, and even the White House, to spare the life of his one-time leader Zulfakar Ali Bhutto, this action was an unmistakable message to the Western world that they had a man in Islamabad on the cut of Nicaragua's Somoza, Cuba's Batista, the Shah of Iran, Papa Doc of Haiti, and others whose memories have rotted into oblivion quicker than their corpses.

Before 1981 had ended, approval of the sale of 40 F-15 aircraft to Pakistan was in the bag. By May it was possible to report that "after three hours of intense debate Thursday, the committee (Senate Foreign Relations Committee) voted 10-7 to exempt Pakistan from a law known as the Symington amendment." Of this vote, Senator Alan Cranston of California would remark: "If I were the leader of Pakistan I would assume that this action means that I can detonate a bomb and U.S. aid would continue." That "aid" was earmarked (then) at $100.6 million, but would escalate very quickly to a total of $3.2 billion at Reagan's insistence.

Zia had sent his message and Congress had heard.

At least one American Congressman would denounce this whitewash. Representing a district in New York City where drug addiction, crime and the drug trade are rampant, Charles B. Rangel, Democratic Congressman from Manhattan, cried out: "I just find it astounding that this Administration would consider a 3 billion military and economic aid package to a country that's one of the largest suppliers of heroin to the United States. I'm incredulous!" He pointed out that the flow of heroin to the U.S.A. from Pakistan had increased lately and contributed to the 117 percent rise in drug-related deaths in one year in New York City. (NYT, Sept. 19, 1981.) (Peter Benswinger, head of the Drug Enforcement Administration, revealed that 1,600 tons of opium were produced in that area in 1979—double what was produced in 1978.)

But if the American drug control organizations existing in Pakistan were actually to stop the flow of heroin, they would also have to blow their covers. For they existed in Pakistan, as Alfred W. McCoy would reveal in his *The Politics of Heroin in Southeast Asia,* not to stop the heroin trade but to provide cover for CIA operatives, as well as being a source of ready cash for many of the "holy warriors" engaged in liberating Afghanistan undoubtedly for the sake of Allah—let us grant them this—but for the sake of freely growing the poppy no less.

With the positive vote from Congress finally come home, things were clearing up between the two capitals, and Reagan sent James L. Buckley, undisturbed by death in Harlem from Pakistan's drugs, to Pakistan to go into matters more closely. Buckley, now titled "Undersecretary of State for Security Assistance, Science and Technology," was eminently equipped to talk to Zia. As he would himself confided exultantly when he returned from Islamabad, he found Zia to be a man after his own heart.

Though his title was lofty, it must be inserted here that Buckley's real job was to sell guns, not butter, in pursuance of Reagan's "conventional arms transfer" policy, which Reagan had initiated to replace Carter's policy (even so, observed more in the breach) of supplying arms to military dictatorships only in exceptional cases. This policy of Carter's Buckley dismissed as "theology." He would use sales of guns to "complement and supplement our own defense efforts and serve as a vital and constructive instrument of American foreign policy."* He would go on to explain his political philosophy: "I might confess that I harbor the simplistic notion that on the world's stage today it is possible to divide the principal actors between the good guys and the bad guys. . ." *(Ibid.)*

One of his "good guys" was most certainly Zia ul-Haq. When Buckley returned from visiting Zia in November 1981, his enthusiasm for the man could hardly be contained. Speaking before the United States Economic Council in New York, he assured the powerful men assembled there that Pakistan had become a "frontline state," and reaffirmed that the Reagan Administration was so aware of this crucial role in the defense of democracy that Zia played that the Congress intended to give him $4.3 *billion* (no wonder Zia had kicked Carter's offer of $400 *million* out the door) spread over six years and including the cost of 40 F-15s.

Only Pakistan's refusal to sign the 1968 treaty against the spread of nuclear weapons stood (as we saw, momentarily) in the way of a more rapid and even more munificent "aid". The newspaper account of his speech (NYT, Nov. 3, 1981) would contain the comment: "We firmly believe," said the man whose very existence came out of speculation in oil,** "that the exploration and development of Pakistan's oil and gas reserves can be done by the private sector if allowed the kinds of market place incentives we have in this country"—where "incentives" of the type enjoyed by the oil monopolies could incite a stick to grow in cement!

As for Zia, he has never openly admitted that Pakistan is actually the staging ground for counterrevolution and that thousands of professional

---

* " 'Hi, Mom, will the merchant of death be home for dinner tonight?' his witty children would ask now." (NYT, Mar. 29, 1982.)

** On November 2, 1981, "The company founded by the late oilman William F. Buckley, Sr., was ordered today, along with some associates, to make payments and relinquish royalties totalling more than $800,000..." (NYT, Nov. 2, 1981.)

mercenaries—Soldiers of Fortune*—and others no less mercenary though cloaking their motives in religious covering, are trained there by the Chinese, Americans, Israelis, some in Egypt when Sadat was alive, or that it is from Pakistan that the war is delivered to Afghanistan day by day.

He clings to the fiction that the camps that exist on Pakistan territory are there for "humanitarian" purposes only, to help the "refugees," and if some of these "refugees" choose to return to Afghanistan at night to cut the throats of the local school teachers—well, what could he do? The night is so dark. The mountains are so hard to guard. And though those police who are blind to the passage of *Mujahiddin,* loaded down with bazookas and plastic mines of the latest technical design, into Afghanistan, but who miraculously recover their sight when it's a case of poor Afghan peasants trying to get back home, may indeed have a problem with their eyesight, this is scarcely his business. He is not an optometrist!

Nevertheless, he is not a man to put all his eggs into one basket. Time was when to have the support and protection of Uncle Sam was enough to guarantee political immortality. But such immortals as the Shah of Iran, Batista of Cuba, Somoza of Nicaragua, Ngo Dinh Diem of South Vietnam, and others too numerous to mention proved that even for them, who had the firmest of guarantees, life could still be extremely chancy. To prove that he keeps his distance even from Uncle Sam, Zia confided to newspapermen (Reuters, Apr. 3, 1983) that the U.S.A. had offered him considerable compensations ($3.2 billion) to allow Uncle Sam the right to station American soldiers and to establish military posts in Pakistan, and that he had stoutly turned down the offer. Nobody—especially the Indian government—believed him, but still there was the intent expressed. Nevertheless, "unbribed," he got the money and the F-16s as though he had been.

So Zia keeps his options open even with the Soviet Union, with which Pakistan still has diplomatic and commercial ties (though slimmed down), and even with—as we noted in Kabul—Afghanistan, though also on a minimal basis.

Keeping his options open, especially to the U.S.A., proved to be a good bargaining lever for Zia, who managed to parlay his bets from a measly $400 *million* in 1980 (with Carter) to over (counting everything) 4 *billion* (with Reagan) in hardly more than a year.

A January 10th (1980) story from the United Nations—a kind of teaser of a story—noted that "Asian diplomats here have concluded that Pakistan

---

* "Buy a Bullet, Zap the Russian invader... All funds collected will be donated to an Afghan resistance group selected by SOF staff. These funds will go to the purchase of arms, ammunition and medical supplies..." Advertisement of "Afghan Fighters Fund" in *Soldier of Fortune* magazine, which boasts of easy and continual access to counterrevolutionary quarters in Pakistan.

is dropping its diplomatic support for the insurgent forces in Afghanistan and is moving instead toward recognition of the Soviet-installed government of President Bobrak (*sic*) Karmal . . ." (NYT).

The story went on to say: "But President Mohammad Zia ul-Haq is said to feel now that he is isolated, unable to count on military support from either China or the United States. . ."

That was January, 1980, showing Zia in a pique. A year later Pakistan expelled a Dr. David R. Nalin, an American who headed what was called the "malarial research centre" near Lahore, charging that he was using those facilities to breed mosquitoes, not however to discover how to control malaria as announced, but how to cultivate even deadlier forms of it. Once the formula was found, the educated mosquitoes would be dropped over (or smuggled into) Cuba* and Afghanistan.

If these actions were smoke signals from Islamabad intended to be read in Washington and Peking (as well as New Delhi and Moscow), they succeeded perhaps even better than Zia had hoped.

Not only would American representatives scurry to Islamabad in the ensuing months to reassure Zia that he was not forgotten, and was not alone, but Chinese leaders also hurried (waiting politely until the Americans had left the room) with similar reassurances. For a time the traffic over the Karakorum highway out of China began to grow a bit denser.

Toward the end of 1982, Zia ul-Haq showed up in Washington looking for more money. After assuring Reagan, who seemed easily persuaded, that he didn't intend to build an atomic bomb, he got what he came for. As both stood on the "sun-dappled South lawn" of the White House, quite the best of friends, Reagan told the press there that Zia's role in giving haven to the Afghan "refugees" (at a reported million dollars a day) was "courageous and compassionate"; and, he continued: "We're proud to stand with you, Mr. President ["President" forever—or as "forever" as guns and money could manage to stretch it] helping to provide for these tragic victims of aggression." (NYT, Dec. 8, 1982.)

The satirist stands helpless before that "compassionate" coming from the same lips that decreed millions of American elderly to a future of slow starvation, living (so many of them!) on dog food. Only an old-style cartoon by Art Young could have done justice to the moment.

But Zia's hopes that the Kremlin was showing a "hint of flexibility" his way were dashed almost immediately because of the "conditions" Zia raised for a settlement. "To be crude and direct, we have always stated that Pakistan will not talk to this man (Karmal) who came to be head of the Afghan regime by riding on Soviet tanks. We will not talk to him." (NYT, Dec. 9,

---

* They probably arrived in Cuba as dengue fever in 1981.

1982.) Coming from the man who had betrayed the ruling head of his country, then hanged him, this moral austerity seemed not only out of place but even exotic.

Karmal, meanwhile, speaking to reporters in Moscow, threw cold water on the proposition that a Zia-detected thaw in Afghanistan-Pakistan hostility was nearing, and threw even colder water on the notion that some of the leaders of the counterrevolutionary bands nestled in Pakistan, perhaps Hekmatyar, for one, might be put forward as a leader of the "new" Kabul regime. Said he: "Afghanistan has no tradition of compromising with gangsters." (NYT, Dec. 21, 1982.)

Pravda added the capstone to this "dialog" by taking Zia to task for his "inconsistencies", pointing out that no settlement of the Afghan conflict could come about until some assurances were given that Afghanistan would not be attacked by the counterrevolutionaries. But—Reagan had turned over $3.2 billion to Zia *not* to end the conflict but to keep it going.

In June, 1983, Gromyko made it quite clear that the negotiations going on, through the intermediary of the U.N., were not to be misconstrued:

> The Soviet Union affirms its full support for the program of political settlement set forth by the Democratic Republic of Afghanistan. On this basis it is possible to reach agreement on the solution of questions related to the external aspect of the Afghan rebellion. *Precisely the external aspect,* since internal matters must be solved by the Afghans themselves. (My italics.)

SHOW-BIZ **MUJAHIDDIN**

> No one watching network coverage on election
> night could fail to see from the start that the
> CBS showmen had decided to go all out. Dan
> Rather came on generating electricity from
> every pore. "Anchorman" was far too passive
> a word for him; he was hyperbolically hyper:
> "heart-stoppingly close ... hatband tight ... a
> death duel politically." As a show it worked.
>
> *The New York Times,*
> Nov. 14, 1982

On April 6, 1980, one of the top TV news "shows," "60 Minutes", put
on a seriocomedy which in its way was a classic of the TV genre in that
it managed to sum up in less than 60 minutes everything that is preposter-
ous and at the same time barbaric in American bourgeois journalism.

The "show" purported to be a documentary in which a CBS "anchorman,"
Dan Rather, disguised as well as the CBS make up men could disguise him
as an Afghan, passed in darkest secrecy and at considerable expense to CBS,
into Afghanistan "behind the lines," where he filmed himself observing a
"war."

For most non-Americans, Europeans and Asians, who cannot possibly
grasp the logic motivating the behavior of such people as Dan Rather by
the rational means available to them, and even for some Americans, it's necessary to provide some background explanation to this case of TV derring-
do.

When early in 1981 Walter Cronkite, long-time "anchorman" of the CBS
Evening News program, announced that at long last he was going to retire,
it is alleged that the nation reacted to this stunning news with almost the
same traumatic recoil that their grandparents experienced, a couple of generations earlier, to the announcement that "America's sweetheart," Mary
Pickford (then in her 40s) was going to cut her curls! America aged overnight when Mary Pickford grew up. Similarly, when Cronkite informed the
American public, which had told innumerable public opinion polls that
they believed Cronkite above any other television or political personality in
America, that he was going to go—his nightly audience was an estimated
19 million—those 19 millions of Americans are supposed to have suffered
momentary cardiac arrest: Papa was deserting them!

His going, on March 6, 1981, left a big gap. Who can replace Papa, when Papa goes? The Eye of the Corporation, in surveying the field, fell rather hesitantly on Dan Rather, not entirely unknown to the TV audience but never seriously looked on as the heir to Cronkite. An instant chill fell over his presumptive image, and millions (3,800,000) of the faithful who had worshipped at Cronkite's altar now deserted to other TV stations—in fact, CBS lost 20 percent of its audience. This amounted to four Nielsen points, rating losses which translate immediately into money losses. For one Nielsen point is worth (in 1981) about $50 million a year. A 4-point loss therefore showed somewhere near a $200 million loss—not peanuts in even the rarefied airs of high finance. (NYT, Dec. 5, 1981.)*

To lose 20 percent of one's audience at one blow is not only a traumatic financial loss, however. It could mark the beginning whose end could be counted out in a line of rolling corporate heads.

The problem, as the CBS saw it, boiled down to this: "The CBS sources say that although they believe Mr. Rather is a good anchor, they have to create a program that uses more of his skills. 'Cronkite has developed an image, and we have to help Dan Rather develop his own image,' one source said. 'He ought to be in settings that are more informal and more relaxed, that allows people to see him as the likeable, positive personality he is.' " (NYT, Dec. 5, 1981.)

"The CBS sources said there was general agreement the program was dull and slow-paced. 'We want to keep it as interesting, rapidly paced, with more spontaneity and serendipity, almost like all-news radio,' one official said." (*Ibid.*)

There had been other losses which had shaken CBS officialdom. Heavy problems, as they used to say, had accumulated overnight. But there are no problems without their solutions hiding somewhere, and CBS had some expert help in finding where. America is the only country in the world which genuinely accepts the notion that "news" is something "created," packaged and "sold" like any other consumer product, and that if it's packaged attractively one will inevitably sell more of it (sell more news) and get paid handsomely in return, with no damage inflicted on the integrity of the "news" in the process.

The second line got some top-level help from a one-time radio reporter, later a B-Hollywood actor and, in by-now logical progression, the president of the United States—even though the "advice" came after the fact. He was all for packaging the news; in fact championed the idea with great enthusiasm. Speaking at ceremonies marking the 40th anniversary of the Voice

---

* Although these newspaper revelations are made after Dan Rather's escapade in Afghanistan in April 1980, they obviously hold good retroactively.

of America, whose chronic problem was its confusion between truth and the other thing, and whose emergence from the closet as a CIA creature had been quite recent (and not voluntary), Reagan—for such it was—declared, to the appreciative laughter of those in his audience who understood him only too well, that the "truth" must be "attractively packaged," but—and he wanted this to be clearly registered—not compromised with.

In still "other words," a lie will serve when the truth falls short. Just doll it up with bells and balls and ribbons!

If there is any proposition that is closer to the heart of corporate TV it is that one. For it, truth is indeed in the eye of the beholder, and it is up to TV to fill that eye, which is the window to the soul, or better still, the pocketbook. CBS is TV and it deals with "packaging the news." Its sports style of reportage à la Reagan manages to invade its news style and vice versa. In any case, it knew how to package the truth with a delicacy that didn't noticeably damage it in the process, and it had the future blessings of the White House into the bargain. The trouble was that the game was not a baseball game in a sleepy mid-Western town. It was a game with our lives.

By April 1980, CBS knew that Dan Rather wasn't going over very well and something had to be done to increase his "appeal," to show the people that he was really "likeable," so that those strayed 20 percent of the audience might not make a permanent habit of what was hopefully only a temporary aberration. After all, one could not afford to forget that while "selling the news" Dan Rather would be expected to sell toilet cleansers and hemorrhoid ointment as well!

It was out of this dilemma that the idea of sending Dan Rather to create his own war in Afghanistan was born.

He arrived there late in March. Like Jim Gallagher of the *New York Daily News* and others before him, he had to ask the natives to show him where the war was, and was appalled to learn that it just wasn't where it was supposed to be. Or what was the same thing: it wasn't there where it could be most glamorously photographed.

What to do? He couldn't turn right around, go back home and tell his Cronkite audience that he couldn't find the war that Carter had called the "most dangerous threat to peace since World War II." So, like many another TV *varieté* buccaneer before him, he figured that what so obviously *ought* to be would *have* to be, and the mere inconvenience of a fact could not be allowed to stand in the way of the truth—and so he ordered one custom-made for himself.

According to reports from Afghanistan published in *Haqiqate Engqelabe Saur* (The Truth of the April Revolution), organ of the Central Committee of the PDPA, the most authoritative newspaper in Afghanistan, published in Pushtu and Dari, Dan Rather, dressed in peasant robes, his face darkened, had "slipped" into Afghanistan (along with his camera crew) to film the war. But the "war" turned out to be no more than a series of interviews with "rebels" who made anti-Soviet charges without bothering (as is the custom) to produce proof.

Colorful as these interviews were, they are not good enough for TV, which must have visual, not spoken "images." Rather told them that he was there not to record *talk* but *action,* the war itself, and so they went out and like good bird dogs found it and brought it back to him.

They obligingly raided an Afghan village, Kathekhabab, captured (kidnapped) three villagers who had been working on an irrigation canal. The three were brought to the village square where they were duly filmed. But that too wasn't enough. Just filming three terrified peasants didn't produce the footage that would win back those four Nielsen points, that 20 percent of the audience, that $200,000,000 black ink!

So, according to the report in *Haqiqate Engqelabe Saur,* whose editor, Mahmood Baryalai, a seasoned revolutionary I had met and interviewed, Rather told them that it would make a better TV story if the captors acted out their holy anger against the infidel scum, dramatizing their hatred, in the sacred cause of the defense of Islam, for the American TV camera and thus help solve Rather's rating problem for him. So they went right ahead— stoned them, then cut off their heads. Rather got his footage, they got his thanks—and pay in accordance with the going rate (as that "freedom-fighter" Hekmatyar had already established.)

That section of the film was never shown on TV. (The Sunday "60 Minutes" comes around supper time.)* Rather denied that it had taken place at all. But he could not deny that it was customary for TV entrepreneurs to stage episodes for the camera that were then shown to the public as unrehearsed, genuinely spontaneous moments of drama happily caught by the camera which, just as happily, managed to be there at the right moment! Later in 1983, at a trial in California for slander (which was dismissed as unproven), the jury was shown outshots of a show Rather had produced in which the desired episode was shot several times with the "actor" meticulously rehearsed in his lines and his "spontaneity."

"The '60 Minutes' camera lingered adoringly on the star of *Mr. Rather Goes to Afghanistan.* There he was in his civvies, walking through a town. There he was again 'disguised as one of them,' wired for sound as he approached a band of Afghan refugees. 'Perhaps I could talk with them here. If we can move right into the refugees here. Hello, my name is Dan Rather!' " *(Ibid.)*

---

* Stomachs are not settled yet.

Hello indeed! "Afghans are stunned even to see a white face," remarks Tyler Marshall dryly later. As to the veracity of the quotes from the genuine Afghan "rebels," or "freedom fighters," one could get a line on that from the piece which appeared in the *Times* by Michael T. Kaufman, who met just such a TV crew in Peshawar just about the time Dan Rather appeared there. Under the headline, "Afghan Guerrillas Wake Up to the Media," we read:

> Over the last three months, some guerrilla units have become more sophisticated in dealing with the swarm of journalists. Several of them are eager for press coverage, implying that through publicity they may establish their claims of leadership and effectiveness. Some have English-speaking spokesmen and at least one of these men talks about "favorable lighting conditions" for television camera crews. Sometimes the groups openly compete for the attention of the correspondents. (NYT, Mar. 27, 1980.)

As for Dan Rather, CBS would announce with quiet satisfaction that by August 1982, Rather's "likeable, positive personality" had brought back those strays who had left CBS when Walter Cronkite had left and, in fact, CBS "had consolidated its position as the most popular evening newscast." (NYT, Aug. 4, 1982.)

Therefore, "Given its now consistent top rating, CBS News has raised its price for a 30-second commercial on the broadcast—from $30,000 to $40,000, which is what the network had been charging before the slide in ratings began . . . in March 1981" *(Ibid.)*.

"Hi. I'm Dan Rather—I'm worth $40,000 a half minute."

ARMS TO THE REBELS?
NO, PERHAPS, AND THEN REAGAN

> In tense situations where the United States is
> suspected of uglier designs, there is always a
> question whether recipients of aid can afford
> the association. But with or without justifica-
> tion, they are often already denounced as C.I.A.
> puppets. Offering open subsidy could hardly
> cause them more damage. There is no reason to
> keep the Americans' ideological preferences in
> the closet, like a shaming secret.
>
> *The New York Times,*
> Mar. 23, 1982

Hardly had word arrived in Washington that the Soviets had entered Afghanistan in December 1979 than Brzezinski leaped to the microphone and told Zia that the U.S. was ready to offer him every kind of aid, including the "use of force", if he felt he needed it.

Carter, more cautious, promised that "direct military assistance to those rebels might be possible later," but in the meantime he wanted to "build a chorus of international criticism of the Soviet move..." (NYT, Dec. 29, 1979.)

Until that was done Carter had to move with some circumspection in sending arms to the counterrevolutionaries in Afghanistan, via Pakistan. So all references to such aid had to be roundabout, and in February, Harold Brown, then Secretary of Defense, made exactly the kind of roundabout reference that seemed to carry out the words of the popular song: "Your lips say no, no, but your eyes say yes to me."

"In Washington, Defense Secretary Harold Brown acknowledged today (Feb. 27, 1980) that rebels in Afghanistan may be receiving arms supplied to Pakistan by the United States, but said that it is 'the Soviet invasion, the Soviet involvement that causes the death and turmoil.'" (Michael Goldsmith, NYT, Feb. 28, 1980.)

In March, *The Washington Post* would come up with: "The United States is reported to have provided some covert aid, including weapons, to the rebels after the Soviet intervention in December. U.S. officials will not speak publicly of the effort, and declined to do so in talks with reporters yesterday." (Mar. 21, 1980.)

Drew Middleton, always described as having a direct pipeline into the inner recesses of the Pentagon, would write in July 1980: "Sources in the Pentagon ... say that the United States is providing arms to the insurgents on a limited basis. This seems to mean enough arms to keep the insurgents fighting in the field, but not enough to provoke Soviet retaliation against Pakistan across whose frontiers U.S. weapons would move to Afghanistan...

"White House officials said on Feb. 15 (1980) that the United States had begun an operation to supply the insurgents with light infantry weapons, presumably rifles, light machine guns and grenades. The CIA, a White House source said, had been assigned to carry out the covert mission." (NYT, July 21, 1980.)

Zia had made no bones about the fact that he wanted weapons from the U.S.A., but linked such assistance to economic assistance in general, always denying out of the other side of his mouth that any American weapons given to him would end up in the hands of the Afghan counterrevolutionaries.

That mercenaries had already appeared on the scene was testified to by various reporters. In March, Tyler Marshall was noting (from Islamabad) that "Government authorities are said to be preparing to deport British and American mercenaries drawn to the guerrilla war in Afghanistan by the lure of money and adventure...

"Peshawar is the headquarters of the major Afghan guerrilla groups fighting inside Afghanistan. That the mercenaries were there became widely known only late last week after three of them found their way into the U.S. Embassy club here and boasted to foreign journalists of plans to sell their services to the guerrillas and 'kill Russians.'" (LAT, Mar. 24, 1981.)

From London at about the same time, the novelist James Aldridge would write: "A while ago the British press was full of very proud stories about a handful of mercenaries who had arrived in Pakistan to cross over into Afghanistan where, they said, they wanted to 'kill Russians.' There were in fact two such separate groups of mercenaries and they had set up their 'headquarters' in Pakistan's North Frontier Province of Peshawar. The first group, which was all British, was under the leadership of a man called David Tomkins, who already fought as a mercenary in Angola under that other British mercenary, Colonel Callan, who was executed by the Angola authorities in 1970.

"The second group is headed by an American, called Eugene Shipley, but two of his lieutenants are British mercenaries named John Pilgrim and Hugh Morrison. They claim to have 72 fellow mercenaries ready and waiting, and Pilgrim told reporters in Islamabad that though he didn't get much money out of his profession, he did it because he 'hated communism' "—in March 1981.

In December 1980, the *Philadelphia Inquirer* had run a story describing how trucks arriving at Peshawar on their way to the Afghan border are stopped by Pakistani police there who, after checking their license plate number against a number in their notebook, waved them on with no attempt to see what the trucks were carrying. They were carrying arms to Afghanistan counterrevolutionaries.

In any case, quite early in the game it was an open secret that the United States was "secretly" arming the counterrevolutionaries in Afghanistan. In April 1980, Carter was still hemming and hawing about admitting what everyone knew—including Reagan, who had already publicly declared during the presidential campaign that American arms were reaching the rebels— "I don't think," said Carter, responding to Reagan, "that that is so," but wouldn't dismiss the idea out of hand.

But one year later, in March 1981, Reagan, now in the White House, had dropped all coy disavowals. Appearing on ABC-TV, "President Reagan . . . said in a television interview that if Afghan insurgents fighting Soviet forces asked for weapons he would consider complying with the request."

The cat, which had already been well out of the bag by then, was now officially out of the bag, and later that year Michael Kaufman would report from Peshawar that:

> No longer do representatives of the various factions engage in diatribes about the need of the Western governments to support their struggle with arms and money. Instead, they say they are doing quite well.

And they proved it:

> He [a "diplomat"] said the mujahideen *(sic)* or Islamic warriors had learned to use new weapons, both those captured from Soviet-supported stocks and those acquired from foreign supporters. "They are bringing down some helicopters and in the cities they are using very sophisticated techniques," said the diplomat, who did not want (!) to be quoted by name. (NYT, Aug. 31, 1981.)

To bring down a helicopter you must have *very* sophisticated arms indeed, which cannot be bought in the local bazaars or on the Black Market. There is only one country in the world that can supply weapons to bring down helicopters and not miss them. As for the "sophisticated techniques" employed in cities, these include knowing how to use poison pellets and gas bombs, again gadgets not to be picked up on every street corner, nor the skill to apply them acquired by reading a how-to book one rainy weekend.

That the Chinese also had been supplying Pakistan with arms (and also the rebels) nobody bothered even to deny. Egypt openly admitted—in fact, boasted—of her role:

> Cairo, Feb. 13 (1980)—Some Afghan Moslem rebels are receiving military training in Egypt and will be sent home armed to fight against the Soviet-backed regime in Afghanistan, Egypt's minister of defense disclosed today. (NYT, by Christopher S. Wren.)

Egypt had been getting arms from the Soviet Union for years (and some of them would turn up among the Afghan rebels) but latterly it had replaced the U.S.S.R. as its supplier with the U.S.A.: "The Egyptian Army is getting U.S. armored personnel carriers and improved Hawk missiles." *(Ibid.)* That some of these would become the property of the Afghan counterrevolutionaries nobody would presume to contest.

But to make sure there could be no doubt about it, the ever-obliging Sadat would tell a NBC-TV audience on September 22, 1981, that he would "reveal" his "secret" to them, which was that the moment Amin had been knocked out of power, in December 1979, "the U.S. contacted me here and the transport of armaments to the Afghanis started from Cairo on U.S. planes."

Saudi Arabia had likewise made no real effort to conceal the fact that it bankrolled the rebel forces, who after all were fighting its own feudal cause in Afghanistan. Great Britain, meanwhile, had never given up hope, grown increasingly forlorn, of re-establishing some fragment of her power where once it had reigned almost supreme, and Lord Carrington made various visits to Zia ul-Haq in that quest. Both were mutually interested in maintaining their concept of the "sovereignty of Afghanistan." In any case, money had begun to flow into some rebel hands so abundantly that by the end of 1981, and into 1982, they were complaning not of the absence of cash but of the absence only of enough "sophisticated" weapons. Drew Middleton of *The New York Times* would quote Hassan Gailani as saying: "What our people need is surface-to-surface missiles that will enable us to attack [a newly-built airport] from the cover of a few small hills east and southwest of the base. But they would have to be missiles with a range of at least 20 kilometers."

But if all this was still considered too circumstantial to constitute the kind of iron proof skeptics demanded before they would accept the facts of Western (i.e. essentially American) intervention in Afghanistan, an additional reference may be made to "scientific" books published by the university press and written presumably by men and women scholars who have had the time to sift the true from the false, the real from the fancy, the moral from the immoral. We turn again to *The Struggle for Afghanistan:* "At Pakistan border checkpoints weapons are routinely confiscated. Yet arms sales to Afghans are not prevented. Smuggling across Afghan borders has long become institutionalized. Announced policies against arms movements may therefore serve primarily to avert Soviet retaliation rather than block actual shipments. Iran and Pakistan could cut off supplies to the resistance if they imposed stringent controls. Such evidence as we have suggests that they have not clamped down totally, despite their official protestations."

There is as little moral objection shown here to such doubledealing on this issue as the same writers show toward the use of torture and the murder of schoolteachers. Casual admissions of lying, hypocrisy and corruption had become part of the new candor generally in the press and in academic circles particularly, whose moral essence seemed to be expressed in the handy-andy formula: "Sure, he's an S.O.B. But he's *our* S.O.B."* This seemed to be what Jeanne Kirkpatrick had in mind as she surveyed the shipwrecked world and reviewed its unsteady history, from her perch at the U.N.

When asked by a reporter on CBS News how the U.S.A. justified its backing of the "bad, corrupt" Salvadoran regime, her answer could have been stitched in needle point: "The truth is that most of the governments of the world are, by our standards, bad governments... Most governments are, by our standards, corrupt... We live in an imperfect world. Most people are badly governed, and always have been. We wish we had (only) allies who were democratic and well-governed, (but) we still have to look after ourselves and freedom in the world. Therefore, sometimes we are going to have to support and associate with governments who do not meet our standards. The relations between power and morality are often very complicated..." (NYT, Feb. 21, 1982.)

Kirkpatrick's "hard-headed realism" was only a reflection of the tone already set by the Reagan Administration, whose impatience with diplomatic kitchie-coo had become more and more obvious with every passing day. But *The New York Times*—which now and then tried to place some distance between itself and the more bulldozing tactics of the Administration—also had burst out with a demand, obviously long suppressed, that hypocrisy should be thrown aside, and just as the bald-headed row in the old-time burlesque theaters used to cry, "Take it off! Take it off!"—as the burlesque striptease queen toyed with her G-string—so, too, did the *Times* raise the cry that the Reaganites should drop their last diplomatic G-string as well and come out admitting what they had so shamefacedly denied before.

Since everybody knows that the counterrevolution everywhere in the world is subsidized by American money, and organized by the CIA, why not admit it, for goodness sakes, and square yourself before God and conscience? "There is no reason to keep the Americans' ideological preference in the closet, like a shaming secret." (NYT, Mar. 23, 1982.)

---

* First uttered by Pres. F. D. Roosevelt explaining why it was necessary for the U.S.A. to accept the elder Somoza.

By the beginning of 1983, the last governmental G-string had been triumphantly torn off and the truth was there for all with the stomach to see. By March, 1982, no further attempts to *disguise* open American economic and military support for the Afghan rebels were being made by President Reagan. In fact he even proclaimed an official "Afghanistan Day." This species of candor, whose mother and father are imperialist arrogance, knocked hypocrisy on the head but only to clear the path more efficiently toward the same end as before—but now openly admitted: imperialist domination. In a "badly governed" world, our role was clear...

For months, accusations had been made by the Soviets, the Afghans, and others that American money and arms were being clandestinely supplied to the Afghan "rebels" who, otherwise, unsupplied, would have faded away into the bushes long before. The Carter Administration wouldn't say yes and wouldn't say no. But meanwhile, the arms kept coming, the bank accounts of rebel "leaders" in Swiss banks kept fattening, and the killing of school-teachers multiplied.

But Washington, despite the evidence, kept denying that it was the main backer of counterrevolution in Afghanistan, and stuck to the fiction that it gave only moral support to a captive people who had nobly risen to combat the Soviet invader. But, with Reagan had come bravado, and bravado was taken to be a kind of honesty. By May (1983), *The New York Times* would report:

> The United States has stepped up the quantity and quality of covert military support for Afghan insurgents fighting Soviet forces and the Soviet-backed Government in Kabul, according to Administration officials...
>
> Beginning last December, the officials said, the Central Intelligence Agency was ordered to provide the Afghan insurgents for the first (?) time with bazookas, mortars, grenade launchers, mines and recoilless rifles. One official said shoulder-fired anti-aircraft missiles were also being supplied. Almost all the arms were said to be of Soviet manufacture. [Reports that the brave Afghan guerrillas had supplied themselves with arms by taking them from the bodies of Soviet soldiers they had killed in combat here takes a knock on the head]...
>
> The arms are brought to Pakistan by ship and aircraft and trucked to the border areas...
>
> Saudi Arabia and Egypt are also said to be involved in covert support for the guerrillas. Iran is also reported to be providing a limited amount of arms to the Shiite Moslems in Afghanistan.
>
> The officials said that a large portion of the arms came from old Egyptian stockpiles of Soviet weapons and that the Saudis and the United States were paying the bills. The total cost of the operations is estimated to have been between $30 million and $50 million a year for the last three years, with the United States paying about half.
>
> Told that Soviet officials said in March that the United States had stepped

up the arms flow to the insurgents, a senior Administration official responded, "Good, I'm glad they're feeling it. . ."

Administration officials spoke of an internal debate [on policy] between what they called the "bleeders," or those who wanted *to draw more and more Soviet troops into Afghanistan,* and those who sought a more cautious approach. They said common ground was found last fall in the President's decision to increase the quantity, but more especially the quality, of arms to the insurgents. . .

There are deep doubts among Administration experts about gaining the necessary unity among the Afghan insurgents for a settlement, let alone a basis for an agreed coalition government. . . (Leslie Gelb, NYT, May 3, 1983. My italics.)

Q.E.D., one would say.

THE SAGA OF THE TWIG
AND THE LEAF

> *A tree with a bitter seed*
> *Fed with butter and sugar*
> *Will still bear a bitter fruit.*
> *From it, you will taste no sweetness.*

Abu Shukur of Balk

Hodding Carter 3rd, when he was a State Department spokesman, introduced the charge to newspapermen at a press conference in January 1980. It was that the Soviets were—or *possibly* were—guilty of using chemical warfare in Afghanistan. He put forth the evidence for his charge in a peculiar crab-wise fashion—each accusation accompanied by a disavowal as to its reliability:

> In Washington [UPI reported from New Delhi] the United States said today that the Soviet Union *may be using* lethal chemicals in Afghanistan and charged that such actions, *if they were occurring,* would be "outrageous and inhumane."

Fair enough. As the joke goes: If I had some ham I'd have a ham and egg sandwich if I had some eggs! But to go on:

> "We have *unconfirmed reports* the Soviet Union used lethal chemical agents against nationalist (!) forces in Afghanistan," said State Department spokesman Hodding Carter 3rd. (All italics mine; also the astonished exclamation point. Jan. 24, 1980, from the *Herald Tribune* Agency dispatches.)

What "reports" that were so "persistent" as to really warrant such charges—even put in such a hesitating way—nobody, certainly not Carter, bothered to detail. Such stories had indeed appeared in the press, and it was precisely such serendipity delights that the State Department thanked the tooth fairy for depositing on its pillow each morning.

But skepticism was painfully present in much of the same press that had published those stories. It had cause. That press had been stung too often in its role of trusting purveyors of government handouts, and Garcia-like carriers of messages from anonymous diplomats to hapless readers that always turned out, sooner or later, and usually sooner, to be not only *wrong* but *concocted.* At a certain point of purveying such tainted services its own credibility came into question. And that part of the press flying at least the tatters of independence had no choice but to look with more cross-eyed skepticism than ever before at curious Greeks bearing such curious gifts.

It was, after all, only yesterday that the CIA had been exposed as not only the source of amazing fabrications which the press had obediently spoon-fed to its gullible readers but, impatient of go-betweens, the CIA had itself infiltrated the newspaper world with its own agents, some of whom had penetrated, with little resistance from the top, into *The New York Times* (not to speak of others).

On September 13, 1981, Alexander Haig in Berlin charged that the Soviet Union had been using chemical weapons in Laos, Kampuchea (or Cambodia, as he insisted on calling that tormented country) and Afghanistan.

On November 10, 1981, Richard Burt, Director of the State Department's battle-weary Bureau of Politico-Military Affairs, declared jubilantly that now Haig had spoken, "We have the smoking gun!"

He went on to sermonize: "Over the past five years, and perhaps longer—" but not *too* long because that would run you into the Vietnamese war— "weapons outlawed by mankind, weapons successfully banned from the battlefields of the industrialized world for over five decades have been used against unsophisticated and defenseless people in campaigns of mounting extermination which are being conducted in Laos, Kampuchea and more recently in Afghanistan." (NYT, Nov. 11, 1981.)

Having stated that as flatly as a statement can be stated, he followed it with a puzzling *non sequitur:* "that the United States has 'concluded that chemical weapons are being used in Afghanistan, but we have no evidence.' " (*Ibid.*)

The "smoking gun" had popped in less than a minute! Though promises had been made for months—actually years—that *conclusive* evidence would be produced proving that the Soviets were involved in waging chemical warfare in Southeast Asia and now in Afghanistan, with names, places and episodes scrupulously detailed, all that came out of that shaking mountain of a promise was a tiny mouse indeed: a "smoking gun" that consisted of a "single leaf and twig" allegedly found in Kampuchea but good enough to convict the Soviets of atrocities in Afghanistan!

Though announced with considerable brouhaha by the State Department in November 1981, the "smoking gun" failed to arouse in other quarters the same excitement that it seemed to have aroused there. Waiting for months for more evidence to arrive than that "leaf and twig," *The New York Times* finally (in March) prodded: "Further evidence was awaited with some eagerness." (Mar. 19, 1982.)

Just a few days later that "further evidence" arrived. On March 22, 1982, Haig issued his long-awaited Report. It opened with what was almost a sigh:

Despite a continued flow [initiated, though it was too modest to admit it, by itself] of reports, dating back over seven years, of chemical warfare in Southeast Asia and more recently in Afghanistan and despite the still-mounting physical evidence of the use of trichothecene toxins as warfare agents, doubts as to the conclusive nature of the available evidence have persisted.

Such mule-headedness could be trying. But some idea of what the problem really was might be gleaned from the following report:

Islamabad, Pakistan, March 5 (1980)—Afghan refugees say that Soviet fighter planes dropped lethal nerve gas bombs last week during a combined Russian-Afghan military thrust against Moslem guerrillas in the eastern Afghan province of Kunar, *Western diplomats* [our old friends!] said today.

Many of the refugees described "metal canisters falling from a plane and spewing out blue-green-gray smoke on hitting the ground," a *diplomat* said. "These backward people then describe how villagers acted like madmen, became paralyzed and died," he said. "These people *have been coached* into what to say but there are so many allegations that something must be behind the claims." (John A. Callcott, UPI. My italics.)

But why, if the evidence he was retailing was so compelling, did the "diplomat" refuse to divulge his name when to do so would have given so much more credibility to his charges? Could he perhaps have been the "hysterical" diplomat reporters had already heard ranting about events he could have had no first-hand knowledge of? Was his name possibly Robert Lessard, George Griffin, or even Louis Dupree?

And why, one is curious to know, bring in the phrase "these people have been coached"? *Who* had suggested that they have been? Who would most likely "coach" them? Was "coaching" these "backward" people a normal procedure? And is this why the people and their possible "coaches" remain unnamed?

And here we're told that the "backward" people had actually seen *canisters* falling from Soviet planes. Why hadn't they picked them up, even fragments of them?

Dr. Edward M. Collins, vice-director of the U.S. Defense Intelligence Agency, testifying before Congress in 1980, had already stated that:

The Soviets do have chemical warfare decontamination units in their own organizations and those units are present in Afghanistan. Now there are two reasonable explanations for that. One would be they intend to be prepared to use chemical weapons, which is a very "iffy" proposition, and the other is that in a typical military fashion when you call up a division you call up everybody. So there is no confirmation at all that they used chemical weapons.

And Bruce Clarke, Director of the CIA's National Foreign Assessment Center, would add: "We don't have that solidity of evidence that would enable us to say with certainty that it [the use of chemicals by Russians in Afghanistan] happened."

He was told that a rumor was floating around that the Russians did use chemicals in Afghanistan and he remarked: "I don't see anything wrong with letting that rumor run." (*Center of Defense Information*, Vol. XI, Nov. 1, 1982.)

The issue of the Soviet Union using chemical warfare in Afghanistan, where it would be charged with killing exactly 3,042 Afghans by chemical attacks "attributed to 47 separate incidents between the summer of 1979 and 1981," was huffed and puffed at by the State Department spokesmen, who launched what they hoped was a final shattering blast when the Department issued a 32-page report on "Chemical Warfare in Southeast Asia and Afghanistan" on March 22, 1982.

The "report" was, unfortunately, received with a thunderous lack of belief. As Gene Lyons had commented earlier on just such charges as it contained: "It's hard to fathom what the Administration is up to with its repeated charges of Soviet chemical and biological atrocities in Asia—other than justification for its program to spend $4 billion to $7 billion on a new generation of nerve-gas weapons. For all its shrillness the Government's case would not suffice to convict a purse snatcher."

SMOKING THE GUN

> ... I believe no satirist could breathe
> this air. If another Juvenal or Swift
> could rise up among us tomorrow, he would
> be hunted down...
>
> Charles Dickens,
> *Martin Chuzzlewit*

Hardly had Hodding Carter 3rd, State Department spokesman, left Washington—part of the changing of the bed sheets—as the Reagan crowd came in than his successor picked up on the very next word of the very same script from which Carter had been reading. The accusation that the Soviets were using chemicals in Southeast Asia, a trumpet call uncertainly sounded by Carter, began to sound more stentorianly with Burt, and the louder it sounded the more obvious the reason for it became.

What is so surprising is how obvious it was. The strategy here was no more imaginative, and far less original, than the old dodge of crying "Stop, thief!" as one meanwhile makes off with the squeaking pig in the opposite direction under the cover of the created confusion. The purpose of the charge of chemical use by the Soviets in Southeast Asia was not to force the Soviets to stop using chemical weapons. It was to justify our own use of them.

For it became almost immediately clear that the Reagan Administration, which had stalled all further meetings requested by the Soviets to discuss precisely the issue of limiting and hopefully finally eliminating the production of all chemical and germ warfare weapons, had plans of its own, already thoroughly worked out, that would enormously expand the production of both lethal chemicals and deadly germs.

The United States had been, if not literally dragged at least pushed, and if not screaming and kicking at least grumbling, to the conference table to sign the various treaties that other civilized nations had long ago signed that would ban the use of such weapons in war. The U.S.A. had originally refused to sign the 1925 Geneva Protocol committing the major powers against their production and use. And it resisted all later efforts to sign it until 1975, and then only with its fingers crossed behind its back.

In 1972, when the Soviets submitted a resolution to the U.N. to ban and then destroy all stocks of chemical weapons, the U.S.A. found itself still unprepared to go that far. In 1979, discussions with the Soviets on banning chemical warfare took place in Geneva but were broken off by the Reaganites in 1980 over the protests of the Soviets. (This is where, at this writing, the matter stands.)

The reason for such reluctance is clear. The men who had now come charging into Washington like gang-busters had no intention of killing germs that might conceivably kill Russians, "the focus of all evil." Instead of fully signing any agreement to ban such weapons, they asked for a steep hike in government appropriations to expand and intensify their production, starting off with a preliminary appropriation of $3.5 million to build the so-called binary nerve gas facilities at Pine Ridge.

This $3.5 million was new money piled on old money. "The current U.S. stockpile of chemical weapons includes three million artillery shells, a few thousand serial bombs and several thousand mines. Most of these are filled with G nerve agents, an organophosphorous compound that is odorless, invisible and devastatingly lethal..." (*The Nation,* July 5, 1980.) By 1984 it was planned that $1,400,000,000 would be spent on producing lethal chemicals at six other centers in the U.S.A. (Wireless Bulletin from Washington, ICA, Bonn-Bad Godesberg, Feb. 11, 1982.)

In fact, the U.S. has enough germs in store to infect the whole world, and enough atomic bombs to kill those who survived the infections—or the other way around.

In any case, there is no question that there exists neither a moral nor a practical reason why American power would hold back on the use of chemicals in war (or even in peace.) It could always depend on that synthetically produced "public opinion," hand-shaped by the obliging media, to accept a decision as their own which had already been taken in advance for them.

But convincing world opinion—a need which came upon America with some surprise—was another matter. To go naked into Armageddon was still too chilling a thought for those who were able to think anymore.

In any case, skepticism persisted, despite the "many allegations" and "running rumors." The Soviets would denounce such charges against them, but though these denunciations would escalate and grow more sulphurous with repetition, they remained unheard (therefore unvoiced) in the U.S.A.

For instance, on March 6 (1980), TASS would declare (from Paris) that "The so-called International Human Rights Federation uniting various emigre groups, many of whose members are on the payroll of the United States' Central Intelligence Agency, circulated another anti-Soviet falsehood. This time to the effect that Soviet troops ostensibly used a cerain 'nerve gas' in the Afghan province of Kunar."

TASS didn't mince words: "Although the falsehood in question does not require special refutation, one must nevertheless say once again that the anti-Soviet inventions which are being spread by certain circles in the West lately—the kind of slanderous assertions as to the use of nerve gas or destruction of people in Afghanistan by Soviet troops—all are unpardonable lies."

Since it was challenged so directly—being called a liar to its face, so to speak—the cue for the State Department here was to produce the damning evidence forthwith and catch its opponent dead to rights. But it might have had some difficulty explaining this little item:

> Washington (Sept. 18, 1980)—Brushing aside Pentagon objections that the action was premature, the Senate has voted 52 to 38 to start building a chemical warfare facility that could begin producing nerve gas and other poisonous weapons as early as 1984... The House had overwhelmingly approved the same $3.15-million funding measures last month on a voice vote...
>
> Supporters of the measure sponsored by Sen. Henry Jackson, D.-Wash. focused on the Soviet chemical arms capability, *citing the reported use of tear gas and incapacitating gases by Soviet troops in Afghanistan,* as well as Vietnam's use of chemical agents in Laos and Cambodia. (LAT. My italics.)

There had been "reports," in fact "persistent" reports of Soviet use of chemicals in Afghanistan (like the one above) but never any "smoking pistol" proof. Nevertheless it was considered sufficient to cite such intangible "reports" in the press to justify launching an enormous, very concrete program aimed at killing off as many future enemies of Senator Jackson as dared to lift their heads over the wrong horizon. That these "reports," frail though they were, were, even so, forged by the CIA and then planted in the ever-hospitable columns of the free press nobody even bothered to deny. It was common knowledge. The charade entered into by the various players, all of whom played their parts "independently" of one another, could not be characterized as a deliberate plot to deceive the public. What happened was more subtle and at the same time more sinister than that. All the "players" had a common key—and with it they needed no precise instructions as to how to play. The "key" was their common anti-Sovietism.

As for the charges themselves, the simple assertion of Soviet guilt was considered sufficient proof of it. Would an American State Department spokesman lie about the Soviets? That the Soviets didn't visibly deny the charges was even more proof that they were guilty. But the fact was that the Soviets did indeed deny the charges, as we have shown, and would continue to deny them.

In April 1982, the Soviet government would consider the charges made against Soviet forces in Afghanistan, Laos and Kampuchea serious enough to issue an official "note," sent to the United States government, in which it declared: "For a certain period of time a slanderous campaign is being conducted in the United States with the participation of governmental bodies with the aim of imputing to the USSR complicity in the supposed use of chemical weapons in Laos, Kampuchea and Afghanistan ... the USSR has never resorted to the use of chemical weapons anywhere itself and neither has it handed over such weapons to other countries... The United States ... needed all this slander to conceal its reluctance to conduct talks on the conclusion of an agreement prohibiting the development and production of chemical weapons and the destruction of stockpiles of them... More than that, the Government of the United States is working to undermine the existing accords in the field of arms limitation and blocking the attainment of new vitally important agreements..." (*Pravda,* Apr. 6, 1982.)

The feisty Soviet weekly, *Literary Gazette* (Apr. 8, 1980), would run a story exposing a story by the already-mentioned Michael Barry, whom it called "a highly professional misinformer"—I suppose that means liar—"and provocateur" who had charged [published in *Le Monde* (Paris), the *Christian Science Monitor* (Boston) and other news agencies] that "people are being poisoned from helicopters by gases of three varieties and are being burnt by napalm" in the village of Shinkorak, Kunar district in Afghanistan. The paper sent its own correspondent there to question villagers who reported no such incidents. Later, Mohammad Gulabzoi, Minister of the Interior for Afghanistan, would state that "I categorically reject the malicious concoctions which he also has made about the alleged abduction of Afghan women and children to the Soviet Union... I have already officially refuted the unscrupulous lies of that Michael Barry..."

It was no doubt on such "persistent" reports of the use of chemical warfare (not to mention the "abduction" of women and children) by the Soviets in Afghanistan that both present spokesmen for the State Department and ex-spokesmen, but still sentimentally attached, like Hodding Carter 3rd (as we shall see), referred to when they claimed to have found the incriminating evidence that warranted a fundamental change in U.S.-Soviet relations—"changed" though they already were.

For the layman, these wheels turning within wheels could only end up by giving him political vertigo. If your government lied, if the newspapers lied, if *you* lied even with your hand on the Bible, who was telling the truth, how could you *tell* what the truth was, and in any case did it really matter? One could still go on living one's life without knowing *exactly* what was true about Afghanistan, for example...

So there was confusion. But though there was confusion, and if precise knowledge of the facts didn't exist, at least skepticism about the facts presented to the public did exist. And it was this "persistent" skepticism, like a poltergeist, that General Haig couldn't abide, and explains why now, like

Lady Macbeth (or a frustrated dry-cleaner), he rode around the world crying, "Out, damned spot!"

All that could be done was increase the "flow" of stories charging the Soviets with using chemicals in Southeast Asia. If the quality of the proof fell short of convincing, perhaps the sheer volume alleging it existed might do the trick.

The target for such fabrications is not the Soviets alone. It is the American people as well. And that is the reason why Americans should not shy from pressing a case that seems to exonerate the Soviets when in fact it saves the American people from untold tragedy. For it is the American people who are inundated with "Russian" yellow rain and the "rain" that fell on their heads (and into their brains) is no true rain, and the same lie that endangers the peace of the Soviets endangers the peace of the Americans no less.

GAS!

> Facts were never pleasing to him. He acquired them
> with reluctance and got rid of them with relief. He
> was never on terms with them until he had stood them
> on their heads.
>
> James M. Barrie,
> *Love Me Never or Forever*

But if the enormous resources of the U.S. military intelligence proved unable to come up with any substantial evidence that they "could put on the table"* despite the fact that literally hundreds, if not thousands, of "witnesses" had "seen" gas attacks, little Afghanistan had no such problem at all.

In fact, you might say the evidence was brought to the Afghans unsolicited—dropped on their tables without being asked. Not only did they have "projectiles" and "bombs" to "put on the table", they were overburdened with such evidence and preferred not to have so much thrust on them.

On June 6, 1980 (and even an earlier incident in May), it was reported (and gleefully confirmed by rebel sources) that a combined total of 2,069 of Kabul's schoolchildren had been gassed and their drinking water poisoned. Not only that. Those guilty of the crime—five men and two women— were caught in June. The evidence of their criminality was produced at their trial in October 1980. They confessed. They were brought before the journalists. They told the world press that they had been working for the Islamic Alliance for the Liberation of Afghanistan, how they had been recruited, what they had done and where they got hold of the poison pellets to poison the drinking water with.

Samples of poison vials (with markings showing that they originated in the U.S.A. and also some in China) were lined up. False passports were produced. Foreign currency was unearthed. Short-wave radios. And other paraphernalia which all well-coached sabotage teams are routinely equipped with by the CIA and other intelligence coaches falling over each other's heels in Peshawar to be at their service.

---

* In the November 1980 issue of *Soldier of Fortune* appeared this ad: "$100,000 Reward from Soldier of Fortune for the first Communist Pilot to defect with intact samples of chemical and/or biological warfare agents." Still trying.

All this evidence which could be seen, touched and—if one was moved to—tasted was the kind of evidence the entire U.S. Intelligence had been trying to get their hands on for years! All they needed to do, of course, was to go to the same sources as these caught saboteurs did—themselves.

On March 25, 1980, some 60 kilometers from Herat, a unit of the Afghan army blundered upon a group of counterrevolutionaries in a bus. The counterrevolutionaries panicked, opened fire, and most of them were wiped out in the exchange. Inside the bus they were riding, the Afghan government soldiers found crates of grenades, which on further examination turned out to be gas grenades. The aim of the counterrevolutionaries had been to use them in Herat. These grenades were marked: "Manufactured by Federal Laboratories, Saltsburg, Pennsylvania, U.S.A., 1978."

An Afghan chemistry expert, Gulyam Djelani by name, explains: "The grenades contain CS gas, a multipurpose toxic agent. A burning sensation in the eyes is followed by tears, salivation, vomiting and pains in the spine. The victim is rendered helpless." (Press Conference in Kabul, April 10, 1980.) (If indeed the Soviets had been "detected" as bringing decontamination equipment into Afghanistan, as Hodding Carter, 3rd, was to charge so ominously in January, this would be the reason for it, among others.)

Bagram Ali, one of those captured, is asked: "Are these the grenades you had on the bus?"

"That's right."

"Did you know that they contained toxic chemicals?"

"Yes, they showed us how to handle them."

"They" were his teachers back in Pakistan, most likely CIA experts or those trained by the CIA. Though these details are from *Pravda*, facts are given, names are named, the whole of it amounting to considerably more than a "leaf and a twig." More than that, of course, was the fact of the poisoned and gassed children who were taken by the hundreds to the hospitals. Charges of U.S. complicity in these crimes were made by the Afghan government and routinely denied by the American government. Nevertheless, further reports of the use of nerve gas in and around Herat would "persist," with accusations being made by the Afghans that Herat had been deliberately chosen by the CIA as a proving ground to try out such weapons in May, June and July 1980.

American correspondents, while sure that the Soviets were using chemicals against the rebels, bemoaned the fact that no "canisters" could be found to prove it. This flaw in the flow of accusations somehow never seemed to embarrass but only to vex the perpetrators.

And yet, wherever chemicals had been used, *really* used, the evidence was not only there for any with eyes to see, it couldn't be avoided, and not just for a moment but for years to come. The State Department spokesman

Richard Burt had carefully specified that no Western country of the "industrialized world" has used chemicals to kill "unsophisticated and defenseless" people for "five years." He didn't explain the five-year cut-off date, but of course even unsophisticated Westerners (not to speak of the "defenseless" Easterners) knew why: an earlier date would run into the "syndrome" of Vietnam.

Evidence? Here is what the U.S.A. did in Vietnam, as Ha Van Lau, the Vietnamese delegate to the U.N., would detail it in December 1980:

The U.S. had dropped "14,500,000 tons of bombs and shells, 100,000 tons of toxic substances, including chemical means of affecting the environment ... were used for the sake of promoting a policy aimed at burning, wrecking and destroying everything. Forty-three percent of the country's arable areas was contaminated by poisonous chemical substances."

Said Assistant Secretary of State Dixon Donnelly, U.S. Government spokesman, during the Vietnamese war:

> Chemical herbicides are being used in Vietnam to clear jungle growth and to reduce the hazards of ambush by Viet Cong forces...

More than ten years later, the use of chemical warfare in Vietnam by the U.S.A. was still there to be seen in the denuded jungles, in the children born with biological defects. Yevgeny Verlin, TASS correspondent, who visited Vietnam in 1982, would report:

> The trees are like ghosts, without leaves and often without branches, just bare trunks. Dead groves, and woods that give no shade and no cool. The scene has an eerie ghostlike atmosphere about it.
>
> Yet it is the reality in the province of Tay Ninh in South Vietnam, whose people and nature were the victims of the Pentagon's operation code-named "Ranch-Hand." In 1961-71 about 100,000 tons of military purpose chemical defoliants and herbicides were dropped on Vietnam soil...
>
> In a group of pre-school children nearby we see a girl with accreted (joined) fingers on her hands. She will reach school age in autumn and will never be able to hold a pen... As I left the place it occurred to me that I had not seen a single butterfly to add to my collection... (*Moscow News*, No. 18, 1982.)

Facts and more facts. On July 26, 1981, Fidel Castro charged in a speech that a plague of dengue fever, which had swept over Cuba in 1981, killing 113 people of 300,000 who fell ill, "may have been introduced into Cuba by the CIA."

Newsday reported on January 8, 1977, that "with at least the tacit backing of U.S. Central Intelligence Agency officials, operatives linked to anti-Castro terrorists introduced African swine fever virus into Cuba in 1971," which forced the slaughter of 500,000 pigs. (Quoted by *Counterspy*, Nov. 1981-Jan. 1982.)

Laos was sprayed with chemicals in 1965—200,000 gallons of herbicides were dumped on those, as the sensitive Mr. Burt of the State Department would call them, "defenseless, primitive peoples"—on orders from General William G. Westmoreland, the National Veterans Task Force on Agent Orange would reveal in January 1982.

General Haig, who served in Vietnam, knew all about chemical warfare. He was there when the U.S. occupation forces practically drenched parts of Vietnam with lethal chemicals that left behind unparalleled devastation, not only poisoning the wells and the streams but human genes.

Haig was also on the staff of General MacArthur in Japan after World War II, and helped cover up Japan's biological and chemical warfare atrocities committed by Japan's Kwantung Army Unit 731 and Unit 100 under Lieut. General Ishii Shiro which operated under such disarming titles as Water Supply and Prophylaxis Administration, Hippo-Epizootic Administration, and so on. In actual fact, Unit 731 had 4,500 incubators which produced 45 kilograms of fleas in about 4 months. It also lovingly cultivated an army of 13,000 rats and planned to raise the rodent population under its care to 3 million. Unit 731 was so efficient it could boast of producing 30 billion germs in one production cycle, which broke down to 300 kilograms of plague germs, 600 kilograms of anthrax, 900 kilograms of typhoid and a ton of cholera germs a month!

These grisly details of Japanese wartime crimes have come to light in the West only lately, particularly with the publication of a book, *Devil's Gluttony,* by Seiichi Morimura in Japan in 1982, some of whose revelations were echoed by CBS' "60 Minutes" on April 4, 1982, under "War Crimes," with Morley Safer reading the script.

The Japanese secret chemical warfare program rivaled the Nazis (with whom they were allied) and was no doubt inspired by them. In any case, their victims were mainly Chinese and Soviet prisoners of war. *But also some American!* None survived. All records were obliterated except those captured by the Soviets at Anta Station in Manchuria. Twelve captured Japanese officials in charge of the program were brought to trial by the Soviets at Khabarovsk in 1949. One of the accused at that trial, Chief of the Medical Administration of the Kwantung Army, General Kajitsuka, would reveal that "Ishii told me . . . that it was much more effective to drop bacteria not in their 'bare' shape but in conjunction with an insect medium, fleas in particular. Fleas, being the most tenacious insects, were infected with plague and dropped from aircraft, and the plague germs, remaining in the fleas, successfully reached the ground with them." He added: "Ishii told me that in the research in this field the germs of cholera, dysentery, typhoid and partiphoid were being used, and that vegetables, fruit, fish and meat were so infected." (From *Materials on the Trial of*

Former Servicemen of the Japanese Army Charged with Manufacturing and Employing Bacteriological Weapons, Moscow, 1950.)

Though the Soviets invited the Americans to proceed with trials of their own based on evidence already in the hands of Americans, they found the Americans extremely reluctant to do so. During the trial of Japanese war criminals in Tokyo in August 1946, evidence of Japanese atrocities, especially the criminal experiments of Unit 1644 (Tama), was cut off with the American statement: "We do not at this time anticipate additional evidence on that subject;" and when Joseph B. Keenan, chief American prosecutor, was handed further information by the Soviet prosecution of Japanese chemical warfare crimes, he ignored it. Nor was the chief organizer of the whole criminal program, Lieut. General Ishii Shiro, ever brought to trial, nor was the Emperor Hirohito, who had given the order for the program in the first place.

The reason why Ishii Shiro was never brought to trial was because he had already struck a bargain with the Americans. In return for his safety he readily cooperated with the Americans in transferring the Japanese experience to the Americans and, in fact, remained in charge of the American program at Fort Detrick until he retired.

POISONING THE U.S.A.

Fair is foul, and foul is fair:
Hover through the fog and filthy air.

William Shakespeare,
Macbeth

That the United States, or rather the political factions that shuttle in and out of the White House, has no moral compunctions or principled objection to the use of chemicals and biological weapons that could kill masses of people, nobody even bothers to deny today.

Genocide has been established since at least 1945 (though it had its precedents in the destruction of the tribal system of Indians years earlier) as acceptable American policy with the atomic bombing of Hiroshima and Nagasaki. This policy was confirmed in the later attempt to destroy vast areas of Vietnam and Cambodia. Even in the still earlier Korean war (1950-53), accusations of the use of chemicals and biological weapons against the Korean people were voiced.

Such charges were contemptuously dismissed by the American press at the time. But much has happened since that cannot be so facilely shrugged off. For though crimes in foreign countries where the witnesses are all suspect may be covered up, it's not as easy to cover up crimes committed at home on thousands of Americans, living (and dead) witnesses all. Exposes in the 60s and 70s of secret government records—records that were never supposed to see daylight—revealed behind-the-scenes "tests" conducted by the military through the 1950s and 1960s on selected sections of the American population, who were turned into unknowing guinea pigs—experiments of a magnitude and irresponsibility that even now boggles the imagination. "In the 1977 testimony to a Senate health subcommittee the Army said that 80 of 239 tests included some sort of disease-producing agent. The tests were conducted in Washington, New York City, Key West and Panama City, Fla., and San Francisco. . ." (Bill Richards, WP, Sept. 17, 1979.)

That information—as well as other—came to light under the freedom of Information Act as requested by the Church of Scientology. The plan was contained in a 71-page report of the Army's Special Operations Division at Fort Detrick, Maryland.

When still other closed doors of the open society were reluctantly opened, they would reveal that both the military and the CIA had engaged in an extensive program, completely secret, in which an entire range of experimental chemicals was tried out on the unsuspecting guinea-pig public.

"Wash. Sept. 2 (1977)—The Central Intelligence Agency said today that it had discovered 10,000 additional documents describing its secret research on control of human behavior, which was conducted from 1943 to the mid-1950s. The discovery vastly increases the amount of information to be made public about the research projects, code-named Bluebird and Artichoke."

Not the least remarkable thing about these "projects" was that, though they involved dozens of universities, their laboratory staffs, university heads and eminent professors, all of them assumed their roles in the conspiracy as if rehearsed to it, and though the secret experimentation was known to literally hundreds, if not thousands, no word got out to the general public. All involved in them knew the experiments were illegal. All personnel accepted their roles without apparently much interior struggle. The only thing necessary to convince most of them that it was permissible to perjure themselves, to commit fearful crimes in a conspiracy against their own people, was an appeal to their class loyalties, disguised as "national security." [Those looking for the "secret" to the earlier German moral corruption that led to later crematoria need look no further: it is to be found in their own living rooms.]

At no time was the use of chemicals by American armed forces in Vietnam a deep secret. Government officials would be quoted, early in the war, as saying, with the air of experts, that one killed buffalo meant that nine Vietcong who depended for sustenance on the buffalo were put out of commission. But by the time war against Vietnam had become a public fact, with the forged Tonkin Bay Resolution of 1964 (the war had been conducted secretly and illegally for years), those who had consented to spreading disease germs over San Francisco *(Serratia maraescens)* had no moral compunctions about killing off "gooks" in Vietnam by the same process. The subsequent devastation in Vietnam was of genocidal proportions (10.6 million gallons of Agent Orange sprayed over large areas of South Vietnam), though, as we shall soon see, easily dismissed by government spokesmen as nothing more invidious than the "sins"* that a mischief-loving people might unwittingly commit when their penchant for practical jokes and boyish hijinks got out of hand.

Again, though Vietnamese suffered (as did the victims of Hiroshima and Nagasaki) and will suffer unto the tenth generation,** if they endure

---

* "Sins" which are expiated in the confessional box quickly make way for a "syndrome" which is expiated on the analyst's couch—you pays your money and you takes your choice.

** Dr. Bui Chi Hung told journalists (Jan. 21, 1982) in Ho Chi Minh City that congenital malformations had increased five times over 1950, miscarriages 10 times, and stillbirths by two or three times. He was speaking of Vietnam.

that long, Americans, too, suffered, and Agent Orange became almost a household word in the 80s, some ten years after the end of the Vietnam war. Like many other aspects of life about which most Americans preferred to remain in studied ignorance (like how to determine if your 13-year-old son is on drugs), being forced to learn why Vietnamese veterans produced deformed children long after they had left Vietnam was not a part of their education that they took much pleasure in acquiring. The air had been poisoned in Vietnam which only the Vietnamese villagers were supposed to breathe. But American soldiers (95,000)* also breathed it.

The American drive—it was almost a palpable ache—to convict the Soviets of the use of chemicals in Southeast Asia, particularly Afghanistan, after such a record of their own in Vietnam, took on a special, practically macabre urgency with the advent of Reagan to power in Washington, and with him the super-fixer of all time, Alexander Haig.**

But it seemed that his efforts, while he was still in charge of such efforts in Washington, and the efforts of his successor, were fated to be frustrated, and not because the Soviets had managed to come up with a devastating rejoinder to the accusations made against them (though they made their protests, unheard here). But for another, even more powerful reason: capitalist contradictions. The grave they dug for the "enemy" they fell into themselves.

As long as a mutual understanding existed between the government and Dow Chemical corporation, which manufactured Agent Orange, as well as other potent chemicals used against dark-skinned, alien peoples, nobody who didn't need to know was told. In any case, who is there in America, sitting among the breakfast dishes, has a tear to shed for a Vietnamese mother whose child was born armless and eyeless and legless because she had breathed the American chemical by Dow whose Stock Market quotations made such pleasant reading?

But when it affected *American* boys, it was entirely different matter. Sleeping moral cells leaped into action. By 1973, it was acknowledged that thousands of Vietnam veterans had indeed been poisoned by Agent Orange

---

* AP, Oct. 28, 1982—More than 95,000 Vietnam veterans have gone to Veterans Administration hospitals for exams out of concern that exposure to the herbicide is damaging their health or causing birth defects in their offspring. Washington, May 3, (AP) [1983]—Vietnam veterans have made more than 369,000 visits to Veterans Administration hospitals for illnesses that could have been caused by Agent Orange, the Veterans Administration said today in its first report on the chemical's possible effect on American soldiers in Southeast Asia.

About 9,400 veterans were ill enough to require hospitalization ... the figures cover treatment from February 1982 to February 1983.

** Who had engineered the deal which got Ford into the presidency and Nixon out of jail.

while they served "their country" in faraway Vietnam. Finally, as their pleas for compensation fell on deaf ears, some 20,000 Vietnam vets in a class action suit charged Dow Chemical with having poisoned them and their children, now and in the future.

By this time, the entire country had been aroused to the fact that their environment had been poisoned by the criminal misuse of chemicals. The Love Canal case in Niagara, New York (1980), where a whole community had to flee their contaminated homes, became only one of many notorious cases of similar poisonings.

Dow Chemical, in answering the brief filed by the Vietnam Veterans, and facing enormous financial losses if found guilty (and juries were not friendly to such killers), declared that "at least two years before the United States halted the use of Agent Orange in Vietnam in 1971, both the Defense Department and the company were aware of evidence indicating that dioxin, a contaminant in the herbicide, might cause birth defects in the children of women exposed to the defoliant. . ."

The brief went on to say:

> Dow's motion also contended that in 1967 Secretary of Defense Robert S. McNamara referred to the joint Chief of Staff a consultant's report that said the fear of Vietnam peasants about the toxins of Agent Orange "was founded partly on actual experience, not solely on Vietcong propaganda." The recommendations of the consultant's report were ignored by the Government, Dow said. . .
>
> The company said the Government continued to spray the dioxin-contaminated herbicides in Vietnam despite evidence of the potential danger because the defoliant program was regarded as a military necessity. The Government justified the program as method of denying the Vietcong food and of clearing areas around American bases.
>
> Dow said that by 1969 it knew about the Government-sponsored animal test indicating that the dioxin in Agent Orange might damage the unborn children of exposed women. . .

So both were guilty—Dow Chemical and the "government" which bought the chemicals from them for a pretty penny. Dow Chemical lied in their public statements about the lethal nature of their chemicals, and not until the Veterans threatened to drag them into court, where they stood to lose millions, did their officers suddenly feel the impulse toward honesty that they were now overflowing with—or the kind of thing that passes for "honesty" in our day: when thieves fall out. . .

At Nuremberg, Nazi criminals who also gassed people had ended up swinging from a rope. In the U.S.A., to lose some money is considered punishment enough. To win some money is also considered retribution enough: morality can be cashed.

As for the deformed children. . .

IS THE U.S.S.R. ALSO IMPERIALIST?

> I have not become the King's First Minister
> in order to preside over the liquidation
> of the British Empire.
>
> Winston Churchill
>
> ...imperialism is the eve of the socia-
> list revolution.
>
> V. I. Lenin
>
> The policy and psychology of colonialism
> are alien to us.
>
> L. I. Brezhnev

The Soviet Union's real intentions toward Afghanistan—and the answer to the question: "Is the U.S.S.R. also imperialist?"—are to be found in its economic relations with that country.

Babrak Karmal, speaking at a Kremlin dinner in October 1980, remarked:

> The history of Afghan-Soviet relations is in the ascendant, being carried forward as it is day by day with new developments in the promotion of brotherhood, friendship and cooperation, advancing in an unprecedented way. There are many remarkable signs of this historic friendship of our peoples on Afghan soil.

In June 1981, *Kabul New Times* reported that 170 major industrial projects were being built in Afghanistan with the help of the Soviet Union.* With 57 percent of the nation's general production coming from agriculture, and another 11.5 percent from handicrafts, industrial production in Afghanistan before the 1978 Revolution was typically (typically for a backward country) extremely low and distortedly one-sided. Per capita income was well below $200 annually. The contribution of industry to the GNP (Gross National Product) amounted to a mere 3.2 percent. (No wonder that there

---

* In 1983, *New Times* (No. 16) would report:

> "Eighty of these are already successfully operating. Among them are the 100,000 kw Naghlu hydropower station, a nitrogen fertilizer plant at Mazari-Sharif with an annual capacity of over 100,000 tons of carbamide, an automobile repair works, a prefabricated housing factory and a mechanical bakery in Kabul, a gas pipeline from the Shibarghan areas to the Soviet border, an irrigation system in the Jalalabad area, several state farms, an oil storage at Hairaton port on the Amu Darya, the Lotus satellite communications station, motor roads, etc."

were only about 60,000 industrial workers in the country all told). Some 71.6 percent of the able-bodied worked in the countryside, though half of the cultivatable land in Afghanistan remained chronically untouched. Usury took most of the income of the peasants—who were required to pay 45 percent annual interest on their loans. One-third of the nation's peasants owned no land whatsoever but worked for the large landowner in a purely feudal relationship.

But this crippling one-sidedness, which reflected Afghanistan's dependence on a market dominated by imperialism, is being corrected today with Soviet planning and assistance, and some balance is being struck. Most Soviet aid has been aimed at constructing the industrial foundation on which a future industrial-agricultural society could be erected. Most such industrial enterprises, built with Soviet funds and technology, pay for themselves (as in the case of gas) by their products or in trade of other products which Afghanistan readily produces.

In May 1980, the opening of the new gas deposits in Jarkuduk was announced. Built with Soviet aid (Soviet geologists had located the deposit in the first place), the new works produced up to 2,000 million cubic meters of gas and nearly 15,000 tons of condensates a year, that is, doubling Afghanistan's annual production of these products.

In building the complex at Jarkuduk, "more than a thousand" Afghan specialists were also trained by Soviet experts. Production of gas from this new deposit made it feasible, for the first time, to pipe gas for home use in Afghan cities, as well as for producing nitrate fertilizers and other derivative products for industry and agriculture.

So profitable is Afghanistan's sale of natural gas to the Soviet Union that income from that source alone rose from 15 percent of Afghanistan's total revenues in 1978 to 21 percent in 1979, and to 34 percent in 1980. In making these figures public, Hafeezullah Navabi, President of the Afghan National Oil Company, pointed out that the high profits from such sales to the Soviet Union were made possible not only by prices pegged at world prices but because no great distances had to be traveled to deliver the gas, which flowed through pipes under natural pressure without the need of compressors. On March 30, 1981, a 30-percent rise in the price of gas was announced, reflecting the general rise in the price of gas throughout the world.

By July 1980, over 1,500 kilometers of Afghanistan's 2,800 kilometers of asphalt and concrete roads had been built with Soviet help, including the streets of Kabul itself. Soviets had been building roads for Afghanistan—which lacked railroads—since at least the 1950s. They had also had a hand in constructing a motor repairs works in Kabul, the airport, and in setting up pre-fabrication home-building factories. This last was particularly pressing in a country where most housing was not only substandard by civilized standards, but considered to be hardly more than hovels even by the standards of the peasants themselves. Housing was a crying need. New construction began soon after the 1978 Revolution, and with the advent of Karmal to power the pace stepped up.

Typically, in creating new projects and industries the Soviets not only supplied blueprints and materials and experts. They also trained Afghans on the job. Before and after the 1978 Revolution, by 1980 more than 72,000 Afghan workers had received on-the-job training at projects jointly built by the Soviets and Afghans. Meanwhile, hundreds, then thousands of Afghan students were sent to the U.S.S.R. for higher training, at the same time that the Soviets built and turned over to the Afghans the Kabul Institute of Technology where Afghan specialists were also trained. Before the revolution, tens of thousands of Afghan workers went abroad looking for work, much as workers still leave Pakistan and other countries.

Afghans export to the U.S.S.R. cotton, wool, raw hides, dried fruits, nuts, gas and other products abundantly produced in their own country—all of which pays for Soviet technology.

The Soviet Union has no transnational companies which not only "invest" in foreign countries but often take them over completely—economically if not always politically as well—and extract huge super-profits from the exploitation of low-paid labor.

> It is estimated that in 1981 the underdeveloped countries of Asia, Africa and Latin America paid the capitalist powers about 30,000 million dollars for the "acquisition" of technology. (Roberto Alvarez Guinones, *Granma*, Aug. 29, 1982.)

Contrasted to this, most Soviet foreign projects are financed by Soviet capital but are paid back by the Afghans, for instance (but this is typical of all repayments from Third World countries), in the *products* manufactured by these same newly-built industries.

That this is indeed typically the way in which the Soviet Union carries on business with socialist and developing countries nobody has been able to refute. Louis Dupree, generally considered an expert on Afghanistan, where he spent considerable time in various American governmental capacities (some of a dubious character), has admitted quite candidly, while he was still free to do so, that there was a profound difference in approach to Afghanistan between the Soviets and Americans, not only in social and cultural matters, but most pointedly in economic, in trade.

In his book, *Afghanistan* (Princeton University Press), he put it plainly enough. He was referring to pre-revolutionary Afghanistan (before 1978) when the Soviets had even less motives for generosity: "The primary difference between Soviet bloc and American loans is that the Afghans pay off many bloc debts in barter goods, whereas Western loans must be repaid in cash. Afghan barter payments include wool, food, oils, grains, cotton, goat and sheep skins and fresh, dried and canned fruits and nuts."

If one can pay for what one buys with those products one has a good supply of—*and not with cash*—how can anyone find fault with such an arrangement?

After listing many projects built with Soviet technological assistance, including vast irrigation complexes, all of these *before* the revolution of 1978—under both King Zahir and Prince Daoud—Dupree comments:

> Many foreign observers still believe that the Soviets wish to trap the Afghan economy, but I believe that Soviet patience, their liberal terms for loans, and their occasional extension of payments due belie this hard-core Cold War belief. Afghan exports to the U.S.S.R. still account for only about 40% of the total, and imports almost equal exports annually. The figures do not seem much out of balance when one considers that about 60% of all foreign assistance comes from the U.S.S.R., and that in the current Five-Year Plan (1967-1972), Russian aid accounts for 40% of the annual development budget, or about $32 million in 1967-68.

And what did American trade relations with Afghanistan look like?

> Somewhere in the mythology of (American) foreign aid arose the idea that all foreign assistance constituted give-away programs. Nothing could be further from the truth. Foreign aid, however, has always been a great boon for American businesses and educational institutions, as well as benefit of the recipient nations. Most of the money never leaves the U.S.A.... In addition, the products purchased in the U.S. almost always cost more than similar items purchased elsewhere ... many aided nations now actually repay loans or interest on loans into the U.S. coffers.

And the Soviets?

> On December 18, 1955, Moscow newspapers announced the Soviet Union had granted a $100-million long-term development loan to be used for projects determined by U.S.S.R.—Afghanistan survey teams...
> The official agreement, signed on January 28, 1956 stipulated the loan would be repaid *in barter goods at 2% interest* over a 30-year period in 22 equal installments. (My emphasis.)

In all the charges against the Soviet Union as "imperialist," "expansionist," etc., nobody bothers to explain just what it is *within* the Soviet Union —within its economic system, its social system—that *compels* it to an "expansionist," "aggressive" course. It seems to be taken for granted that the reason is self-evident: it is expansionist because it is Soviet. Does one have to explain why the Devil is evil?

At best, in advancing no rational reason for their charges, the accusers (whose hands are so dirty it's surprising to see them in this court) simply

236

let it be taken for granted that past bourgeois history sufficiently explains present socialist history. All great powers in the past were imperialist. The Soviet Union is a great power. Ergo, it is also imperialist. Q.E.D. A syllogism does for analysis and proof.

This theory—or lack of it, rather—explaining the motive force behind Soviet foreign policy is infinitely sterile in contrast to the Marxist theory accounting for the historical origins and development of Western imperialism and its aggressive colonialism and periodic wars of conquest for the division of the world's markets. Marxist theory, based solidly on a materialist reading of history in its dialectical development, documented meticulously in various major economic works, starting chiefly with Lenin's classic *Imperialism, the Highest Stage of Capitalism* (1920), proves that imperialism grows inevitably out of that last stage—its monopoly stage—in the development of capitalism when its drive for maximum profits—which is its true *fatum*— moves it to export capital to those areas of the world where maximum returns can be expected, and in the process creates the conditions that inevitably lead to colonial revolts. "Where your treasure is, there will be your heart also," according to St. Mark. He could have added: and your troops, Peace Corps, CIA, and various Sixth and Seventh fleets as well. In contrast, the U.S.S.R., in 1960, moved a resolution in the U.N. for universal decolonization, which was overwhelmingly approved of.

But "imperialism" is not just a curse; it is an economic phenomenon with a precise history, which can be observed objectively. To be taken seriously those who call the Soviets' entry into Afghanistan "imperialist" and not the response of a friendly neighbor coming to the assistance of another in grave peril from outside marauders, have the burden of proving not only that the Soviet Union *exploits* Afghanistan (or any other country it has economic dealings with) but that socialism itself gives rise to imperialism— if true, an historic discovery with profound consequences indeed!

There is *no* dominant class in the U.S.S.R. that *must* expand its rate of profit or die—no *fatum* like Britain's need to trade that drove her to foreign conquests so world-embracing that the British could finally boast that the sun never set on it.

There is no proof whatsoever that the wealth created by the Soviet people through their own efforts is appropriated by a native exploiting class in its—opposed to the people's—own interests. As a state of the whole people, as a society with no antagonistic classes, the wealth created by the whole people is disposed of by the whole people in its own interests. That this is truly so is a fatal blow to world imperialism. For *if* the Russian revolution had indeed gone into a Thermidorean reaction and had reconstituted Czarist imperialism in a new guise, there would have been no particularly difficult problem in this for world imperialism. Like it or not, still the reality could be accommodated to. But the visceral hatred which imperialism bears for the Soviet Union is not because the Soviet Union is a new rival for the old colonial pie, already divided up, hungrily wanting to wrest a share for itself from those who already have it all. But the Soviet Union, in ending its own Czarist imperialism, struck a body blow to imperialism in general. Imperialism—German imperialism—was weakened fatally in World War II (as were Japanese and the nascent Italian), and in thus proving that these imperialisms could be ended the Soviets opened up a great new vista of hope for those colonial countries throughout the world still in thrall to Western imperialism. It stands today as an inspiration—and the word is no rhetorical exaggeration—to those neo-imperialist-dominated countries still struggling for their real freedom, though they have an ostensible political independence they can boast of.

From its very inception as a more or less independent country, certainly since 1919 when Afghanistan, under the Emir, declared its independence, it has leaned on the Soviet Union for the necessary economic and military means to ensure that independence *in fact*.

The chain of hostile states on the southeast border of the U.S.S.R. which stretched from Turkey through Pakistan and then to Iran needed only Afghanistan to be complete, and the aim of American foreign policy, certainly since Dulles began erecting his CENTOs and SEATOs in the 50s, has been to complete that chain and confront the U.S.S.R. with a permanent threat there.

Any leadership in any country which ignored such a peril to their country's security would be considered criminally irresponsible, and when Daoud, in the 1970s, began to depart from the country's traditional non-aligned policy which was based on friendship with the U.S.S.R., he knew that this step was fraught with great danger for himself as well. Even so, there is no evidence to prove that the Soviets had any connection with his overthrow in 1978, any more than there is proof that the Soviets masterminded the overthrow of Somoza in Nicaragua or had a finger in the JEWEL movement which brought Grenada out of the shadows of American imperialism, though once in power the revolutionary forces in both these (and other) countries turned to the U.S.S.R. for aid and support.

While genuine imperialist countries take over—or heavily influence—the banking and financial systems of the subject countries they deal with, and with their transnationals determine what kind of industry and commerce will prevail in those countries, this is not so with the U.S.S.R. where "banking and financial interests" do not form an independent, autonomous and most powerful force determining, in the last analysis, political decisions. Thus, even to qualify for loans from the International Monetary Fund and World Bank (dominated by the U.S.A.) "heavily indebted countries" (mainly the Third World) must "agree to a long period of economic belt-tight-ening. . . What it means is a set of measures for debt-plagued nations that are intended to increase their foreign exchange earnings and thus their ability to repay debts, but at the expense of such things as subsidies for food, housing and other domestic social programs." (NYT, Sept, 11, 1982.) The U.S.S.R. is not a member of the IMF or World Bank nor, for that matter, is it a member of any Stock Exchange, domestic or foreign: it has no stocks to sell or buy.

Imperialism does not aim to create an industry owned and operated by native forces serving national ends. Nor is it keen on giving birth to a working class in backward peasant countries, knowing by now that it is this modern working class, equipped with a revolutionary vision, which is a mortal threat to colonial power. Imperialism aims to create an economy in its "client" countries which remains weak and dependent on its own power, and has as little of a working class as it possibly can and yet produces a profit for itself. It "drains" off the native intelligentsia, sometimes trained at home, sometimes abroad, and in a profoundly vital sense deprives the subject countries of those scientific and educated forces without whom progress is impossible —this, too, is a grim species of colonialism, though it flaunts the flag of generosity. To staff American hospitals with doctors from India and Pakistan while in those countries millions go begging for medical aid is not an act of generosity but a form of trafficking in stolen brains.

In its January 31 (1981) issue, the Cuban newspaper *Granma* noted that over the past 15 years alone the capitalist states had lured away from their native, mainly Third World, countries about 300,000 scientists, engineers, physicians and other specialists badly needed at home but where they could not earn as good a living as was possible in the Western countries. The United States, Britain and Canada have absorbed 245,000 of that total. The United States alone has saved some $5 billion in educational and training costs over 25 years of such "brain drain." Latin America annually loses eight percent of its technical specialists, and 20 percent of its specialists in the natural sciences, in this way.

But imperialism not only directly drains subject countries of profits, brains and labor. It also takes over the means of education, communication and mass culture. The American UPI and AP between them "service" (in 1980) 114 and 110 countries respectively with "news." In fact, the four great Western news agencies, which include Reuters of Britain and Agence France-Presse, maintain (in 1980) 48,000 offices around the world and provide 90 percent of the international news that's either printed or broadcast. The non-aligned countries, for instance, take 65 percent of their TV and radio programs from the West (mainly the U.S.A.) and most of their news.

Called, not surprisingly, "information imperialism," just as in the past (and still) the cross followed the sword into the colonial world, today TV follows capital investment. Though the idea of millions of ex-colonial peoples, still barely literate, watching "I Love Lucy" on their local TVs, with dubbed-in dialog in their native languages, might warm the cockles of the corporate and imperialist heart, it takes no tyro in education and mass culture to suppose that such children, taught in such a way to accept American bourgeois values by the most powerful educational influence in history, are not to be envied. "The more a ruling class is able to assimilate the foremost minds of a ruled class, the more stable and dangerous becomes its rule," Karl Marx had already noted.[*]

Not only were Third World countries caught in a scissors (low prices for their raw material for export and high prices for finished goods they imported), which mercilessly sheared them of their wealth ("The estimated external-debt service payments owed by many of them in 1983 is more than 100 percent of their revenues from exported goods and services." Robert S. McNamara, NYT, May 27, 1983), but they also served as a dumping ground for products condemned in the U.S.A. as menaces to the health of the American public.

In addition to making money from poisoning the people of their host country, American entrepreneurs profited in other ways. The low wages they paid native workers, plus the preferential tariff charges, made it possible to knock down an additional profit from goods sold *in the United States* from which they had fled with the devil of decent wages and decent environmental provisions pursuing them! This arrangement had the added charm of undercutting the wages of American workers—those still employed—thus driving the standard of living closer to the survival bone.

In any case, the ex-colonial world was not profiting however the loaf was sliced. It was fast slipping behind in the race for food production; it kept losing position after position in the world market, where the price of its products was cynically manipulated by the powers in the capitalist countries.

Jeffrey E. Garten, a vice-president of a New York investment banking firm, writes: "The debt of developing nations has reached an untenable $500 billion.[**] Prices for their exports, adjusted for inflation, are the lowest in 30 years. The future looks bleak... Third World countries will need more than $100 billion this year and again in 1983 to pay for essential imports and to pay off debts. Foreign leaders, reeling from bad loans, will not soon turn on the tap." (NYT, Aug. 29, 1982.)

---

[*] *Capital*, Vol. III.
[**] "Developing nations owe roughly $600 billion to governments and commercial banks." (NYC, Apr. 19, 1983.)

It would seem that in such a situation any self-effort to get out of such a quagmire would be welcomed by those countries blessed with cooler suns, who find poverty confined to the "southern" parts of the world and affluence to the north. But every concrete effort to do so by these small ex-colonial countries turned out to the the wrong effort. In today's historical context the struggle for political independence is the struggle for economic independence—one is impossible without the other. But each such attempt to break loose from crippling, sometimes strangling economic chains was (and is) resisted by all imperialist powers, and most fiercely by the U.S.A., which has taken on itself the onus of world policeman.

What concretely is the Soviet Union's economic relationship to the countries it has dealings with? For here is where the crucial difference is to be found between nations, and will prove whether in fact they are predatory—imperialist—or have established a mutually beneficial, equal relationship, friendly in form and essence, i.e. socialist.

At a press conference in Moscow, March 2, 1981, Vadim Zagladin, first deputy head of the International Department of the Central Committee of of the CPSU, told foreign journalists (including myself) that "the U.S.S.R. gives aid to a number of developing states, including military aid. We do not and did not have any bases on the territory of Third World countries. We do not create any military outposts. We assist the people of those countries in defending their gains.

"Sometimes we are reproached by those who say that the Soviet economic aid in percentage ratio to our national income is allegedly smaller than the aid which is rendered, let's say, by the U.S.A. This is not true. If you take all the developed countries to which we are giving assistance and among them are such states as Mongolia, Vietnam, Laos, Kampuchea and Cuba, and if you take the sum total of our aid—it is greater in percentage terms than the U.S.A. aid to the developing countries. Its characteristic feature is that we do not make investments, do not strive to capitalize. The whole of our aid is aimed at assisting the people in their economic development."

Zagladin's claims seemed to be substantiated, if indirectly, from that same McNamara, who in February 1982—in words significant for a former Defense Secretary—would say:

> The Reagan Administration's response to the needs of the third world was challenged in a report published today by the Overseas Development Council, and by the Council's chairman, Robert S. McNamara, former President of the World Bank.
>
> The report ... says that the United States should make a greater commitment to development aid and place less emphasis on military or strategic considerations.
>
> The report, "U.S. Foreign Policy and the Third World: Agenda, 1982", says the United States has fallen almost to the bottom of the list of 17 donor

nations in the Organization of Economic Cooperation and Development in the ratio of development aid to gross national product... (NYT, Feb. 28, 1982.)

While the frantic search for "security" began to reach paranoic levels, as a river of "credits" to foreign countries, followed by the establishment of military and naval bases—about 1,500* of them in 39 countries (500 major ones) as the 80s opened—threatened to put half the world's military on Uncle Sam's payroll, exploitation of ex-colonial, "poor" nations did not cease. While plundering the workers and peasants of the Third World countries with one hand, the other hand was kept busy buying off their ruling juntas. But the plundering continued, as can be seen by comparing the following interest rates—to only cite those—charged by the various plundering "industrialist" countries and those charged by the Soviet Union.

Interest on Soviet credits to all socialist and developing countries currently (1982) range from 3.25 to 5 percent. West German interest (in 1980) came at a rate of 13 percent, the British took 14 percent, and Uncle Sam the biggest out of all—18 to 20 percent. The Soviet Union has a special rate for some countries—for the Cubans the interest on their debts is 0.5 to 2 percent.

But, as already noted, investments or loans to developing countries also differ. The loans from Western banks (including the World Bank) go to those enterprises that are profitable, often tied to the military, but not necessarily basic to the country's real needs. Soviet loans go to develop basic industry, without which no country can hope to build an independent economy.

By the end of 1981, interest on the Third World foreign debt, according to estimates by the World Bank, stood at more than $62 billion, most of it owed to U.S. banks. In the months that followed, the situation continued to get worse. Third World countries paid 23 percent of their income from exports for debt service. "The trend toward deterioration of this situation is also seen in the increase in the interest paid, which averaged 30.3 percent from 1971 to 1981 and rose to 33.7 percent in the last two years, when floating interest rates climbed from 12.3 percent to 18 percent." A one-percent rise in interest rates reflects a rise in debt service costs by $2 billion. "In 1980, 39.6 percent of the foreign debt was concentrated in the Latin American countries; 18.1 percent in Southeast Asia; 16 percent in North Africa and the Middle East; 13.9 percent in sub-Saharan Africa; and 12.4 percent in southern Asia... At the same time, every dollar invested made a profit of 2.37 dollars which went to the developed countries." (Dr. Jose Luis Rodriguez, Asst. Editor of the Center for Research on the World Economy, *Granma,* Sept. 26, 1982.)

---

* U.S. forces abroad totalled 543,400 in 1982.

242

The very opposite is true where the U.S.S.R. is concerned. Typically, the Soviets concentrate their aid on those basic industries which are essential in any country for establishing an independent economy. It consciously helps to bring a working class into existence and then helps to train it, not only to run its industry but to rule the state as well. This is not theory. Abundant experience has accumulated to prove that this is applied policy which has worked well (Mongolia is a dramatic example).

In a speech delivered to the 68th Inter-Parliamentary Conference in Havana, September 15, 1981, Fidel Castro, in his capacity of Chairman of the Movement of Non-Aligned Countries, made the charge that the relationship between the undeveloped, backward, "Third World" and developed capitalist countries has dramatically worsened for the Third World in the last 10 years.

Among other things, he pointed out that in the underdeveloped world the number of undernourished who live in acute hunger amounts to 570 million; there are 800 million illiterate adults, 1.5 billion who have no medical care, and 1.3 billion with an annual income of less than $90. Some 1.7 billion cannot expect to live to 60. Some 1.03 billion live in unfit housing, and some 250 million children never go to school at all. The unemployed total stands at about 1.103 billion.

Those who split hairs in their view of what moral rules such countries should be allowed to follow before earning their approval should be forced to answer the question: in what way do their "democratic" "human rights" standards apply to the billions of people the world over who never reach the voting age?

The illiterate, superstition-ridden Afghan peasant can hardly care who is up or who is down, who is king or who is majority-elected president if his lot never improves under any of these. Imperialism is a reality translated into hunger and early death for him. *Every* attempt to save a child from starvation inevitably strikes a blow against American imperial interests. The reason why Americans are rich is because the millions they keep in economic subjection are poor. The simple fact is that for humanity to survive it *must* combat American imperialism: this is the sad state to which capitalism has brought America.

WHEN PEACE COMES

> I labor for peace, but when I speak unto them
> thereof: they make them ready for battle.
>
> *Psalms*

Reading the American press on Afghanistan in the years since Karmal came to power, one gets the impression of a country divided into two lopsided halves: nine-tenths of it dominated by the "holy warriors" who control the countryside apparently populated with murdered teachers and dead cattle and landscaped with burnt fields; and the other one-tenth—or rather the two or three blocks in central Kabul—occupied by a band of terrified Russian puppets, themselves divided into deadly enemies but jumping to the Soviet whip, and yet so ineffectual that they can't even shoot themselves when they try!

Wherever the Russians are there is rape, killing, pillage—apparently they take turns with the *Mujahiddin* in devastating the countryside. Though equipped with enormous firepower, gas and diabolical chemical weapons, they are totally ineffective against the freedom-fighters equipped with hardly more than speeches by Ronald Reagan. Fanatical peasants, sent nobly into battle by their masters from Peshawar, die happily with "God is great!" on their lips—and visions of 12-year-old wives in their minds' eyes!

That being the case, there's very little a canny opposition is called upon to do except wait until the whole thing collapses of its own evil and then go in and erect a democratic system à la South Vietnam of recent memory and South Korea of still more recent. And yet, though Christmas always seems near and the sugar plums of victory are practically in one's grasp, why is it that Report No. 9 issued by the U.S. State Department in December 1981 notes (though demurely) only that "the Afghan nationalist movement has made considerable progress in consolidating its position in Afghanistan and improving its military capabilities"? But, that "It continues, however, to be highly fragmented, and therefore lacks the advantage of centralized strategic planning and the international stature of a viable alternative national political movement"?

What's this? Why is it, if the cause is so holy, and the internal opposition so weak, that the "holy warriors" remain "highly fragmented" and unable to present the world with a united, "viable" movement with "stature"—and this, not just after two months of trying but after *two years?*

Every one of the six (sometimes seven) leading counterrevolutionary gangs has its specific origin, its supporters, its beliefs, but all have the same aim: to come out on top. They view each other with deep suspicion and consider the other's ambitions as a direct threat to their own. In their rivalry for power the "enemy" tends to grow dim. In fact, if it seems that one group would most likely benefit from "victory," it is that group that becomes the nearer enemy. "Victory" is not, in any case, their real aim, and "victory" would undo them. For most of the "resistance groups" in Afghanistan the defeat of the Karmal government would mean defeat for them as well.

American officials responsible for American policy in Afghanistan continue to put on a positive face to the problem, but the cold fact is that there is no feasible exit from the Afghan dilemma that will warm their hearts. In fact, as time wears on it becomes more and more obvious that they know this and don't expect anything to evolve out of the conflict that can be called "victory." What they hope to do is to wreak as severe a "punishment" on the Russians as they can, keep the pot boiling in Southern Asia for whatever political benefits can be steamed out of it, and hope, if they stick to it, events will hang some unforeseen serendipity favors on their Christmas tree after all.

From practically the moment Soviet troops entered Afghanistan, Leonid Brezhnev was saying that it

> is absolutely false ... that the Soviet Union has expansionist plans with regard to Pakistan, Iran or other countries in the area. The policy and mentality of colonialism are alien to us. We do not covet the lands or wealth of others. It is the colonialists who are attracted by the smell of oil. (*Pravda*, Jan. 15, 1980).

He put the Soviet policy clearly:

> When making the request to us, Afghanistan proceeded from the clear-cut provisions of the Treaty of Friendship, Good-Neighborliness and Cooperation, concluded by Afghanistan and the U.S.S.R. in December 1978, from the right of each state, in accordance with the United Nations Charter, to individual or collective self-defense—a right that other states have exercized many times.

He might have added that Amin was the head of the Afghan government at the time—that same Amin whom Carter would call the only "legitimate" president of Afghanistan—thus making the request for Soviet aid even more "legitimate." Whatever happened to him later cannot erase the fact that in making his original request for Soviet aid he was acting legally.

Said Brezhnev:

> It goes without saying that there had been no Soviet "intervention" or "aggression" whatsoever... The national interests of security of the United

States of America and other states are in no way affected by the events in Afghanistan.

In fact, Brzezinski had said as much in April 1979, when he told the *U.S. News & World Report* that Afghanistan "was remote from the reach of U.S. power," although by then a Marxist government was already there, presumably as "menacing" to American interests as seemed to become much more the case when Karmal came to power just a few months later. Was it possible that Brzezinski's complacency about Afghanistan's danger to the world had "solid" ground to stand on as long as Amin was in power?

In any case, Brezhnev would point out that "the events in Afghanistan are not the true cause of the present complication of the international situation. If there were no Afghanistan, certain circles in the United States, in NATO, would surely have found another pretext to aggravate the situation in the world."

What had happened was that a political decision had been taken in the West to "draw the line." Carter would draw the line in Afghanistan and Haig would draw it later in San Salvador, where it was as impossible to hang revolutionary complicity on the Soviets (though he tried) as it was to deduce a policy of chemical warfare from a stem and a twig.

"We can only regard the actions of the American Administration as a poorly weighed attempt to use the events in Afghanistan for blocking international efforts to lessen the military danger, to strengthen peace, to restrict the arms race, in short for blocking the attainment of aims in which mankind is vitally interested," Brezhnev would point out. *(Ibid.)*

The Soviets had declared at the moment of their entry into Afghanistan that they would leave when the danger to the Afghan government had ended. In June 1980, they had taken some units of its army out of Afghanistan as a gesture of goodwill inviting the Americans, in the first place, to match this action by withdrawing counterrevolutionary forces from Pakistan. The invitation was refused.

Fred Halliday, who paid a visit to Afghanistan in 1980, seems to come as close to the reality there as nobody. He writes:

> The Russians certainly are facing difficulties in Afghanistan... Yet Soviet casualties are tolerable. The economic investment is large but should be repaid by development of Afghanistan's mineral exports in the next few years. Although the rebels may roam much of the countryside, these were areas never strongly controlled by any Government. Soviet control of the main cities and communications is something the rebels cannot challenge... Above all, the Russians have a strategy: to build up the central state machine and to develop the more accessible parts of the rural economy, leaving the wilder mountainous regions to their own devices. In a significant recent decree designed to broaden support, the Afghan Government announced that tribal

chiefs and army officers would not have their excess land confiscated—provided they cooperated with the regime...

The idea that the Afghan resistance can inflict such a military cost on the Russians that they are forced to withdraw is baseless. Hardly less founded are hopes that, in the course of battle, the feudal opposition groups can come together.

And Halliday sums up the alternatives: If the West (the U.S.A.) continues to oppose not the presence of Soviet troops in Afghanistan but the Karmal government, then the Soviets will stay in Afghanistan until that government is secure, and he feels that this possibility is quite feasible. "The Russians will leave when the Afghan state is stronger..."

The Russians will not allow the Karmal government to be overthrown, he says. "The Russians will not let that happen." Pakistan, with Zia, no doubt finds the situation to its liking. "This serves Pakistan, which has used the 'Afghan card' to ensure massive new American aid. And it benefits those in the West who call for 'spoiling operations' against Moscow."

And he says: "Some Western diplomats admit in private that this is what they favor—continuing to stir the Afghan pot, while asking the Russians to negotiate on unacceptable terms."

Brezhnev had already said it on February 22, 1980:

The U.S.S.R. will withdraw its military contingent from Afghanistan as soon as the reasons for their presence there disappear and the Afghan government considers it no longer necessary. The United States is clamoring for the withdrawal of the Soviet troops while in effect doing everything to put off such a possibility by continuing and stepping up interference in Afghanistan's affairs. I wish to declare most emphatically: We shall be ready to begin withdrawal of our troops as soon as all forms of interference from without directed against the government and people of Afghanistan are completely discontinued. Let the United States together with Afghanistan's neighbors guarantee this, and there will no loger be any need for Soviet military aid.

On January 8, 1980, Carter had said:

We will let them (the Soviets) know that they will indeed suffer now and in the future for their unwarranted invasion.

Things had not improved under Reagan.

Money and arms for rebels were no longer the problem. These came in amounts sufficient to arm a dozen counterrevolutionary armies, including huge funds allocated for the private needs of the various leaders and their retinue, whose loyalty to Allah needed something more substantial to guarantee their loyalty to them. Once victory was won, that cornucopia conceivably could dry up.

Still, though much was siphoned off (and a peek into the Swiss banks would be educationl), enough remained to pay off an army of mercenaries, not all of whom wanted to be an instant *shahid* (martyr), though they were promised that in Paradise all their earthly sins would be washed away. The fact was that their pay as cutthroats was beyond what they could hope to make as peasants toiling on the land. In addition, they were free to buy and sell hashish at $50 a kilo (Jere van Dyke, NYT, Oct. 17, 1982), which eventually ended up in New York City worth thousands of dollars more on the street.

The terms that Washington laid down for a settlement of the Afghan war ranged all the way from the hope that Karmal would be assassinated (voiced by William Dyess when he spoke for Reagan) to establishing a "neutral and non-aligned Afghanistan government" without Karmal and the PDPA.

Selig Harrison, already quoted, would list the options for a political settlement to the war that he had rounded up by the middle of July (1982), particularly in the wake of meetings conducted by U.N. intermediary Undersecretary General Diego Cordovez in July 1982.

In his view, the options, based on the belief that the Karmal forces could never win a victory, boiled down to establishing a form of "Finlandization" in an Afghanistan whose neutrality would be guaranteed by the U.N. But "Finlandization" was based on an acceptance of Soviet interests in Afghanistan. He also wouldn't rule out the return of King Mohammad Zahir in some future political "rearrangement" in Afghanistan that allowed it to become neither fish nor fowl, and particularly not good red herring.

No resolution on the proffered "options" was reported. The U.S.A. did not want an Afghanistan that was committed in advance to a policy that would spell no danger to Soviet interests. The reason why the Americans diddled at all in Southern Asia was to create danger to Soviet interests! There was no other reason why they were there.

Meanwhile, the Soviets, while clearly stating that a political settlement of the issue had to be made, made it equally clear that it could not be at the expense of the present Afghan government. The freely-voiced invitation to betray the Karmal government, based on the notion that cynicism is all that motivates politics, had about it the character not of serious negotiations but of provocation. It was also based on the idea that there could be *no* military solution, and that the Karmal government could *never* consolidate its power over the country, or that its power had no validity behind it.

Those talks, and later talks with Pakistan, came to little, though looked upon hopefully. The assumption that "Moscow wants to find a face-saving way out of Afghanistan" was clearly based on a wrong assumption. Moscow indeed wanted to get out of Afghanistan—and negotiations themselves implied this—but there was no reason to believe that the cause was lost there, and that the only problem was how to get out with some tatters of dignity to cover one's nakedness.

Historically, the cause of counterrevolution is out of date. No matter what forces were there to prop it up, fighting for Allah and a kilo of hashish are not aims worthy of a noble cause but much closer to the aims of the Mafia, who are also reputed to be as God-fearing as they are efficient traffickers in drugs But the fight between imperialism and freedom is contemporary. And the forces that complicated the war had little to do with feudalism but much to do with imperialism. Win or lose, feudalism—the cause of the *Mujahiddin*—was already lost.

But the State Department remained stuck in its position first voiced by Carter early in February 1980: "The president reiterates that the United States supports the restoration of a neutral and non-aligned Afghanistan government, a government that is responsive to the wishes of the Afghanistan people." (IHT, Feb. 20, 1980.) Carter was further quoted as saying that the U.S. was ready to back a "transitional arrangement" in Afghanistan.

There was something extraordinarily disingenuous in this "position." For from 1919 on *every* Afghan government had been a "Finland." *Every* Afghan government had built its foreign policy on the demonstrated solid foundation of friendship with the Soviet Union, coupled with a policy of non-alignment. It was *only* when the Americans, not content with a country that actually abided by a policy of *real* "neutrality" and "non-alignment," tried to tilt Daoud away from his own pledged policies that the trouble began. When the devil was sick the devil a monk would be. After sowing the wind by arranging for the assassination of Afghanistan's revered Mir Akbar Khybar, American policy reaped the whirlwind of revolt in the overthrow of Daoud himself.

Being too greedy it lost everything. But now that the Devil was sick, it put on the pious face of the monk it would be and demanded now (it always demands) that the *status quo ante* be restored—Daoud be dug up and put back on his seat again, as though nothing had happened.

Yet nothing more rational than the "Finland" theory in the way of a settlement was proffered. True, the dilemma that confronted the State Department superfixers was clear enough. To have been more realistic would have meant to invite open rebellion from all those on its payroll.

Of the six (or seven) leading counterrevolutionary contenders, *none* agreed with this proposal, which most likely would have eliminated *them*. The State Department had no concrete program to which all the factions agreed. Though attempts were still being made to knock together some kind of unified group which logically could use the same stationary, little came of it, including one as late as April (1982) called *Ittihad-e-Islamiye-Muja-hideen*.

But whoever they are and whatever they claim to represent, nothing is clearer to any observer of the scene than that the "aims" of the American State Department(mainly rhetorical) are the sixes against their sevens. For what these men want is not an ersatz "democratic" state dolled out with "presidents" and "vice-presidents" but an *Islamic* state which, in power, would restore the feudal land to their feudal "owners," force women back into illiteracy and the veil, and put an abrupt end to delusions that ordinary peasants have a right to own the land they themselves till. Progress, even on a minimal basis, would be ended.

There was no ambiguity about where they really stood. The two Islamic conferences (in 1980) in which Pakistan and Saudi Arabia played a leading role were represented by states that were themselves caricatures of states that could be called "free" or "democratic," or "responsive" to the wishes of their own peoples (*vide* Pakistan) by even the most indulgent of standards.

Summed up, however, their published views came to the following: "the immediate and unconditional and total withdrawal of all Soviet troops; respect for the inalienable national right of the Afghan people to choose their own socio-economic system and form of government without outside interference or coercion; respect for the national independence, territorial integrity and non-aligned status of Afghanistan; and the creation of conditions in Afghanistan that would enable refugees to return home in security and honor."

By such standards both Pakistan and Saudi Arabia would be in deep trouble! But even so, the U.S.A. could not take too much comfort in these provisions which were always thrust out at the world as one prong of a fork that had another, not so pleasant, prong: "Islamic foreign ministers reaffirmed their opposition to the Soviet military intervention in Afghanistan but directed the brunt of their condemnations against the United States for its recent actions in Iran and its support of Israel on the Palestinian question." (NYT, May 21, 1980.)

In an interview with the Australian paper *Age* (Sept. 16, 1981), answering the paper's question as to whether world tension had increased with the Soviet entry into Afghanistan Indira Ghandi declared: "Oh no, it has been there before. Afghanistan was in a way inevitable. I mean, not that it happened in Afghanistan, it could have happened anywhere. But once the Soviet Union felt itself encircled, you see, originally there was Iran, Pakistan and, of course, the other Europe and so on, where the Soviet Union felt American influence was strong. But once they [U.S.A.] made friends with China, it sort of made the encirclement more complete. And it was obvious that the Soviet Union would retaliate somehow or another."

On May 14, 1980, the Afghan government had called on Pakistan and Iran for talks aimed at normalizing relations between themselves and Afghanistan. It also proposed a political settlement, with no prior conditions except the stipulation that subversive and armed attacks against the Afghan government should cease. The Afghan government was already non-aligned. It had no intention of changing its character. "The people want a peaceful life, they have got tired of the murders, plunder, and violence being perpetrated by the counterrevolutionaries. There is ever increasing support for the measures of the Party and the government on the part of the popullation. Those who were deceived by the hostile counterrevolutionary propaganda clamor and with arms in their hands tried to struggle against the DRA are now with each passing day becoming ever more convinced of the wrongness of their actions and are laying down arms," Babrak Karmal would say in a speech at the Kremlin dinner in October 1980.

At meetings with Ulemas (Islamic scholars) in July 1980, and with "elders, chieftains and representatives of the Pushtun tribes of Vazir, Otmanzay and Saraghi," in March 1981, and with officers and men of the Afghan army in Jalalabad in April 1981, Karmal would reiterate his government's conditions for reaching a political settlement to the war, but without altering "the main historical task now facing the Afghan people," he told the army officers, which was "to bring to a victorious conclusion the national-democratic, anti-feudal, anti-imperialist revolution." (Apr. 22, 1981.)

There would be no backtracking on that. And at the Party conference held in Kabul on March 14-15 of 1982, Karmal would repeat that the aim of his Party and government was "the complete elimination of the armed counterrevolution, further stabilization, fortification of more confident revolutionary power in the areas where the undeclared war of the reactionary forces is still continuing and the ensurance of a stable peace all over the country; it constitutes the most important and urgent task of the Party and the revolutionary power."

An Appeal adopted by the delegates to the Conference stressed that "Victory over the forces of counterrevolution, free-booters and bandits requires of us the complete mobilization of all our strength and material resources, courage, staunchness and stamina. Victory can be won if we fight for it all together, all in common. . .

"Our aims are clear and understandable. We want what the overwhelming majority of the people want—the flourishing freedom and independence of the motherland. . .

"Persistent action in defense of peace in our region and the rest of the world is the main thing in the approach of the PDPA and revolutionary power to international issues. The DRA Government reaffirms its invariable adherence to the principles of the non-alignment movement.

"We shall continue efforts for holding talks between Afghanistan and its neighbors—Pakistan and Iran."

There is now no chance that counterrevolution will prevail. And although it might take more time and effort than the Soviets or the Karmal government would like to give to it, the eventual defeat to the counterrevolutionaries is certain. Just as it's impossible to non-invent the wheel, so it's impossible to return to a status in life *today* when serf bows to master after the serf had tasted freedom even for a moment.

THE PROSPECTS OF PEACE

I speak of peace, while covert enmity
Under the smile of safety wounds the world.

William Shakespeare,
King Henry IV

All during the summer of 1983, hopeful signs multiplied that a formula for ending the hostilities in Afghanistan might actually be within reach. The U.N. Secretary-General's personal representative, Diego Cordovez, had met with representatives from Pakistan and Afghanistan in Geneva in June. Reports that other, informal meetings had also taken place, appeared in the press. More meetings were scheduled. Andrei Gromyko saw in the negotiations "a step in the right direction." In April such "indirect negotiations" between Afghanistan and Pakistan had registered, according to the U.N. mediator, "substantial progress," which Selig Harrison, an Afghan-watcher, would characterize in June, 1983, as having "resulted in agreement on most provisions of a 20-page 'comprehensive settlement'." And he added: "The United Nations mediation effort on Afghanistan has now reached a make-or-break state."

Then, suddenly in July, Secretary of State George P. Shultz (still on a sabbatical from Bechtel) descended on Islamabad with both feet, and that ended it. The progress in peace talks which had been conducted by the U.N. special representative Diego Cordovez for months with Foreign Minister Shah Mohammad Dost of Afghanistan and Foreign Minister Shahibzada Yacub Ali Khan of Pakistan in "quiet diplomacy" went up in smoke.

Shultz had come to Islamabad as a bill-collector reminding Zia ul-Haq that the U.S. had given him some $3.2 billion months before and now Reagan wanted something to show for it. Standing at the Khyber Pass, where months before Brzezinski had stood with his machine gun aimed at Afghanistan, Shultz had cried to the bemused Afghans collected there: "We are with you!"

But "heading where?" the *Times* had asked.

The future Shultz was projecting looked bleak indeed. "With you" was more than just a phrase promising warmer and warmer State Department—press department solidarity. It meant money and real guns, more burnings and more killings, a pledge of further devastation and continued destruction. The one thing it did not promise was the end of the war.

In fact, no pretense was made then, earlier or afterwards, that an end to the war could be expected. In December, Reagan was still mouthing the Cold War rhetoric which had become a reflex action of his Administration including his charge that "we have convincing proof of chemical weapons (that) have been used by the Soviets against the Afghans," but produced none. In fact, later the Administration would have to concede that months of "looking for the Godot" of chemical warfare in Afghanistan had come up with no more than a leaf and a twig in ... Cambodia!

It was obvious to anyone with moderate political eyesight that *the Reagan Administration did not want the war to end.* Shultz in Islamabad in July, putting the whip to Pakistan's foreign minister, made it clear that the war, which nobody else wanted, the U.S.A. wanted.

It was now Reagan's war.

To make it all quite clear the *Wall Street Journal,* in April, 1984, would quote "one U.S. intelligence source" who admitted that "The professionals say (the Moslem rebels) aren't going to win. The most we can do is give them incremental increases in aid, and raise the costs to the Soviets." (WSJ, Apr. 9, 1984.)

The U.S.A. was already sending the "rebels" an admitted "$80 million annually" *(Ibid.)* in "covert" aid, which by 1984 had come to a nice round figure of $300 million. But "unadmitted" aid amounted to millions more.

This money had bought guns, paid for the upkeep of 100 camps in Pakistan, for military assistants and trainers, for propaganda, and payoffs to the various "rebel" leaders across whose outstretched palms the flow of silver never ceased, though the amount, in their eyes, was never large enough. "What," one of them, Sibjhafulla Mojadedi, had cried after looking at what Washington could spare for him, "You're making us die cheap!" *(Ibid.)*

Not that he was in great personal danger of dying that way. He owned a big motor company called the Mojadedi Transport Company in Pakistan that had cost him $750,000. He was also rumored to have thousands more tucked away in various banks—a detail, which, in fact, all of the leaders of the "rebel" groupings had providentially taken care of, and, in fact, as their American paymasters expected them to do. Speaking of their earlier prototypes in South Vietnam, also on the American payroll, an "unnamed official in charge of refugees" had this down-to-earth observation to make: "The U.S. embassy was always aware of who was making big money in Saigon and who was relatively honest. We went along with Vietnamese corruption as the price paid for their loyalty." (NYT, Nov. 22, 1972.)

Indeed, in December, "the leader of the main resistance alliance fighting the Soviet-backed Government of Afghanistan today denied a charge that he was misusing its money in a struggle against rival guerrilla groups.

"The charge against Abd-i-Rab Rasoul Sayaf, president of the Pakistan-based Islamic Alliance of Afghan Mujahiddin, was made Saturday by the leader of a key group in the alliance, Yunus Khalis." Yunus Khalis, as we know, is the man who couldn't tell the Afghan leaders who his true father was, but in any case, he trusted his fellow "holy warriors" so little in the sight of money that he forthwith "pulled out of the Alliance of seven guerrilla groups." (Reuters, Dec. 11, 1983.)

In May, 1984, Khalis was still "out," though, according to another leader of "holy warriors," Professor Burhanuddin Rabani, of Jamiat-e-Islami, and "head of the Defense Committee of the Alliance," Yunus Khalis' exit from the Alliance represented no more than "teething troubles," and he remained with them in spirit and he promised that "his complaints. . . will be looked into." Rabani also added that "Now the Soviets have deployed troops from Cuba. . ." in Afghanistan! (*Arabia,* May, 1984.)

"We get some exaggerations and contradictions," Dr. Sayid Majrooh, head of the Afghan Information Center in Islamabad, would comment blandly on the "information" flowing from his mimeograph machines that was so quickly contradicted by events. (NYT, June 30, 1983.) And: "A major problem for reporters early in the war (and late in the war!) was that the Afghan guerrillas' accounts were found on inspection to contain considerable amounts of exaggeration and wishful thinking. The reason for this, Mrs. (Romney) Fullerton *(Daily Telegraph,* London) said, was that the purpose of their accounts was less to inform than to promote enthusiasm and morale among the guerrillas. This 'singing the song of the jihad,' she said, is part of the long tradition of Afghan balladeers." *(Ibid.)*

And not only Afghan! Almost four years of a kind of war had brought the situation in Afghanistan to where a "study" by the Senate Foreign Relations Committee, which somehow boiled itself down to the impressions of one man, John B. Rich, 3rd, could say, in April, 1984, that a"stalemate had developed in the Afghan war, with both sides more or less stymied. The "report" went on to add: "The Soviet-backed regime of Babrak Karmal continues to maintain dominion over the major Afghan cities and logistical centers. . . But the resistance meanwhile has gained and held control of some 80 to 90 percent of the country, while showing steady advances in organization and fighting ability." (NYT, Apr. 8, 1984.)

In this "report" there is also no hint that a settlement of the war is either possible or desirable. No reference is made to the May 14, 1980 and August 24, 1981 policy statements of the Afghan government which outlined a reasonable and viable process by which the war could be ended, the Soviet troops withdrawn, and the refugees returned. No reference is made to the U.N. negotiations and why they were torpedoed.

The Senate report, on the contrary, recommended further arms and more money, further hostilities, further burnings and killings, further "cheap deaths," and raised the possibility that (once again!) the counterrevolutionary bands (now minus one Yunus Khalis) could still be knocked into some kind of unity which could then be dubbed a "government-in-exile" much after the fashion of the *Mukado's* Poo-Bah who was a whole government rolled in himself. But once such a "government" could be proclaimed and solemnly "recognized" by Reagan, the moneys and weapons now supplied by covert action then would be supplied just openly.

As far as one can determine from the report, war is to be a way of life in that part of the world, and only peace is to be feared.

Despite repeated warnings published in the American press that everything coming out of the propaganda caves of Peshawar should be taken *cum grano salo,* the American press blithely continued to repeat all the "exaggerations and contradictions," sing the "song of the *jihad*" lustily as though no such warnings had ever been uttered. Not only had Jeane Kirkpatrick declared in her inimitable style that the Russians had booby-trapped children's dolls all the better to blow up children, but John B. Rich, 3rd, in his thrilling report to the Senate, would charge the Soviets with "destroying crops and bayoneting women and children." Why? They're Russians, isn't that enough of a reason?

Echoes of the "song of the jihad" were to be heard in an editorial of *The New York Times* ("Remembering Afghanistan") a few days after the report to the Senate came out. It is a rather remarkable editorial for its unzipped language, if not for its logic. "So Afghanistan is still not pacified after all. In more than four years of direct occupation, the Soviet Union has yet to broaden the appeal of the puppet regime. Most of the countryside remains in control of the insurgents. Three regimes have been unable or unwilling to negotiate a face-saving withdrawal on lines proposed by a United Nations negotiator. Perhaps they really believe the nonsense that only help from the West through Pakistan keeps the angry rebellion alive." (April 26, 1984.)

This book has answered these jeering accusations I would imagine clearly enough, citing book and verse, mainly their book and their verse. But the "song" continues as though the whole world had gone tone-deaf. Surely, after Shultz had descended on Pakistan in July with Reagan's ultimatum that there must be no settlement, it's no longer possible to speak of the Soviets being "unwilling" to negotiate (let's forget that bit about face-saving)? They had been "negotiating" with expectations of coming to an agreement, right up to the last moment! It was Bechtel's Shultz who knocked that on the head.

And, as for the "nonsense" about believing that "only help from the

West" is what "keeps the angry rebellion alive"—what can one say about that? Try drying up the source of Abi-i-Rab Rasoul Sayaf's income and see how long *he* stays "angry" at the Russians! And the others, whose high life styles aren't paid for by afghani or rupees but by the American dollars.

And, as for the "telling" point that "after more than four years of direct occupation", and so on, the "Soviet Union" had not yet managed to gain the love and affection of the Afghan people, one can only point to the facts already recorded in the earlier pages of this book, reminding the reader at the same time that the "Russians" are not an occupying power, and any visitor of Afghanistan could substantiate that. It is the Afghans themselves who are struggling to settle their problems. The evidence is abundant that people like Karmal or Keshtmand or the students I dealt with who had spent their whole lives in dangerous revolutionary struggle, could never accept the role of puppets for any reason whatsoever. Despite institutionalized cynicism in the West about all things socialist, the *fact* is that the relationship of the Soviet Union toward the Afghan government is now, as it has been for decades, a friendly one—a brotherly one. The Soviets are in Afghanistan to put up a shield against the depredations of mainly foreign-inspired and foreign-paid mercenaries who, with no hope of "winning," continue the war, and will continue the war, as long as they are paid to do so.

As for the charge, which is not new, that the "countryside remains in control of the insurgents," that is, to be more specific (which is dangerous to be in this game) "some 80 to 90 percent" of the countryside, one can even cite Marco Polo on this matter. He had found, some two thousand years ago, that much of the country (though it was not then as it is not even now a country) being "destitute of every sign of habitation, the people having fled to strong places in the mountains, in order to secure themselves against predatory attacks by lawless marauders, by whom these districts are overrun."

Not much had changed in the following two thousand years as Karmal would indicate, noting that

> ...except in the capital, Kabul, and some of the cities, after the independence of Afghanistan (1919), something under the name of a local government came into being, but in all other districts, villages, and rural areas, and other corners of the country, the local organs of state in its reality did not exist at all. (*Kabul New Times*, March 5, 1984.)

Where Marco Polo found destitution in the plains and flatlands, today farms are functioning there, and with all the cities and "logistical centers" in the hands of the government, real control over the country is in their hands: what else can that mean? Nor is it true that the "resistance" is all converged in the mountains of Afghanistan (it is mostly converged in the military camps in Pakistan), nor is it true that that "resistance" has been only against the Karmal government. For local chieftains fought against the marauders coming in from Pakistan quite as fiercely, for these "liberators" started out by demanding a tax from them and shanghaied their sons to return with them to Pakistan for military service, and they weren't all that eager to comply with such demands.

In fact, it was precisely the "predatory attack of lawless marauders" that finally convinced many of them to make their peace with the government, which actually had treated them with a laissez-faire hands-off policy, talking with them, when possible, and waiting for experience itself to teach them who was friend and who was enemy.

Not only did they make peace but so did many other local "bandits" who had run out of counterrevolutionary steam. The new government's policy (as distinguished from the Taraki government as Amin administered it) of universal amnesty, of promises of free land, of the restoration of the property of the "middle peasants" and small proprietors, of assurances that the country remained Islamic and all were guaranteed freedom of worship, began to show results even in 1980 and later more so, especially as it became clear that those who "surrendered" or "came back" were, in fact, not arrested and not punished (real criminals did not surrender or come back). "The (surrender of bandits) is one of the fundamental phenomena of the growth of our society and our revolution," Karmal would declare in March 1984. (*Kabul New Times,* March 5, 1984).

By the end of 1983, some 200 such "bandit" leaders, with 21,000 of their followers, had indeed surrendered with their arms, and some had promptly been reorganized into people's militia units and sent out to battle in a *jihad* against their erstwhile "holy warriors." At the same time the return of nomads and other "refugees" continue, though the obstacles erected by the Pakistani authorities grow more brutal, as in this instance reported by Bakhtar News Agency (Aug. 6, 1983): "The Afghan fugitives in the Surkhab camp in Pakistan's Baluchistan province have announced recently their collective intention of returning to their homeland. But the Pakistani authorities responded to their demonstration by sending in large detachments of police. As a result of the clash many fugitives in the Surkhab camp were injured and some were arrested."

It would take a hard-shelled skeptic indeed not to believe that many of the so-called "refugees," regardless of how they originally got into the camps, wanted to spend their lives there and didn't yearn for the chance to come home, and wouldn't take that chance when and if it came their way.

258

In any case, by February, 1984, the government felt it had the situation well enough under control to institute a system of local government throughout the country. The country's infrastructure had been functionally restored —in some places established for the first time. Universal suffrage was introduced for the first time as well. Local authority came into existence with the right of all citizens to serve in office beginning at the age of 18.

Key to the restructuring of the economy even in the middle of war is the land reform. By February, 1984, the Karmal government could claim that some 300,000 formerly landless peasants now owned their own plots of land (which had been enlarged up to *six jeribs*). Along with land comes water— and vast new irrigation systems have been (or are being) built with Soviet help. Once the peasants were convinced the land actually belonged to them, it took no special pleading on the part of the government to persuade them to organize self-defense units to repel the marauders. And, indeed, "Thousands of people have voluntarily joined self-defense groups, defenders of the revolution, and local and tribal militia. By so doing they consciously risked their lives," Karmal would note. If one can't see the logic in this, then he is permanently blind to reason. What effect did the charge that the Russians wanted to take over and occupy the land as a permanent foreign presence have on the mind of the peasant who was digging his own land? Land, by the way, which his ancestors had dreamed of having for literally centuries before with never the slightest real possibility of ever obtaining any?

One tests the truth by biting it, smelling it, eating it, fondling it, and— waking up in the morning and finding it's not a dream. This is exactly the process by which thousands of peasants have been led to change their attitude from skepticism that Karmal's promises could be true to picking up a gun and defending the reality of those promises!

This brings us to the charge that the Karmal government does not trust its own people and keeps them disarmed, a charge that, as the opening pages of this book reveal, I had had refuted for me the first day I set foot on Afghan soil.

Speaking to the First Assembly of Cotton Growers in Kabul in February, 1984, Karmal would tell them that "you should have arms in one hand to defend your land and in the other a shovel for implementing the land reform." (KNT, Feb. 2, 1984.)

The problem was not to keep the people disarmed for fear that if armed they would turn their arms against the government, as the *Times* more than implied. The problem was to convince the peasants that they could really defeat the marauders if they met them with gunfire. And once they went through their first baptism of fire, they constituted themselves into permanent people's militias. One report of a local action put it this way:

259

"Our brave armed forces launched their operations against the criminals, and they ran like rats. But we crushed them." (KNT, Feb. 12, 1984.)

In his speech titled: "For the Intensification of the Combat Against Counterrevolution," Karmal raised the cry; "Go on the offensive—flush the enemy out of their hideouts!"

With a political settlement vetoed so autocratically by the Reaganites in July, 1984, there was no alternative left for the revolutionary forces but to take the war to the enemy in earnest and wipe out those who resist. Up until that point, the government had been more or less satisfied to control the cities and transportation facilities, leaving the bandits up in the hills or in Pakistan to rot. If a peace settlement could be arrived at, they could be taken care of at leisure. It was this policy which the State Deparment "analysts" interpret to mean that a "stalemate" existed in Afghanistan because the government forces were not strong enough to eliminate the opposition.

But this is a serious miscalculation. The very first action in 1984 by the government forces against the "rebels" holed up in the Panjshir Valley was a stunning defeat for the counterrevolution. Up until then an armistice had been in effect between the leader of the counterrevolution Amad Shah Masood and the government which had been hoping that, with a political settlement, force would not be necessary to liberate the area he claimed. Masood meanwhile, raced to Peshawar where he "won" the battle he had lost in Panjshir via press releases. The remnants of his forces have dispersed among the hills dreading the approach of winter.

More and more battles took place in the hills as the local militia backed up by the regular troops who, in their turn, were given assistance by the Soviets with helicopters and armored vehicles, went seriously to work to eliminate the opposition which had enjoyed a charmed life until then— a kind of tolerance born of the belief that time was on the side of the revolutionary government and the successes of the government would erode the resistance, as indeed would have happened if it had not bee⁻ ⁺or the intervention of the Americans who brought much money, more guns, and the psychology of desperadoes who have no thought of erecting a new social system but only of pillage, marauding, killing as a way of life.

The most extraordinary stories about Afghanistan continue to appear in the press. Even before the supreme humiliation of Grenada, an adventure from which the Reagan forces kept the American press, the situation that the Western press created itself had become critical, and opposition to the arrogant power of the Western press as "information imperialism" had mounted everywhere. It must be said the press did little to help change its deteriorating image. Take these stories chosen at random from *The New York Times*:

March 13 (Reuters)—Many Army Desertions Reported in Afghanistan
March 20 (*The New York Times*)—Mutiny Is Reported in Afghanistan
March 27 (AP) Afghan Communists Reported Slain

Not even a fragment of substance backed up these headlines!

The game of numbers had continued relentlessly since I was there in January when it first began its giddy ride. The whole thing has since passed beyond partisanship. It verges on lunacy. To take one example. According to the figures solemnly published in the press as *facts,* there should be no Afghan army left today, and the Soviet troops too should be a mere shadow of themselves having been decimated over and over by losses and desertions. Hekmatyar's—what shall we call them?—ravings? are repeated by the press with admirable tolerance and parotted by the editorial writers of *The New York Times.* In his most recent hashish dream, he sees that "during the last four years some 25,000 Russians have lost their lives." And, while the State Department is still stuck with its figure of 105,000 Soviet troops in Afghanistan (God knows how they got that figure), Hekmatyar has already raised the number to 200,000. He put the Afghan army at 40,000. (*Arabia,* May 1984.)

Does it help to refer again to Karmal on this question? "Despite the propaganda of the enemy, our armed forces are quantitatively several times larger and more powerful than they were in the best of conditions in the past."

And he would tell Western correspondents in Moscow (Dec. 20, 1983) that:

> In fact, today, we can say with pride that the armed forces of the DRA are capable of fighting the bandits, miscreants and terrorists. The limited Soviet contingents are here ... on the invitation of the legitimate Government of Afghanistan.

And, he had noted in other places, these Soviet troops would leave the country as soon as it was possible to do so. And that would be when a settlement had taken place guaranteeing the country from foreign assault and invasion—precisely the consummation the Reagan forces most devoutly intend not to see happen.

It has also been suggested in some quarters that it was Karmal himself who stood in the way of a settlement. In the same press conference in Moscow, Karmal would answer this point:

> As a matter of fact, on the basis of our ideological principles, such a question is not a real one. I have not come to power like this or that military ruler as a result of some conspiracy or coup d'etat, arranged by the imperialists and reactionaries...
>
> A revolution took place in Afghanistan under the leadership of the People's Democratic Party of Afghanistan, with the help of the armed forces of the

DRA, and on the basis of the long-standing historical needs, hopes and desires of the Afghan people...

In our country, the leadership is collective. It does not belong to this or that individual and not to myself. I obey the policy of the Party and of the State and of the will of the people.

And as for those who think the clock can be turned backward:

The PDPA leads the state of the DRA and exists as a living, dynamic, organic and real force, and as a hard fact... (The people) will not take even one step back from the revolutionary path chosen by them.

Meanwhile, the editorial of the *The New York Times*, which has kicked all this off, goes on to say: "And unlike Afghanistan's Marxists, the Sandinistas are confident enough of their support to arm large numbers of their own people."

The not-too-subtle flattery here, and the contrasting of the somehow more amateur Sandinistas "Marxists" of Nicaragua to the hard-boiled "Marxist-Leninist" revolutionary forces of Afghanistan is intended to divide up the opposition to what is a single world-wide phenomenon between "good" Communists with which we can deal and eventually destroy from within, and the "bad" Communists who put up hard resistance against all our blandishment and "reasonable" proposals and thus condemn themselves to the fate appropriate to anyone who remains part of the "evil empire". As the *Times* has made more explicit in another editorial, a "Marxist takeover" need not be forever.

I have already disposed of the allegation that the Soviets so little trust their Afghan allies that they won't let them have any guns—one of those absurdities so patent that it should have, simply in the nature of reason, no newspaper notice at all. Once it appeared in print, however, it miraculously acquires a kind of reality, after all, and reason must go and hide its head.

In the same editorial, the *Times* lets us believe that while the CIA only "tinkered" with bombs in Nicaraguan ports—as part of the campaign to force Nicaragua to its knees from hunger—the Soviets perpetrated "butchery" in Afghanistan, presumably basing this charge on the hallucinations of Jeanne Kirkpatrick. One, the overzealous but good-hearted Uncle Sam whose blunders in the pursuit of justice are after all understandable. The other, the unregenerate barbarian.

But listen to Daniel Ortega, Coordinator of the Directing Council of the National Regeneration, Nicaragua, speaking:

Acts of political, military and economic aggression and threats of even larger-scale moves have been repeated in the course of two years and eleven months with severe consequences to our people: the assassinations, wounding, and kidnapping of Nicaraguan citizens, and the destruction of schools, hospitals, first-aid centres, bridges, fuel depots, civilian airports and building equipment.

The U.S.A. doggedly seeks to still further lengthen this already endless list of evil deeds. (*Barricada*, Dec. 5, 1983.)

Here's Karmal on the other side of the world:

After receiving military training in Pakistan and Iran, the Afghan miscreants are dispatched to the territory of Afghanistan to destroy and burn bridges, roads, health centres and educational institutions. These bandits cut the public highways, impose fines on the defenseless people, and plunder the property and wealth.

They burn the schools and kill the women and children and old men by the order of U.S. imperialism. *(Kabul New Times,* Feb. 11, 1984.)

If the language sounds almost eerily alike, it is because both leaders are describing the exact same phenomenon: the hand that is wreaking havoc and murder in Nicaragua is the same hand wreaking havoc and murder in Afghanistan.

In December, 1983, Sibjhafulla Mojadedi, leaving his command post just outside of Washington, D.C., turned up in Tegucigulpa, ostensible capital of Honduras, where he exchanged experiences and information with his natural friends, the CIA-trained-and-equipped Somozaistas in a forum sponsored by a group in Paris, also ostensible in all its identifications, called "International Resistance." Like seeks out like. Both CIA groups met and compared notes aimed at fine-tuning the counterrevolutionary art of murder and arson even more subtly than before. Those who burn and pillage, who flay prisoners alive, who kill schoolteachers and their students, are all paid by the U.S.A., without benefit of the sanctioned approval of the American people and totally disregarding the provisions of the War Powers Act.

Time magazine (June 11, 1984) casually begins an article on Afghanistan: "The CIA spends around $75 million a year supplying the rebels with grenades, KPG-7 rocket launchers and portable surface-to-air missiles, as well as with radio equipment and medicines. . ."

And, as a kind of low-level gents' room joke: "Politically the CIA's main challenge has been to avoid linking its operation to the government of Pakistan, President Zia ul-Haq ... (who) has repeatedly denied Soviet charges that his country was directly supplying the Afghan rebels in any way... 'We're going to keep Zia's hands clean,' CIA William Casey told a top aide. . ." This man Casey who lied about his income, is up to his neck in Wall Street investments (including in those firms where as head of the CIA he had inside information) and who is, at this writing, trying to explain how he managed to get Pres. Carter's campaign notes which he passed over to candidate Reagan who then, with an expertness that had aroused the astonished admiration of the entire world, read off the answers to Carter's sharpest points with ease and relish!

Thieves, arsonists, murderers, simple liars, brazen liars, cute liars, coy liars—you pays your money and you takes your choice. They have only one rule, and that they lifted out of the world of Lewis Carroll: "What I tell you three times is true." *(The Hunting of the Snark.)*

But even if they tell you a million times it's still not true! The world is dealing with fanatics of a familiar basis stripe but with specific American trimmings. Having re-located the "focus of evil" in the Soviet Union where Hitler last saw it—and indeed it was the last thing he ever saw—Reagan and his confederates (and whoever succeeds his cabal of White House quarters) declare that they have found the key to understanding all things on heaven and on earth, simplified into one formula. Cato had his *"Delenda est Carthago!"* "Carthage must be destroyed!" Reagan and company have theirs: the "empire of evil" must go!

All bourgeois knowledge comes to a dead stop at this point, and all science and art remain frozen in the ice of this formula—infinitely sterile. Afghanistan *is* Nicaragua. The peace of one is the peace of the other.

Afghanistan Revisited - 1986*

[Phillip Bonosky had just returned from a visit]

Six years later the situation can be summed up in this way: (1) The Democratic Republic of Afghanistan has successfully defeated a sustained counterrevolutionary attempt, backed by the U.S. and other imperialist powers, to overthrow it by "force and violence." (2) On the basis of its actual control of the country, the DRA can claim that the war has, for all logical purposes, ended and all that remains is for the imperialist side to concede this fact. (3) If hostilities nevertheless continue, it is only because outside forces, notably the USA, do not want to establish peace because of what are, in Reagan's eyes, important strategic reasons.

As a CIA source told the *Wall Street Journal* (April 9, 1984), "The professionals say that [the Moslem rebels] aren't going to win. The most we can do is give them incremental increases in aid, and raise the costs to the Soviets."

On July 28, 1986, Mikhail Gorbachev announced that the Soviets would *unilaterally* withdraw six regiments of the Soviet army from Afghanistan, preliminary to withdrawing *all* of them if a political agreement can be reached. Peace-minded people who may have been baffled by how to understand the Afghan situation, with its specific complicating features (the presence of Soviet troops) should now see it precisely for what it is. It is not a case of Soviet invasion and occupation, followed by a stubborn refusal to leave the country, keeping it oppressed and exploited (the way imperialism does). It is an imperialist ploy to keep the pot boiling, part of a policy of maintaining a constant threat against the USSR, and also India and beyond India all Southeast Asia.

Thus the resistance of the Afghan patriots to counterrevolution is an important contribution to the security of that area and to the peace of the world.

Reagan's answer to Gorbachev's declaration that Soviets troops would return to Soviet soil was typically arrogant, the same insolence with which he greeted Gorbachev's continuation of a moratorium on Soviet nuclear tests. Reagan torpedoed the "proximity talks" that had been going on in Geneva between Pakistan and Afghanistan through the office of UN representative Diego Cordovez. These talks had been in process since 1980, and had reached a certain measure of agreement on key questions, including the withdrawal of Soviet troops. Even before scuttling these talks, Reagan had signaled his intentions by publicizing a meeting he held with Afghan counterrevolutionary leaders, pledging money and arms to them, and hinting that, at an appropriate moment, he would recognize them as the leaders of the "genuine" Afghan government.

These acts make all talk about wanting peace in Afghanistan so much hot air. The lips move, but they are out of sync with the action. The fact is that Reagan *does not*

* Adapted from Political Affairs, Sept. 1986.

want to permit the Soviet Union to withdraw its troops from Afghanistan. The propaganda plums to be gained from their presence are too valuable. Only on the Afghanistan question does the U.S. find itself in the majority at the UN. While posing as a champion of "peace and democracy," the Reagan Administration makes sure that a situation does not develop which will permit peace and democracy.

Meanwhile, there is a crescendo of the grossest kind of propaganda against the Soviets and Afghans. It observes no limits or proprieties.

In 1985, acting through its Commission on Human Rights, the UN appointed Felix Ercora to head an "investigation" of human rights in Afghanistan. After two visits to Pakistan, where he "interviewed Afghan refugees," Ercora came back with a report, duly issued by the UN, which found that the Afghan government violated human rights.

Unpublicized was the fact that this same Felix Ercora, an Austrian national, had voluntarily joined Hitler's forces early in his career. And this was no wayward impulse. He continued his pro-Nazi activities after the defeat of the Third Reich as a member of the "Organization of Germans from the Sudenland." His "investigation" of "human rights" in Afghanistan is a mockery of every word in the assignment—"investigation" and "human rights."

Not to be outdone, Helsinki Watch also came in with a report, predictably mimicking Ercora's. Helsinki Watch is the brainchild of Robert L. Bernstein, who has reduced the once prestigious Random House publisher to a conduit for anti-Soviet propaganda carried on in refined, hypocritical style.

What is the Afghan reality? Is there any fire where there is so much smoke? How much truth is there in the allegation that the Soviets are "invaders," that they came into Afghanistan against the wishes of the people, who oppose their presence and run for their lives to the safety of Pakistan? What is the reality of the military situation? Can the Afghan situation be settled independently of a general political settlement—a new detente—between the USSR and the USA? Is it true, as the *New York Times* claims, that

> Even by this century's standards, the occupation has been notable for its violence. A devastated land remains unpacified, the party remains divided and the puppets in Kabul remain universally despised. (May 6,1986.)

Is it true, as this same editorial claims, that the situation in Afghanistan, which "has been all but formally annexed" [to the USSR], remains hopeless—that "the Soviet hope of quickly raising a loyal Afghan army was dashed long ago"?

In another editorial it accepted the former Nazi Ercora's "report" at face value, and in its parson's prose opined:

> Equally devastating has been the world's judgment of Soviet barbarities in Afghanistan. In its first inquiry into the crimes of a Communist country, a UN commission [Ercora's, they mean-P.B.] confirmed the use of toy bombs to cripple children and savage tactics to slaughter and starve

civilians.... This dirty war has so far cost 500,000 lives and driven tnree million Afghans into exile. Even so, most of the country refuses to lie subdued. If the Soviet Union's war bleeds on, it will say nothing new about the behemoth that launched it. But it will tell a good deal about the stature of the Soviet leader who inherited it. (Ibid.)

So, cheers for Gorbachev's withdrawal of Soviet troops as a step toward ending the war?

Don't hold your breath . . .

Refutations of these slanders were forthcoming from authoritative sources, including general secretary of the People's Democratic Party of Afghanistan, Najib, in answers to questions I asked during the week I spent in Kabul [July, 1986].

To begin with the most crucial—where does the war stand? Who's winning, who's losing?

Answers came from Brigadier General Abdul Hao Ulem. Gorbachev had just made his announcement that the Soviets would take out six regiments, and the natural question was: How would this unilateral action affect the military situation? Could the Afghan army handle it alone if the entire Soviet army finally departed?

Yes, was his answer. If all the Soviet soldiers left tomorrow, the present Afghan army could easily take care of the motley group of *dushman* (bandits)—on condition that American and other foreign support to them is ended:

> Our [Afghan] army is today much bigger than it was in 1980 [put then at 80,000 by bourgeois sources, which claimed that it was later cut in half by desertions.—P.B.]. On the other hand, the quoted number of Soviet troops—120,000 to 140,000—is wrong; there are far fewer Soviet troops than that.

He added that the present Afghan army is a disciplined, organized and effective fighting force, highly motivated, a true people's army. The Afghan army carries on the main burden of the war—a point which Najib also stressed—with the Soviet troops acting mainly as backup. The Soviet presence discourages those who dream of sending a professional army across the border into the country. Relations between Soviet and Afghan army personnel are good, the general went on: the Afghans learn from the Soviets, who remain visitors in a country which they came to help.

In addition to the regular army, the general pointed out, Afghanistan is truly an armed nation. There are, at present, some 120,000 civil defense units, which include armed workers who protect their factories and armed peasants, who stand guard over their fields, irrigation systems and crops. To these forces must be added the militia and the police. Women take an active role in the country's defense and so do the youth.

A development which has tilted the balance to the government side, he pointed out, is the decision of the tribes on the Pakistan-Afghan border to move from passive resistance to the counterrevolution to active resistance. This past year, a High Jirgah (council) of Nationalities and Tribes of the Frontier Area was held in Kabul, with 3,700 representatives. A decision was made to mount an offensive against the incursions of the *dushman* forces. Sharp clashes with regular Pakistan army units have taken place. In December, the Pakistan army invaded the "gray area" between the two countries, and attacked the Afridi and Shinwari Pushtun tribes, which had begun to harass counterrevolutionary bands passing though their territory into Afghanistan proper. This army was badly battered. Some of its Pushtun soldiers refused to fire on their brother Pushtun tribesmen, and the army had to be withdrawn. More and more instances of "rebels" joining the government side are recorded as life in the so-called refugee camps becomes ever more intolerable.

A small item in the Times in May 1986 noted:

> Although there is widespread sympathy for the Afghan refugees who have fled to Pakistan, there is also concern that they compete with Pakistanis for jobs. Recently, there have also been concerns that the refugees are engaged in smuggling, drug manufacturing and other illicit activities.

Unnamed among these illicit activities is black marketeering and the buying and selling of girls (as young as 12) for prostitution. Bitter gun battles between rival factions have intensified, expressed also by repeated bombings. Actually, most Pakistanis would like to see an end to the camps and the war.

Internal security has tightened considerably since I was last in Kabul. Today visitors to public places, including parks, are frisked by guards. Then it was possible for counterrevolutionaries to slip in an out of the city almost at will, plant their bombs, or pour their poisons in the drinking water of school children, and skip off again to Peshawar in Pakistan to report to their CIA instructors. Supplied with stinger missiles, they would fire rockets at random at populated areas, killing men, women and children, destroying buildings, schools, mosques, planes, etc. Bombs were planted in shopping centers, movies, trolley buses. In September 1984, a bomb exploded in Kabul International Airport, killing 11 and injuring 22. Others wreaked property damage amounting to an estimated 45 billion afghani.

General Abdul Hao Ulem contemptuously dismissed the charge that the Soviet and Afghan government forces booby-trapped children's toys, a charge made by, among others, Jeanne Kirkpatrick when she was Reagan's mouthpiece at the UN. Children's toys were indeed booby-trapped—by the counterrevolutionaries, for whom terror is the only weapon. "We are a humane army," the general said simply. The *fact* is that all over Afghanistan, hospitals staffed with Soviet doctors have tried to put together children blown apart, not only by booby-trapped toys, but by bombs aimed at their schools by the Mujahadin.

The hills around Kabul show the jagged profiles of guns aimed at the distant mountains, and from time to time you can hear a *boom* from them, a continuing reminder of what awaits counterrevolutionaries. Helicopters send out flares as they patrol the hills to head off and detonate heat-seeking Stinger missiles which, as Andrew Cockburn writes, have proven disappointingly ineffective:

> Recent reports from Afghanistan show that out of as many as 18 Stingers fired at enemy warplanes, not one has downed its target. (*New York Times*, July 22, 1986.)

(Actually one did, but about this, later.)

In July, Afghanistan was completing an extraordinary period in its new life—a nation-wide election. Carrying out a nationwide, grassroots election for the first time, even in peacetime, is difficult. In wartime it represents something of a gamble. The decision to hold the elections at all showed remarkable confidence of the Party in the people, a conviction that the tide had indeed turned from the neutrality typical of the majority of the people in 1980 to active support of the revolution now.

This confidence is tied to a second remarkable achievement of the revolutionary forces since 1980. In a country where almost everybody is a Moslem, the counter-revolution banked heavily on being able to marshal the religious beliefs of the people against the revolution, which it characterized as anti-Islamic.

Six years ago when I met with Islamic clergy, it was plain they felt menaced, if not surrounded, by counterrevolutionary assassins. They talked about how many mullahs supporting the government had been assassinated (50 in Kabul then, and later 965 altogether throughout the country). Often their mosques were burned to the ground. I read in the Western press after leaving Kabul in 1980 that the brave Islamic scholar Abdul AszIa Sadegh, who had been a spokesman for the loyal mullahs, and whom I had interviewed, had been killed. But the present head of the Organization of Islamic Affairs, Maula Abdul Walk Hujah, told me that Sadegh had been to see him that very day.

The government has not only repaired destroyed and damaged mosques, but supports several *madresses* where some 3,241 students with 229 teachers are studying. They also made a point of informing us that much of the anti-illiteracy campaign is conducted by *mullahs*, many of whom have themselves just learned to read and write.

Islam has accepted secularization of schools, now in force in the cities and gradually being introduced in the countryside. Also solved is something which had been a sticking-point for years—teaching both girls and boys in the same class. This is a dramatic change from the past, in which girls adopted the *chari* at the age of 13 and no male outside the immediate family ever saw their unveiled faces in public!

"One of the biggest changes that has occurred in the last few years," Maula Abdul Walk Hujah told me, "has been the change of mullahs from opposition to the government to support of it. This is indeed a great political victory." This turnabout had effectively spiked the plans of the counterrevolution, which counted on blind belief by the mullahs and peasantry that the revolution was an enemy of Islam.

One of the key indices of the moral health of any society is how it treats its children. One can say that to Afghanistan each child is infinitely dear. A significant portion of the state budget is allocated to protect their health and promote their education and welfare. In a country where it was taken for granted that every second child would die before the age of five, it is a profound psychological experience for mothers to realize that *most* of their children will live!

A determined effort has been made to make education universal—extending the educational system even into the remotest mountain villages, where counterrevolutionary raids on schools are most common.

There are now 784 primary and middle schools and 332 high schools in the nation, and there would be even more if the counterrevolutionaries had not burned so many. Some 9,000 girls and boys have graduated from Kabul University since April 1978.

Since the anti-illiteracy campaign was launched in 1980, some 1,150,000 illiterates have learned to read and write. The noble aim of the counterrevolution, which they've proven by focusing their attacks on schools and teachers, is to return the nation to ignorance and superstition: an ambition worthy of the Harvard-educated trolls of the State Department Afghan desk!

Today all children go to school and stand up courteously when a stranger enters the classroom. They've been vaccinated against diseases and study their ABCs under the scrutiny of doctors and nurses. Hospitals and clinics, many set up under Soviet guidance, exist to care for them. All are well fed. None are homeless. Visiting schools, parks and orphanages for children whose parents have been murdered by the counterrevolutionaries, I found nothing but care and consideration for the children.

Today Kabul has an air of tranquility, despite the fact that one is frisked when one enters a public building, including schools! To charge that childrens' toys are booby-trapped by their own people or by the Russians—apparently for no other reason than to enrage the people—is not merely nonsense but vicious nonsense. Toys *have* been booby-trapped. But it's not done by people who vaccinate children and rescue them from early death by disease.

Visually, Kabul, now with a population of 1.5 million (the national population is put at 15 million) is a bustling mad kettle of noise. Its streets are jammed with vehicles of every make, from cars seen only in museums elsewhere to the latest Toyota models fresh from Tokyo. Interwoven with them are still the irreducible burros, the plodding camels, the women in *shadri*, following their husbands by ten paces and carrying bundles which he does not deign to touch.

On Chicken Street, where tourists once went, the tradesmen who in 1980 confided openly to me that they hoped the counterrevolution would triumph and who shut their doors in a strike supporting an attempted counterrevolutionary *putsch*, now spoke to me much more modestly. Gone is the atmosphere of naked huckstering. The government has set up shops with fixed prices. Stores are well-stocked with products whose origins are New York, London, Paris via Pakistan. It was surprising to come upon Lux soap and ball point pens from Japan. On the whole, prices are kept in line. But in July, Sultan Ali Keshtmand, Chairman of the Council of Ministers, voiced concern that prices of a few staples, particularly the basic rice, were rising and a means to stop this had to be found.

This time I noticed more women working in the factories. I remembered the statement of Anahita Ratebzad—then Minister of Education—that the social emancipation of Afghanistan's women could not proceed independently of their economic emancipation. At factories making machines and prefabricated slabs for housing, I questioned women, chosen at random, as they stood at their machines. What they told me substantially confirmed what I already knew. Their pay was the same as the men's, which averaged (in the prefab concrete plant) 3,500 afghani a month (somewhat above the general average), plus about 12,000 more annually as a bonus for good work.

To judge how far such an income stretches one has to know that a month's rent for a very tolerable flat runs about 300 afghani. Since husband and wife both work, their combined income allows them to live quite comfortably.

Led by the chief engineer for the prefab factory, Hami Raofi, I visited both the plant where the slabs are made and nearby homes built with factory profits. The request to see these homes was a spontaneous one, and at the complex I came to, I flipped a coin to choose which apartment to descend upon, unannounced.

This particular apartment—three rooms, not counting bath and kitchen—rents for 300 afghani, has running water and electricity, and houses eight people, including grandparents and in-laws. Questions to the tenants elicited answers already familiar to me: all workers were eligible for vacations, pregnant women had longer periods off, literacy classes were run by the factory. Some 420 workers at this plant were enrolled in the self-defense unit which patrolled the grounds and inside of the factory around the clock, and, in fact, had uncovered a planted bomb and defused it some months before.

It was important for me to follow up on the successes or failures that had been registered since 1980. At that time, many new organizations were nothing but gleams in the eyes of the Party. Today they are a reality—unions for journalists, writers, cinema workers, hospital workers; women's organizations; youth organizations; artists (6,000 of them nationally); organizations for tribes and nationalities, the extension and spread of unions for production workers—all these now exist and function under the umbrella organization, the National Fatherland Front, which today has a membership of 800,000.

Still, since Afghanistan is primarily a nation of peasants, the land question is crucial. Quite literally, to defeat the counterrevolution the individual peasant has to be convinced that he is *entitled* to the land he tills. And once that is managed, he has to be persuaded to adopt advanced methods of farming, using better seed, taking advantage of government-organized pools of tractors and harvesting machines. The peasant will join a cooperative only after the most painstaking demonstration proves that it is to his advantage to work with other farmers. Some 300,000 peasants have been *given* land—6 jeribs at first, raised to 30 later. For the individual peasant to feel that he *owns* the land on which he and his ancestors have been nothing but tenant farmers since time began, burdened down by inherited usurious loans and heavy taxes (now annulled) is no small psychological transformation. There are cases of counterrevolutionary peasants on whose dead bodies grants of land were found—they couldn't believe this land was theirs and died fighting against it.

Middle peasants who fled to Pakistan after Amin came to power in 1978, and even those who were better off than that, were invited to return by the present government, which assured them that both land and compensation would be theirs, that they had a place in the social and political life of the nation (as long as they supported its program). Many returned.

To make its land policy succeed, the government has to provide water (new irrigation systems are being built) and to prove that it can repulse the marauders who, early on, were able to swoop down out of the hills on the working peasants and haul away or burn their crops, exact a money tax, and kill those who resisted. Also, the peasant has to be convinced that he now has legal power. While I was there, the nationwide grassroots election process was winding up during which villages elected their local governments as well as (in later elections) their national representatives.

One must remember that in Afghanistan one is dealing with men and women who had had no experience in self-government (or, minimal experience, confined to a small class segment). They had, in fact, just learned how to read and write. They had to learn to work by dock time, not by sunrise and sunset, by summer, winter, fall and spring. This represents a major shift in psychology. It was a major psychological jolt for men to have to look upon women as equals, almost as hard for women to dare to think of themselves as equals.

At the office of the National Fatherland Front, leaders explained to us how this organization (established in June 1981), which joins 17 national organizations, including the Party, under one umbrella, now functions.

Abdul Rahim told us that there now 3,340 jirgahs (councils) functioning and of these 2,953 are located in villages. The Front has no executive power. It proposes candidates for office, but not all of its recommendations are accepted. In Kabul, for instance, 73 of 653 were rejected.

Some 89 per cent of the voters of that city went to the polls.

The general secretary of the People's Democratic Party of Afghanistan, Najibullah, or Najib as he is more often called, lacked 15 days to his 40th birthday when I interviewed him. Like many other Afghan revolutionaries, he was born into a civil servant's family. Like many, too, he is a Pushtun (an exception: Sultan Ali Keshtmand, a Hazara). In 1964 Najib graduated from the Habibia Lyceum, and in 1975 he graduated from the Medical Faculty of Kabul University. But he never practiced medicine. By 1975 he was already 10 years a member of the Party, and his revolutionary activities had earned him two jail sentences.

At the 18th plenary session of the PDPA Central Committee in 1986, he was elected—on Babrak Karmal's motion—general secretary of the PDPA, replacing Karmal in that office.

Najib denies that his election implies either basic disagreement with Karmal's policies or a basic shift in the Party's orientation. When he assumed his position in May, his major criticism of the past focused on "lack of energetic action." He went on to say, "We have a well thought out and balanced strategy but are weak when it comes to putting it into practice. Many good ideas and plans are drowned in verbiage and remain on paper." Vigor is the key to his style. He places great emphasis on the need to accelerate all social processes and to insist on efficiency, honesty and dependability.

Najib quickly answered questions I had brought. The main question was whether an end to hostilities could be expected from negotiations, then going on in Geneva. (Soon to be abruptly stopped by Reagan.) Gorbachev had announced that some Soviet troops would be unilaterally withdrawn from Afghanistan. Najib pointed out that this confirmed the position always held by the two countries—that as soon as the situation warranted, Soviet troops would be withdrawn. He underlined the fraternal assistance the Soviets had rendered them in their hour of need. It was an instance of international solidarity, he pointed out.

Najib stated that the only differences in the Geneva negotiations were over details of the proposals for Soviet troop withdrawals. Other sources report that the Americans (through the Pakistani negotiator) wanted an immediate withdrawal, while the Soviets called for a phased withdrawal, testing whether their leaving the scene would encourage new, hostile incursions into Afghanistan by Pakistani army units.

Najib denied that the change in general secretary had any bearing on the negotiations. He dismissed the suggestion that any settlement could be reached at the price of significantly modifying the revolutionary essence of Afghanistan.

Najib repeated what others had already made dear. The Afghan army could wage the war on its own if imperialist backing was removed from the counterrevolutionary bands. As for the Soviet "limited military contingent," in principle the Soviets were committed to full withdrawal, beginning with the return of the six regiments.

He pointed out that despite the war, social progress had not stopped. Some 335,000 peasant families have so far received title to land free of charge.... From March 21, 1981, to March 20, 1986, state and cooperative sectors of the national economy have grown 47 per cent. Industrial production has grown by 25 per cent.

So far more than 1.5 million people have learned to read and write. Women of our country not only participate in production, administration and culture but also, shoulder to shoulder with men, work and struggle in the armed defense of the homeland and revolution. There has been a considerable change in the orientation of the tribes in our country toward the defense of our revolution. The local elections establish grounds for the realization of true democracy.

Probably no single episode characterizes the Reagan Administration's rogue-elephant role than the fate of Charles Thornton.

Ostensibly a reporter for the *Arizona Republican*, Thornton was recruited by one Dr. Robert Simon, ostensibly of the University of California. Actually, as Thornton tells in his diary (recovered after his death), he worked for the CIA. That was at the end of 1985.

If you wanted to go illegally to Afghanistan, Dr. Simon was the man to know. His specialty was recruiting "volunteer medical teams" to go to the assistance of wounded Mujahadin. Oddly enough, instead of carrying medicine, the "doctors" carried guns. Their aim was not to heal but to kill. Dr. Simon had already sent about 200 such "teams" on just such strange missions of mercy. Dr. Simon knew all the ropes.

Thornton, with Dr. Judd Jensen and John Moughan (a male nurse), both Americans, and Peter Schluster, a photographer for an Arizona paper, slipped illegally across the Pakistan-Afghan border early in September 1985. They were equipped with West German passports (which you don't pick up at the local grocery) and, led by an Afghan counterrevolutionary, Malanga by name, they spent 17 days "behind the lines" near Kandahar.

They had chosen the right kind of leader in Malanga, for when the village of Kaare-Nainje, where he used to hold sway, was liberated, Afghan government forces found two wells stuffed with human heads. This 29-year-old "holy warrior" expressed his religious fervor by beheading his victims and stuffing their heads in wells. He would have been delighted to give Dan Rather a sample of his technique if Rather had been there then, instead of in early 1980, when Rather had to content himself with having the local heroes stone peasants for the benefit of his CBS cameras.

Did Thornton and his "humanitarians" witness an exhibition of Malanga's skills? Afghan sources say they did. On Sept. 4, 1985, an Afghan airliner was brought down as it left Kandahar. Among the dead were seven women and six children. Afghan sources claim that the Stinger missile that shot down the civilian plane had been brought by Thornton and his friends, who actually filmed the firing and the crash of the plane.

To his diary at least, Thornton confided his real aims and opinions. Early in his trip he wrote in his diary that it was not medicine he intended to bring to the "rebels" but guns. On September 11 [1985], for instance, he told his diary (which he never expected to fall into the wrong hands): "At times I sort of shudder when I think of the people around me whom we call our friends."

Well he might have shuddered—if he called Malanga a "friend"! Next day he was writing:

> The longer I live among the mujahid rebels, the greater is my belief that they'll never succeed. Time is not on their side. Villagers are becoming increasingly disillusioned with their methods, which bring nothing but bombs and violence. When the children of these peasants grow up and finish school, it will be the end of the mujahid fighters.

Earlier, September 7, he had recorded the opinion of Karl Freigang, a West German posing as a representative of the German-Afghan Committee:

> Freingang believes that the ringleaders are mercenary and their mullahs corrupt. He refers to them as bandits, says victory for them is out of the question, and ridicules their statement as to the extent of territory under their control.... Mujahid rebels have degenerated into gangs of marauding rabble.

Thornton paid with his life to learn that. One of the "gangs of marauding rebels," led by a local gangster by the name of Nabib, a rival for Malanga's turf, ambushed the party near Shahwalikot, in Kandahar province, and two Americans, including Thornton, were killed.

This isn't the end of this grisly tale. It seems that Thornton's body disappeared from the scene. In due course Dr. Simon got a message from a "religious lunatic" who claimed he had Thornton's body and was holding it until Dr. Simon forked over the dollars he had promised this "lunatic"—to build a clinic.

Dr. Simon eventually washed his hands of the whole affair, complaining that Habibullah Akhund had "inaccurately represented his authority, had zero control over the area and lied to us about the mujahadeen under their control." And, he added somewhat huffily: "We have no intention of meeting his demand. We intend to ignore it entirely." (*New. York Times*, April 12, 1986.)

Thus ended this glorious episode, so typical of the entire squalid business.

Anyone who pretends for a moment, as Helsinki Watch cynics maintain in the face of all the facts, that there is a "democratic" stake in Reagan's Afghan policy, are not only deceiving themselves but are luring others like Thornton to their deaths. They are as guilty of the barbarous crimes committed in Afghanistan as are the cutthroats on the scene.

The Reagan Administration made it clear that it did not intend to reach any settlement. A spokesman for the President even went so far as to say that the coming summit, [US-USSR] if ever it transpires, the American side does not intend to focus on arms control—which it dismisses as a "single issue"—but instead intends to stymie the meeting on discussion of "regional issues," especially Afghanistan.

Reagan declared,

> We want to talk about arms control but not exclusively because we want to talk about regional issues. We mean, what is the Soviet Union doing in Afghanistan if they are such peace lovers? What are they doing in Afghanistan and when are they going to get out? (*New York Times*, August 21, 1986.)

This from a man who had just announced that he was going to train contra cutthroats to take over Nicaragua!

Had anybody told him that Gorbachev had already announced the removal of six regiments from the country? Is it possible that he and his Neanderthalian advisors really think that by raising "regional issues they can deflect world opinion from the "single issue" confronting mankind today—disarmament? Solve that and everything else follows....

The Afghan government and Party today look forward to (1) sealing their borders to counterrevolutionary bands; (2) extending the Revolution's popular base to include all classes of Afghans except the out-and-out criminals; (3) widening grassroots democracy so that every village in the country elects its own representatives; (4) speeding up industrialization and accelerating solution of the question of land and water; (5) making further efforts to solve, the national question by persuading all Afghan tribes to participate in social life.

What is required of American public opinion is to take a new look at Afghanistan and, with Thornton in mind, draw necessary conclusions.

1996

When I opened up the *New York Times* the morning of Sept. 28, 1 was shocked to see, there on its front page, a photograph of two Afghan leaders, one the past president of Afghanistan, hanging from a lamppost in what was identified as a public square in downtown Kabul.

One of the faces was familiar to me. It was the face of Najibullah!

When the Taliban finally closed in and the end was near, Najib escaped to the protection of the United Nations compound in Kabul, with his brother and bodyguard. The Taliban broke into the UN compound, murdered Najib, his brother and his guard. Nobody in the UN Commission either objected or resisted the Taliban murderers.

At no time did U.S. government want a truly democratic regime in power in Afghanistan if it was not hostile to the USSR.

One of the great crimes of the Gorbachev and Yeltsin crews in Moscow was how profoundly they have sacrificed the security of their nation, surrendering it almost literally to the United States. It is vital to a nation to have friendly neighbors on its borders. The USSR had a friendly Afghanistan. Now Russia has an unfriendly one, whose guns are aimed across the Amu River, whose plans include "overturning" the Moslem countries in one-time USSR, in the relentless drive of American power to reduce and dismember Russia itself into a thousand villages.

The *NYT* tries to make the murder more palatable by characterizing Najibullah as "cruel" without ever citing any specific act. This charge of "cruelty" has to be put in the same category as Hitler's charge against the Communists in Germany as having murdered the pimp Horst Wessel, whom he proclaimed a martyr.

It was Najibullah's job in charge of the nation's security to frustrate counter-revolutionary plots and intrigues, most of which had their origin in the American embassy, which had no other function in Kabul.

After all, none of the "rebels" would be in Kabul today if the United States policy hadn't put them there.

INDEX

I

imperialism, 12, 176; discussed, 237-43
International Communications Agency, 105
International Human Rights Federation, 220
Iran, and CIA, 34, 46, 59; SAVAK in
  Afghanistan, 23, 40 counterrevolutionary bases
  in, 181
Islam, 108-09, 131-32; Quadiriya sect of, 179
Islamic Alliance, 224
Islamic Foreign Ministers Conference, 169
Islamic parties and movements, 172, 173, 179,
  181, 255; fuedal Afghan state their goal, 250

J

Jackson, Sen. Henry, 221
Jalalar, Mohammad Khan, 85, 129
Jamiat-e-Islami, 174-75, 176, 177, 189-90
Jamil, Palvasha,86
Japan, and chemical warfare, 227
Javits, Sen. Jacob, 188
journalists, Western, false reports, 22, 135, 138,
  141, 144-49, 153, 155, 168

K

Kadir, Gen. Abdul, 106
Karmal, Babrak:
—on Great Britain 10, 26
—on counterrevolution, ill
—policy of, 37
—progress under, 89, 92
—on refugees, 165
—on Soviet aid, 48; Soviet-Afghan relations,
  233, 236-37, 261 see also Afghanistan
Karmand, Fouroug, 85, 128
Karigar, Azam, 86, 117
Kasin, Mohammad, 148
Keenan, Joseph B., 228
Keshtmand, Karima, 117
Keshtmand, Sultan Ali, 23, 86, 91-92, 147; interview with, 95-98; in 1986, 271, 273

Khakin, Abdul, 148
Khalis, Yunus, 181, 255
Khan, Emir Amanullah, 32-33, 47
Khybar, Mir Akbar, see Afghanistan
Kirkpatrick, Jeanne,101, 202, on realism 212;
  262, 268
Kudus, Nimat, 86

L

Laiyek, Suleiman, 37, 85; on "refugees," 159
"Lawrence of Arabia," 33
Lenin, V. I., 35, 40; and Afghan independence,
  46-47; on imperialism, 237; on peasantry, 66-
  67; on revolution, 50, 68, 78; on self-criticism,
  89
Lessard, Robert, 50, 144; and disunity of
  "rebels," 182, 183
Livar, Shahzar, 117
Lyons, Gene, 218

M

McCullough, William, 188
McNamara, Robert S., 241
Maddock, R., 168
Maiwandwal, Mohammad Haskin, 34, 40
Majrooh, Dr. Sayiat, 255
Mansoor, Nasrullah, 172
Maoist ideas, 64, 65-66, 93
Mao-oriented groups, 182
Margan, Sakhi, 113
Marx, Karl, 6; on British in Afghanistan, 12, 13,
  14, 47; on class domination, 240
Mashal, (Lal Jan), 189
Mazyar, Daoud, 113
mercenary troops, 209-10
Middleton, Drew, 209,211
Moafar, Zahir, 86, 117
Mohammadi, Maulavi Nabi, IRM, 172
Mojadedi, Sibjhafulla, in Honduras, 254, 263
Mojadedi Transport, 254
Moneer (author's guide), 69, 79-80, 114, 140,
  146
Mongolia, 93
Moslem Brothers, 173, 177, 181
Mujahiddin 8, 65, 71, 202, 209, 255, 263, 171,
  249
mullahs, 71, 72; and black market,158-59;and
  counterrevolution, 172-73 number of, 93, 130;
  number murdered, 269; and PDPA, 132, 269-
  70; as refugees, 156; and USSR, 132

N

Najibullah (Najib), 273, 276; *see also*
  Afghanistan
Narcotics Control Authority, 67, 184
National Fatherland Front, 96, 272
National Front of the Islamic Revolution, 173
National Liberation Front, 181
Nalin, Dr. David R., 201

Act, reversed, 1997, 198

T

Taghian, Amad Shah, 139, 140, 141
Tahzib, Nizamuddin, 86, 127
Taraki, Noon Mohammad, 10, 23, 24; and Amin, 37, 39; *see also* Afghanistan
Theroux, Paul, 9
Thornton, Charles 274-75
toxic gas, see chemical and germ warfare
trade unions, *see* Afghanistan, Pakistan
Turner, Stansfield, 62

U

Ulem,Gen. Abdul Hao, 267, 268
Ulfat, Aziz, 177
ul-Haq, Gen. Mohammad Zia, 8, 12, 37, 48; and U.S. aid, 208-09; and Carter administration, 199; coup and, 191; executes Bhutto, 191, 198; and Nassery, 168; policies in Pakistan, 194-95
United Islamic Revolutionary Council, 167
United Nations, debate on Afghanistan, 18; Charter, on aggression, 57; inspection of refugee camps, 162-63; peace talks halted by Reagan/Shultz, 253, 265; Security Council Resolution, 57, 77

V

Vance, Cyrus, 9
Voddud, Capt. A., 43

W

Wakman, Mohammad Amin, 179, 180
Watanjar, W. A., 51, 52
Westmoreland, Gen. Wm., 227
Wick, Charles Z., on propaganda, 105-06
Woddis, Jack, on Amin, 49
women, progress of, 271; *see also* Afghanistan
Writers' Union, 104

Yusouf, Dr. Mohammad, 113

Z

Zagladin, Vadim, on Soviet aid, 241
Zahir, King, 27; and Soviet aid, 48
Zahma, Ali Mohammad, 63
Zeyar, Munawar Ahmad, 63
Zia, General, see ul-Haq
Zoyar, 86